For Barb & Ed -

Good friends -

Enjoy Bill's book -

Love -

Pearl Kastran Ahner

3-19-07

Revealed by Fire

Pearl Kastran Ahnen also has written, edited or contributed to the following books:

Daughter of Immigrants
Balancing Act
Legends and Legacies (memories)
Variation on the Ordinary, a Woman's Reader
Heart Song, Poetry Society of Michigan
Voices on Writing Fiction
Kaleidoscope: A collection of poetry and fiction
Masterful Minds in Mini-Cages, The Gifted

Revealed by Fire

A true story of a soldier told in his letters at a time unparalleled in American history—the Korean War 1950–1953

Army Corporal Bill Ahnen
& Pearl Kastran Ahnen

Foreword: Marine Corporal Duane E. Dewey
Medal of Honor

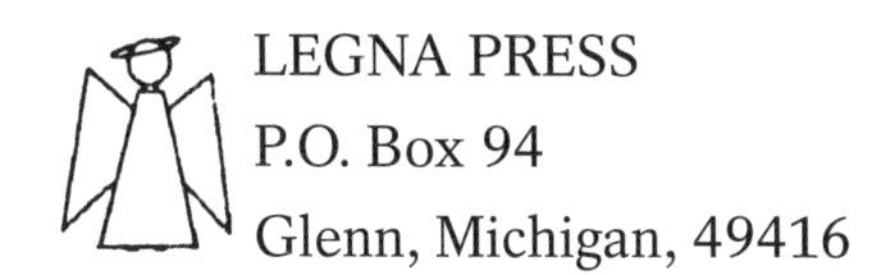
LEGNA PRESS
P.O. Box 94
Glenn, Michigan, 49416

Published by Legna Press

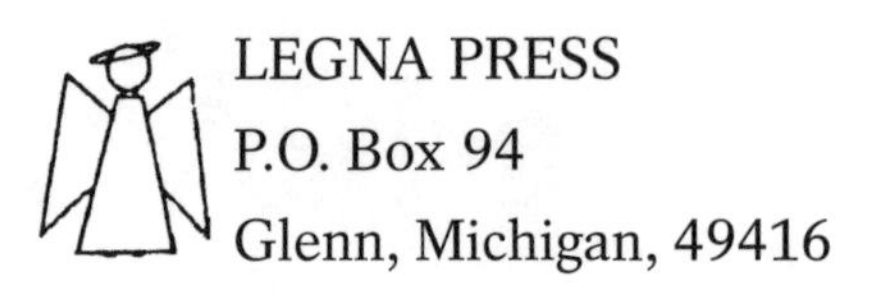

Photos provided by Bill Ahnen, Gust Anton, Paul Balasick, and Duane E. Dewey

Library of Congress Control Number: 2006910312

ISBN-13: 978-0-615-13519-9
ISBN-10: 0-615-13519-6

First Edition
Manufactured in the United States of America

Jacket design by Deneen White, of San Antonio, Texas
Photo of Ms. Ahnen by Deneen White

For the men and women who served in the Armed Forces
during the Korean War—1950–1953.
And in memory of the men, women and children
who died during that war.

"Every man's work shall be made
manifest: for the day shall declare it,
because it shall be **'revealed by fire'**
and the fire shall try every man's
work of what sort it is."

The Bible, 1 Corinthians
Chapter 3, Verse 13

CONTENTS

FOREWORD

When I read the letters that Bill Ahnen wrote during the Korean War, I was awe-struck. This story had to be told, because it brought flesh and blood reality to one man's life during that terrible encounter in Korea that was often called the "forgotten war."

From my own experience, I know that few men talk about what happened to them in a war. But those who wrote home and those who kept their letters have a record of what happened; the nightmares, the terror and the deaths.

"Revealed by Fire" contains more than 300 letters written by Army Corporal Bill Ahnen, of Pontiac, Michigan, to his parents. It tells the true and often frustrating story of one soldier who had a highly classified job in Korea as a member of the Artillery's Fire Direction Center (FDC). Huddled in a tent these FDC men studied maps and charts to determine the enemy's location after receiving messages from runners and helicopters flying in enemy territory. Then they'd telephone the front line to fire.

But the soul of this book is a love story. Bill fell in love with Anita, an Arkansas gal he met while he was in basic training at Camp Chaffee, Arkansas. They promised to wait for each other while he was in Korea.

These valuable historic letters were given to Bill's wife, Pearl, by his mother Martha in 1971 when they returned from their honeymoon.

These letters and excerpts from Bill's journal record the day-to-day ordinary, frustrating and often horrible side of war. They reveal the private thoughts of one young man who was swept into a harsh reality.

Bill's letters commemorate a war that killed nearly 34,000 Americans and wounded 92,134. And when he came home, what did he face but public indifference.

I was there and know what Bill went through. I'll never forget the night several hundred Chinese came at us. All hell broke loose. There were only 80 of us and our ammo ran out. A grenade hit me and put me down.

Bill didn't face grenades, but he faced the terror of enemy planes bombing the FDC tent. Moving the tent was almost a weekly ritual. Of course, the bombings were classified information, and Bill could not write about them in detail. It was only years later that Bill and Pearl were able to obtain the declassified battle information and record them in this book.

The book does not end with the war. Yes, Bill was a happy GI when he learned he was going home to Pontiac. What happened to his romance with Anita is revealed in the book. Although this is Bill's story, if it were not for his mother, Martha, who saved all his letters and for his wife, Pearl, for recording them in book form, all would be lost. The women who kept their loved one's letters played a very important role in history. Bill's letters and all the letters of all the men who fought and died during a war are valuable, historical documents.

U.S. Marine Corporal Duane E. Dewey,
Medal of Honor
Irons and South Haven, Michigan
2006

(The Medal of Honor is the highest U.S. Military decoration, awarded by Congress for gallantry at the risk of life above and beyond the call of duty; established 1862.)

Corporal Duane E. Dewey was awarded the Medal of Honor on March 12, 1953, presented to him by President Dwight D. Eisenhower. The heroic incident occurred on April 16, 1952, in Panmunjom, Korea, when Dewey was a squadron leader during the Korean War. In his words, "It was 11 at night and before I knew it two grenades flew over my head. My ammo carrier grabbed an M-I rifle. All hell broke loose. There were hundreds of Chinese and only eighty of us.

I ran to another machine gun, and as I was returning a grenade exploded at my feet, knocking me down. I lay on the ground, bleeding heavily from my thigh and groin. A Navy corpsman (medic) came to me. We were surrounded. A second grenade hit the ground beside me. I grabbed the grenade and scooped it under my right hip. I thought for a second I could throw it back, but I knew I didn't have the strength, and I might have hit our men. Then I pulled the medic to the ground and I said, "Hit dirt, Doc." The grenade exploded. (The medic was unharmed. Corporal Dewey smothered the deadly missile with his body, absorbing the full force of the explosion to save his comrades.) They got me the hell out of there, dragged me to a bunker that was full of casualties, left me outside. I blacked out. Shock was setting in so they got my feet up and my head down and gave me morphine. There was a big hole in my hip. The next morning they got me to a field hospital (M.A.S.H.). There they found an eight-inch bullet hole in my stomach near my bladder. Finally I was shipped to the states where I would spend three months convalescing. In an Army hospital in Hawaii, I was presented with the Purple Heart."

When President Eisenhower presented Corporal Dewey with the Medal of Honor he said, "Son, you must have a body of steel."

INTRODUCTION

REVEALED BY FIRE

How it Ended for One Soldier

April 2, 1953

Cpl. Bill Ahnen tried to stop himself from remembering what he had left behind in Korea—the fields alive with mines, the starving Korean children, the dead soldiers—finally he shook his head. Yes, he was lucky. It was April 2, 1953, and an hour ago he had received his separation papers at Fort Custer, Michigan. He was a civilian!

But Bill was not aware of the two letters waiting for him at home from his Arkansas girl. He fell in love with her twenty months ago during basic training at Camp Chaffee, Arkansas. Now his immediate plans included buying a car and marrying his gal, Anita, in that order. When Bill was drafted in 1951 and stationed at Camp Chaffee, he was a bony, long-legged twenty-year old. After Korea in 1953, he emerged—tough, muscled and disciplined.

Outside the Fort Custer gate his mother, Martha, waited in front of the family Buick. For a while he simply grinned, and in his mind counted back to when he last saw her, many months ago. Hours later, at home in Pontiac, Michigan, Bill nervously brushed back his sun-bleached blond hair, before hugging family, friends and neighbors gathered to welcome him. When his mother found a quiet moment she handed Bill two letters. They were from his Arkansas gal, Anita. Somehow they had traveled from Korea back to the states and finally caught up with him in Pontiac.

He excused himself, and raced upstairs, flung his bedroom door open and ripped open the envelope of Anita's first letter. Did she still love him? Or was this a 'Dear John' letter? No, the first letter said how happy she was that he would soon be coming home, and she was eager to see him and finalize plans for their wedding. She sounded so excited. Bill grinned and counted his blessings. Anita loved him!

The second letter had a serious tone. In her first sentence she said she had cancer, bone cancer to be more specific. The doctors had told her it was confined to one of her legs and she recently underwent surgery to remove that leg. She had known about the cancer for several months, but did not want to worry him. He had enough to worry about being in Korea.

She had been fitted with an artificial limb. "It's really not that bad," she wrote. She ended the letter by saying she loved him very much and his love was what had kept her going all these months. Bill glanced out the window, the sun was shining brightly. A tight knot encircled his heart. Then there was a cry building up within him, a shrill silent scream that tore him apart. More than anything now, he wanted to erase that last letter. The air was heavy in the bedroom, and pressed Bill down. Limp, he sat on the bed. Outdoors, the sun was lower.

Finally, Bill jammed the letters in his breast pocket and went downstairs. His face set in concentration, his mouth closed in silence, careful not to reveal his thoughts, Bill walked into the living room to join family and friends. Bill had come home.

How It Began

July, 1951

After supper the evening before he left for the Army, Bill sat with his parents at the kitchen table. His mother said, "Son, don't write us letters—talk to us on paper. Promise? And we will do the same—every day." Bill promised to "talk to them on paper" as often as possible. Soon these letters written to his parents, Martha and Nicholas, back in Pontiac, Michigan, became a diary of his life in the Army.

Bill was twenty years old, in excellent health, with blond hair and washed out blond eyebrows that framed sharp blue eyes. He was two inches shy of six feet and weighed 165 pounds. He often dressed in casual plaid shirts and faded blue denims, that had become a uniform for him. He loved to fish in the rivers and lakes of Michigan and hunt deer in the Upper Peninsula woods. Often his hunting companion was his father, Nick.

Bill's stint in Korea marked him forever. He was one who survived and counted himself lucky to be alive. History calls what happened in Korea a "police action," but to this soldier it was war. Korea became a touchstone moment of historic frustration for the men who survived. Perhaps the North Koreans were vulnerable and overextended. Perhaps not. Perhaps the U.S. and United Nation troops supporting the South Koreans were more vulnerable and overextended. Perhaps not. Perhaps the truth was **"revealed by fire"**.

Bill was drafted into the Army in July 1951, a few weeks shy of his twenty-first birthday, August 7. While at Camp Chaffee, Arkansas, for his basic training, he also received instructions to become a member of the Artillery's strategic unit, the Fire Direction Center (FDC). By mid-December he was on a troop ship, the U.S.S. General R.L. Howze, with 4,000 other GIs shipped from Seattle to Japan. The fifteen-day journey saw many of the men below deck spewing their last meal, sicker than dogs.

On Christmas Eve, 1951, when the troop ship crossed the International Date Line, most of the soldiers were oblivious to the fact; they were too sick. Bill, below deck, thought how ironic it was that a ship filled with soldiers was on its way to Korea to kill—in a war that the people back in the states called a "police action."

Once in Korea, his duties at FDC were graphically described by his Major who said, "The crew at FDC bombs the hell out of enemy targets they don't see."

Another duty Bill had in Korea was driving his Major in a jeep to the Front. The following is one of Bill's journal entries: "We got there after a blast exploded and before the medics. One soldier's lower body and legs were burned and bleeding. I stumbled over the body of a soldier—too many bodies, not enough medics to remove them."

Whenever there was a lull at FDC, Bill managed to scratch out a letter to his parents or his girl, Anita, in Arkansas. He maintained his optimistic outlook in his letters, to reassure them that all was well, although there was danger surrounding him.

—m—

(The following are memories of Pearl Kastran Ahnen)

Eighteen years after Bill's discharge, in April, 1971, I married him. When we returned from our honeymoon, his mother gave me a large duffle bag filled with over 300 of Bill's war letters.

When I read Bill's Korean War letters and journal, I often visualized the M*A*S*H television program with its zany antics and heartbreaks. Yes, the Korean War was crazy and young men died in that craziness.

Many years passed and the letters remained in my closet. "I've got to get to them," I'd say. Finally when I did, I hope I retained Bill's voice and his way of "talking on paper." In doing research about the Korean War, I also spoke with many Korean War veterans. Some of their Korean War memories are in this book when they coincide with Bill's Army stint—1951–1953. Later, I obtained information of the battles in Korea and included them. (In 1952–1953 Bill was not allowed to write about them in his letters.)

In recording Bill's letters, I attempted to tell the story of a young man caught in the Korean conflict. This is not a war tale. It's an historical record of one soldier's ordinary, personal letters to his parents, reassuring them that he was all right and would come back home, safe and well. But most of all it is a love story of two young people thousands of miles apart. And finally it is the day-to-day frustrating, terrifying and occasionally mundane experiences in Korea of a young soldier from Pontiac, Michigan.

"Don't make me out a hero." Bill said. "I was just doing my job."

FACTS OF THE KOREAN POLICE ACTION

The Beginning

In 1945, following the Allied victory, Korea was liberated from 35 years of rule under Japan. But the north and south were divided and conflict between the communist North and the democratic South were intensified. At that time, interim occupation governments were established on both sides of the 38th parallel. The Soviet Union controlled the North and the United States oversaw affairs in the south.

Kim Il-sung, leader of the North, began to build up his military strength and his aim was to "liberate the South." With support from Joseph Stalin of the Soviet Union, and the approval of China's Mao Zedong, Kim Il-sung launched an all out attack on the South on June 25, 1950.

That's when the Korean War began. Because the North Korean Communist attack erupted across the Korean peninsula in coordinated assaults, no single soldier or unit could accurately claim to have heard the "first shot fired."

An urgent United Press Dispatch was sent by Jack James, a United Press correspondent in Seoul that day—June 25, 1950, to his home office in the United States. James' cable was received instantaneously at the UP office in San Francisco, where it was sent to New York and a rewrite man on the foreign desk translated the urgent cable into a news story dispatched around the world.

South Korea had 769,353 troops fighting, some 113,248 dead and missing, and 159,727 wounded. The United States had 45,116, dead and missing and 92,134 wounded. Twenty other countries in the United Nations came to the aid of South Korea.

Cease fire on July 27, 1953

(When the Korean conflict began, Bill was working at General Motors' Truck Division, in Pontiac, and had joined the Naval Reserves. At one point, he had gone on a Naval cruise with his unit. However, he missed too many Naval Reserve meetings because as he put it "The meetings conflicted with my social life." So Bill was drafted into the Army.)

(Prelude to Bill's induction into the Army: President Truman was unhappy with the direction General Douglas Mac Arthur was taking as U.S. Commander in Korea, and on April 4, 1951, dictated a memo to his staff announcing the firing of Mac Arthur. Before Mac Arthur heard the news, he and Lieutenant General Matthew B. Ridgeway visited a battlefield in Korea. A few days later, Ridgeway succeeded Mac Arthur as U. S. Commander in Korea. Later, Ridgeway assumed the title of United Nations Commander in Korea.)

First Communication from Bill Ahnen

Postcard dated July 20, 1951
Fort Sheridan, Illinois

Dear Mom, Dad, and Sis Carol,

It sure was good to hear your voices. It made me feel a little less lonesome. I haven't had time to do anything except what the Army tells me to do. This is my first chance. Everything is going swell so far. But we haven't even started yet.

Daddy, have you worked on my car yet? Don't write to me at this address. Wait till I get a permanent one.

Don't have anybody to make my bed anymore. No evening snacks or running around. They may even make a man out of me before I'm through here. I'll write soon as I get stationed. Love to all of you. Miss you very much. Love, Bill

p.s. How's Ollie? *(Bill's parakeet)*

—~—

Fort Sheridan, Illinois
July 21, 1951

Dear Mother, Father and Carol,

We had inspection of barracks this morning and now we are all sitting around and waiting for the results. If they aren't good enough we'll have K.P. or something. Our whole company had K.P. yesterday. We didn't do anything wrong, it was just our turn. I took the dishes after they were washed and put them in their proper places.

We also had our shots yesterday. My arms are sore. As a matter of fact, all the guys' arms are sore.

We have pretty good meals. I can't kick about them very much. All in all the Army doesn't seem too bad (so far). There are rumors going around that we may get sent to Arkansas. I don't know how true they are. We have to get up at 5:00 a.m. each morning, then go through our processing to get us ready for basic. We're usually off about 5 or 6 p.m. I just now got back from a company meeting and I found out for sure that I'm going to Arkansas. I have to go and eat dinner now and then go have our final records checked.

I got a haircut today. I went to the barbershop and I wasn't there over a minute and I was back out. They really scalped me. None of my hats fit anymore. There goes all my blond curly locks, down the drain. Ha! We are getting off today about 3 p.m., I guess. They have a day room next door to our barracks. They got a TV set in there. We've got most of the conveniences of home. Well I've got to eat now. I will write and tell you my new address in my next letter. We are leaving Monday. So long for now, I'll write soon.

Love, Bill

—~—

Fort Sheridan, Illinois
July 24, 1951

Dear Mother,

We left Fort Sheridan at 8:00 Monday morning and reached Camp Chaffee, Arkansas, Tuesday at 4:30 in the afternoon. We came by train through Iowa, across the Mississippi through Kansas City then into the camp. This camp is located about a mile from a town called Fort Smith. The temperature is wavering at 100 degrees. My clothes are wringing wet from sweat. The Battery that I'm in specializes in field artillery. I'm not in the infantry as far as I know. When I get out of Basic, I may continue in field artillery or they may branch me off into something else. I haven't much time to write this. I'll write later.

Lots of love, Bill

p.s. Tell sis to write. Send my address up North to everyone and anyone who wants to write me. I'll probably be pretty busy the next week. Write soon and lots. Give my address to Fred and Bob. Tell them to pass it on.

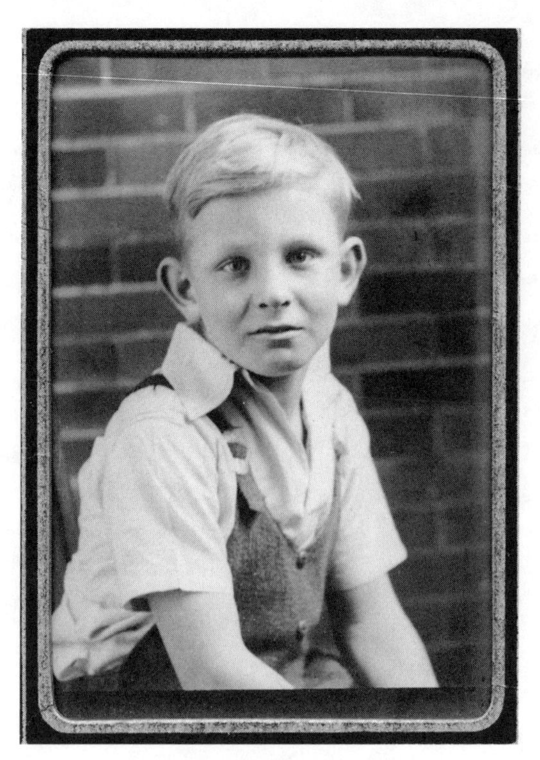

Bill Ahnen age four

CAMP CHAFFEE, ARKANSAS

(Basic Training)

July 27–November 19, 1951

Returning to Camp Chaffee, Arkansas
Bill and Pearl Ahnen, 1987

Bill and I decided to visit Camp Chaffee, Arkansas, to see where he had taken his basic training in 1951. We left Michigan one summer day in 1987. I wanted to see the camp since I planned to record his letters in book form. "Some day your letters will be in a book, honest, honey," I said.

"Sure, some day," he said.

"Tell me a little about Camp Chaffee. Say, I bet you can still fit in your uniform. You're the same size, besides being better looking." I said trying to lighten the mood.

He gave me a shy smile. "That's my girl. Sorry, but the uniform was given to the Salvation Army many moons ago. I wanted to forget about that war in Korea."

He was silent for a while and then the open roads and the lack of traffic this early morning encouraged him to talk. He said the camp was typical of many camps in the country at that time. There were barracks, officers' quarters, a post exchange (P.X.) where the soldier bought cigarettes, candy, beer, etc, a chapel, and the canteen where they hung out and played pool, Ping Pong or cards when they were off duty.

His basic training began the end of July, 1951, and it was hot in Arkansas. They did a great deal of marching and in that heat it "was no picnic, some guys passed out" to use Bill's words. Marching, rifle practice, training, making soldiers of raw recruits did not leave much time for off duty recreation. Finally, when the men did get their first pass they were anxious to leave camp behind them for a few hours. Bill was no exception.

His attention soon turned to the heavy traffic on the expressway as we entered Arkansas. We were both silent while he guided the car through the crush of traffic.

"We're almost there," he said, pulling off the expressway. In a matter of minutes we were at Camp Chaffee, only the sign about the entrance said "Fort Chaffee." There were several large equipment trucks, with the name of a Hollywood movie studio stenciled on them, parked to one side of the entrance. Two military guards were stationed at the gate. We drove to the gate and Bill explained our mission.

"I took my basic training here in '51. Want to see if the place has changed. Is there a chance we can get in and look around?" Bill asked one of the guards.

"I'll have to check sir. We have a company here shooting a film. It's not an active camp anymore. Closed down several years ago. Wait here and I'll see if I can get you clearance," said one of the guards.

In about fifteen minutes the guard returned with a pass to drive through the camp. He cautioned us about the shooting of the film and warned us to obey the "no trespassing signs." We agreed and with pass in hand, Bill led the way driving slowly down the narrow dirt roads. We passed several barracks and then Bill stopped.

"Here's where I bunked," he said. We walked to the barracks and sat on the porch steps for a few minutes while Bill told me here is where he sat in the evenings and wrote his letters. It was cooler there and quieter, he added. Later we got up and Bill tried the door. To our surprise it opened and we walked into a vast empty room. He pointed to a far corner. "That's where my bunk was—all the comforts of home. Not!" He grinned.

We spent some time exploring the empty room and then decided to go to the PX. Bill was sure the PX would be open, especially with all the movie people around the camp. The PX was a short distance from the barracks, and when we entered, he was right, there were several people there from the film company. Bill bought some ice cream and sodas for us and we found a table.

"On my 21st birthday I bought a pint of ice cream and a beer to celebrate," he said.

"I know the story. You've mentioned it to me several times. Remember?"

"Well, here's the place I celebrated, all by myself," he said. Then while we both enjoyed our ice cream and sodas, he talked about camp life.

He said the first time he got a pass he went to Fort Smith, a nearby town, with his buddy, Curly. He met Curly when they were both drafted and reported for duty in Pontiac, Michigan. They didn't like Fort Smith because there were too many soldiers.

"It was a rough town, really not a place to enjoy yourself," Bill said. So the two devised a plan to locate a quieter town. Once back in camp, they pulled out a map of Camp Chaffee and the surrounding area. They placed a pin at Camp Chaffee, tied a string to the pin and worked it in a circle about 50 miles radius from the camp. They were trying to locate a town near enough to hitch a ride, yet not swarming with soldiers. "A nice quiet town." They went to several towns in their quest and finally settled on Paris, a nice quiet town where the people were friendly.

Paris, Arkansas, in 1951 was a typical small country town, with a courthouse in the middle of the town square, a hardware store, a five-and dime and a dry goods store, at one end, a small park facing the courthouse, a movie theater at the other end, and additional stores completing the square. A block down Main Street was the town bank, and several miles down the road a cemetery. There was a roller skating rink at the edge of town and beyond that open fields.

When we visited Paris in 1987 not much had changed. The courthouse was still there. The movie theater was now the site of Baptist revivals and prayer meetings. The other stores remained the same except for the five-and-dime. It had become a "dollar" store. The roller skating rink had been torn down and there was a used car dealership in that location. The bank was still there and also the cemetery. The open fields were filled with middle income housing. Bungalows and two-family frame houses dotted the area.

We walked around the town square, sat on the park bench, listened to the old clock in the courthouse tower chime. Later we strolled to the movie theater and peeked into the lobby. "See that ticket booth. That's where I met Anita," Bill said.

For the first time in sixteen years, he began to tell me about the girl he met in Paris. She worked at the movie theater, sometimes selling popcorn, sometimes at the ticket booth, sometimes as an usher.

"We got pretty close when I was at Camp Chaffee. You might say we were 'smitten with each other.' Every pass I got, I spent it in Paris with her—Anita. She was a sweet kid, nineteen, not too tall, with long dark hair and bright eyes."

Although Bill didn't say, I suspected it was first love and first everything for both of them. Bill was twenty-one and she was nineteen. Later when I finally read and recorded his letters and journal, I witnessed the bumps and trials the love affair took while Bill was stationed in Korea for so many months.

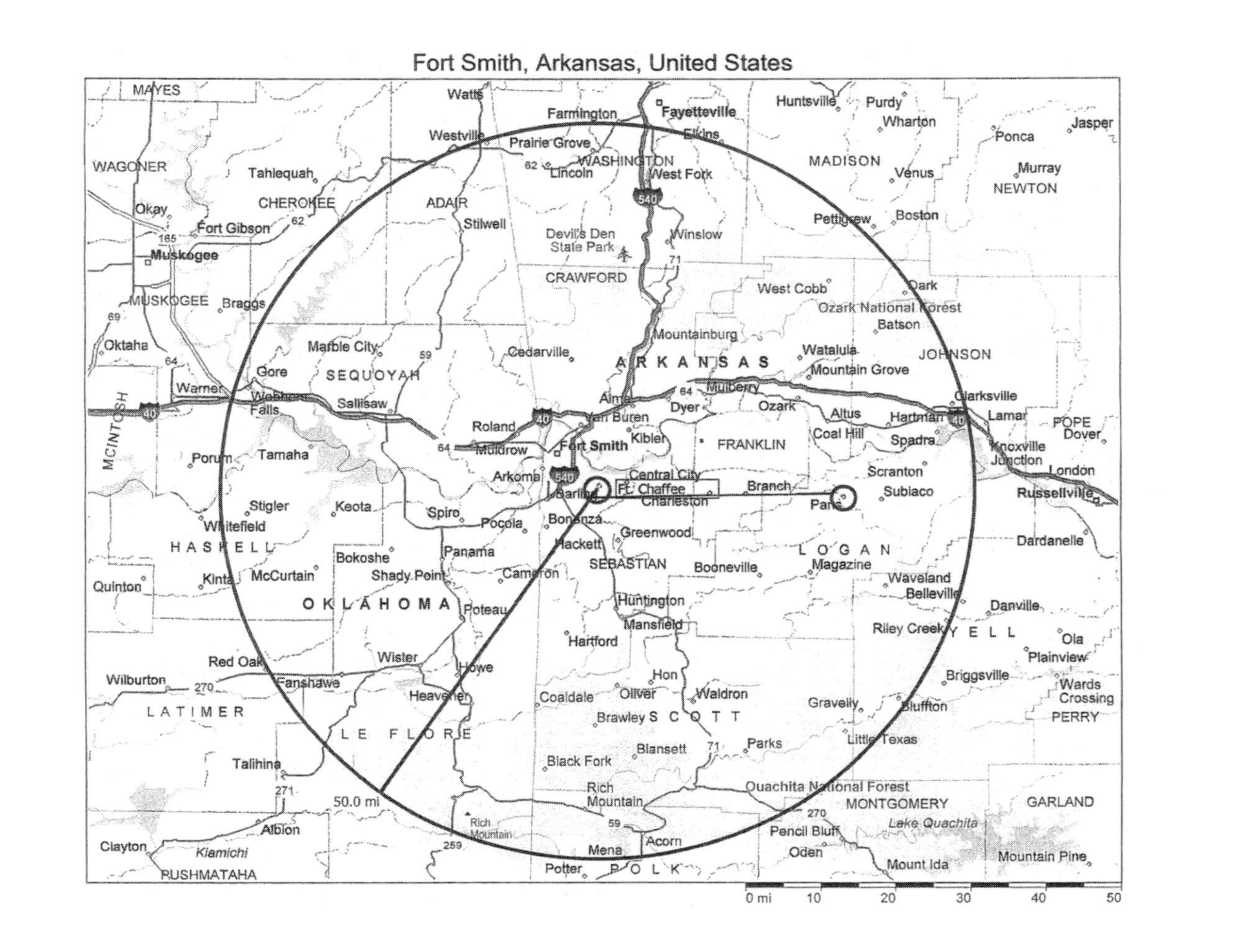
Fort Smith, Arkansas, United States
MAYES
WAGONER
MUSKOGEE
MCINTOSH
CHEROKEE
ADAIR
SEQUOYAH
HASKELL
LATIMER
LE FLORE
PUSHMATAHA
OKLAHOMA
ARKANSAS
WASHINGTON
CRAWFORD
MADISON
NEWTON
JOHNSON
FRANKLIN
SEBASTIAN
LOGAN
POPE
YELL
SCOTT
PERRY
MONTGOMERY
GARLAND
POLK
Fort Smith
Fayetteville
Muskogee
Russellville
Ft. Chaffee
Devil's Den State Park
Ozark National Forest
Ouachita National Forest
Lake Quachita
50.0 mi
0 mi
10
20
30
40
50

Bill beside howitzer (cannon)

Bill's buddies at Camp Chaffee

Bill at Camp Chaffee

(While Bill was on his way to Camp Chaffee, this was the prisoners of war situation in Korea described by Gunner's Mate Fay Gordon Quardokus, of Stevensville, Michigan.)

(Spring, 1951, in Korea: Gunner's Mate Fay Gordon Quardokus, of Stevensville, Michigan, was on an LST 112 and in four or five trips helped haul 10,000 Chinese and North Korean prisoners of war to Koje-Do Island. "The prisoners were among those taken from Puchon and Inchon. It took us about a month and actually some 180,000 POW ended up on the island," said Quardokus. There was a helicopter pad installed on the ship. The helicopters supported search and rescue operations. Both helicopters based on the ship were shot down in June, 1951 by the North Koreans, according to Quardokus.)

—ᴡ—

(July, 1951, in Korea—Marines of the 1st Division hold a memorial service for fallen comrades as the fighting comes to a standstill while U.N. and Chinese cease-fire. Negotiators talk at Kaesong.)

—ᴡ—

Camp Chaffee, Arkansas
July 27, 1951

Dear Mother, Dad and Carol,

Maybe I told you before but I'm restricted for the next few weeks around here. That is for all men when they first enter basic. We can't go anywhere except to the day room and that's just a building where you can write letters. We went out to the field today and had a demonstration on firepower. They shot every kind of gun they had—pistols, rifles, machine guns, bazookas, cannons, howitzers and also threw in hand grenades. We'll be able to get a chance at that in a few weeks. When one of those big guns went off it made more noise than it actually was worth. We were issued our rifles today, too. They are semi-automatic and really a nice little gun for deer hunting. The range is over a mile away.

One thing I have to tell you is if there is any sickness (serious) in the immediate family notify the Red Cross and they will work from there to get me an emergency leave. Don't call here because they'll just have to go back and notify the Red Cross. Notify the nearest Red Cross chapter in town for they have to investigate and get all the details. The commanding officer told us that and told us to be sure and write our parents.

I'd like to call home on my birthday if I can but I haven't very much money till payday. So I guess I'll have to reverse the charges. I hope it's all right. That would be a nice birthday present for me. Stay home that night and I'll call between 6 and 7, my time, your time I think will be 7 to 8 p.m.

Will you send me two white shorts and under shirts, also 4 or 5 white handkerchiefs. Send them in a little box of some sort. Send me those two shorts I've got in my drawer, that is if Daddy hasn't worn them.

Also see if you can get Bob and Fred and a few guys over to the house when I call on Aug. 7. Call Fred and he'll call Bob. I'll try to call as close to 7 (your time) as I can. Tell me just what was wrong with my car? It's about bedtime now so I'd better get over and mail this in a hurry. I miss everyone a lot.

"Come-on-a-my-House," Rosemary Clooney's song, is playing on our little radio here. Things like that make me lonesome for home. Tell me whether you want me to call or not. It may cost quite a bit. I have to stay here but never-the-less I wish I were home.

Love, Lonesome Willy

—~—

July 28, 1951

Dear Mammy, Pappy, Carol (Ollie and Brownie, too)

The Army is treating me fine so far. We haven't been doing much of anything yet. Just enough to keep us busy at all times. I'm waiting for chow now. Supper that is. The food here at Chaffee is good. No kiddin'. Our mess hall is just for our camp. It's kept very clean at all times. Sundays it's my turn to keep it clean because that's when I have K.P. Everyone gets assigned K.P. No one likes it. At the present time we are learning Army discipline and Army courtesy. We'll be doing that for eight weeks. After that we start classes on artillery, learning everything there is to know about certain types of guns.

We are going to train for range finders on the big guns. I was lucky though to get out of the infantry into this because of my high scores on the aptitude tests. Our Sergeant is an exception, by that I mean he's a very nice guy. After my Basic I may go into motor pool or I may stay in Artillery. It all depends where they need me, not where I want to go.

I've learned more in these first few weeks than I thought I'd ever learn. They pound it in your head so you'll never forget it. One of the first things they told us was to quit thinking for yourself. "We'll think for you!" My letter was just interrupted by the Sarge. He called all of us to attention and said, "All right you guys. Let's G.I. these barracks". We all GIed everything till it shined. G.I. means to clean everything with soap and water. I'll guarantee you that we are tired at the end of the day. Our working days end at 4:30 p.m. After that we can do what we want unless the Sarge orders us to do something else.

I'm getting used to being away from home little by little. I still get lonesome for everyone but I guess I always will. Furthermore I can't understand how I'm going to save any money. We have to buy something every time we turn around. I've got $15 left. That's money I brought plus our advance of $20. I was thinking of coming home for a weekend or three days if I could get it later on. But it costs about $80 for round trip by airplane. I can make it in four hours. I start on a Friday night and get there early Saturday morning (all day Saturday and Sunday) and leave Sunday night to get here Monday morning. It would be nice but maybe I'd best wait for my furlough, eh?

I sent my clothes home today C.O.D. If I need money I'll write. I'd better mail this now before it gets too late. Love to all of you. I miss you. Your loving son, Bill.

Write soon!

Aug. 2, 1951

Dear Mom and all,

I don't know how I find time to write around here but I do. Now that was a brilliant statement, eh? We started our basic training Monday morning. Our schedule is—up at 5 a.m., eat at 6, exercise from 8 to 9. Classes from 9 to 11, eat from 11 to noon.

Then dismounted drill from noon to 2 and more classes from 2 to 4 p.m. Then we come to the end of the day. But they usually find extra duty for all of us.

The weather here is fine. It rained once and cooled off to about 90 degrees. Ever since then it's been up to 100 degrees or more. Each night we get back we have to wring out our fatigues. It's hot! Just finished washing my socks and underwear. It isn't too hard once you get used to it. But I'm not quite used to it though.

I'll be home about the last week of November. It'll be for 10 to 15 days. I can hardly wait. I've been writing to Mary and she seems to be a faithful letter writer just as you said she'd be. I find she's a very nice girl, too.

Money goes fast around here the first few weeks. There are a lot of miscellaneous things we have to buy. I'll get about 10 to 15 dollars the 10th of August and then on the 30th of August I'll get a full month's pay and there after the last of each month. I don't see yet how I'm going to save much money. I sent my uniforms to be dry cleaned and that will cost $2.

Did you get my pictures yet? How did they come out? I wonder if you could get a couple of pictures made and send them to me. If they are good I'd like to send one to Mary. Try and do it, eh?

About my Ford: Daddy, I think it would be better to fix my '47 motor than to put the '40 in there because the '40 has a little knock in it just like my '47 motor did. All you have to do is use the '40 transmission if it works and fix the '47 motor. Use your own judgment on that.

My duty hours quit at 4:30 p.m. each day and noon on Saturday and I have Sunday off. It's really not too bad here. I got a card from Mrs. Gross. She didn't say much. I got one pack of cigarettes, stationery, one shaving cream when I left Pontiac. I got five letters from Mary already.

Pat and Carol I'll write soon, and thanks for the letters. Can Ollie talk yet? Tell Pat to teach him. Lights out soon. I'll write soon. Lots of love and kisses, your loving son, Bill.

(add to Aug. 2, 1951)

Dear Mom,

Just a little note because I want you to send my camera to me. I'd like to take some pictures. Send it as soon as possible. Mark it "Fragile". Stick $5 in it too. I think I can use it. Starting next month, I'll send money home. Good bye for now. I'll write a long letter again as soon as possible.

p.s. If I don't call before 8 p.m. Aug. 7 don't wait. I'll call the next day. If you want to give me a watch I can buy it at the camp PX a lot cheaper. Ask Pat about it. A good watch value $50–60, I can get it at the post for $30. I'll tell you in my next letter or on the phone. You can send me money for it if you want or do what ever you want.

What ever Dad thinks is best for my car tell him to do it.

Enclosed is a souvenir hanky. Pretty, eh?

It takes one or two days for air mail and two to three days for regular mail.

Love Bill

—ω—

August 7, 1951, Journal Entry One:

Since it's my 21st birthday I bought myself a present at the PX. It's this notebook, black hard, cover with lots and lots of blank ruled pages. I know there will be some things I can't write my folks, so I'll jot them in this. I did tell them my letters would be sorta like a diary of my life in the Army, but maybe this will be the diary, a record of what really happens to me. We shall see. Now to find a good place to hide it so the Sergeant won't find it. What- cha gonna do?

—ω—

August 11, 1951

Dear Mother, Dad and Sis,

Thought it was about time for me to answer your letters. We've been pretty busy lately and I haven't had much time to write to anyone. Every now and then they give us a few minutes to ourselves. Tomorrow morning we have to rise and try to shine at 3:30 a.m. We're going to march to the firing range to shoot our rifles for the first time. The range is 4½ miles from here. I dread it. It rained today for the first time. It lasted only ½ hour but is sure did cool it off in a hurry. It dropped from the 100s to the 70s. It sure does feel good to get back to the cool weather again.

You asked what type of classes I have. It's called a "directional finders' course." We're the ones who sit back and figure out which way and how far to shoot the guns. All our work is done geometrically. It's a system of triangulation. It works like so: our guns are here, the enemy's guns are over yonder a mile or so. Our scouts tell us the position of the enemy's gun. They radio back to us and we sit in our little tent, with our slide rule and maps and geometrically figure out the exact position of said gun. When we have reached our conclusion we then radio the guns and it's up to them to fix the range I give and fire on the enemy. In other words, I am a key man in artillery. Everything depends on us. If the enemy charges, we'll be the first to be evacuated. That's how important we range-finders are to the success of the artillery. (We're the brains!)

What a birthday I had, marched all day long then went to bed early so I could get up early the next day. Oh well, I'm a man now. The cheapest watch is all right for me. Honest it would only take a day (24 hours) to come down here. I won't say much more about it now. Sunday is my day off. Most of the time I have Saturday afternoon off, too. Send me three or four of the best of my pictures (billfold size) as soon as you can. The meals aren't half as good as those you cook.

p.s. We also marched the evening of my birthday. Somehow we flubbed up and had to march that night. Maybe the word drill would be better. A very wonderful birthday, eh? But I did have some beer (legal at last), and a whole bunch of ice cream.

If you want, you can send me some "goodies" of some sort, cookies, candy, etc. It would be nice. Nothing that will melt, though. Lots of love and thanks for the $20 or should I say watch. Love, XXX, Bill.

—~—

Aug. 14, 1951

Dear Mom, Dad and Carol,

Received your letter this afternoon and I was almost too tired to read it. We got up at 3 a.m. this morning and by 5 a.m. we were marching to the firing range, about four miles out there. The temperature then was about 80 degrees, and at 11 a.m. the temperature was 110 degrees and that's hot believe you me. Sweat, sweat, and more sweat!

We are going to do the same things tomorrow and Friday. I keep my fingers crossed hoping I make it each day because if we drop out we have to make it up on our off duty hours. It's no picnic here that's for sure. Each and every night we have to clean our rifles without fail. We take everything apart there is to take apart and clean it. I don't mind that too much. We shot 36 rounds today and I got 22 bull's eyes out of it. That's pretty good, eh? You have to have 140 to qualify and 160 to be a marksman and 175 to be an expert. I got 166 today. I hope to do better tomorrow.

On all the inspections we've been having I've passed every one so far. Everything has to be spotless and just right. The bed sheets have to be pulled so tight a quarter will bounce on it. I'm doing pretty good so far.

There's a beautiful full moon tonight and not a cloud in the sky. It's almost as light as day. It's also cooled down a little. Now, it's about 75 or 80 degrees. You're up north and wearing coats? Sure wish I were up there.

I have to wash my fatigues and underwear every night because they are soaked with sweat. I have to stand guard duty on Friday night. They are taking us in alphabetical order. We have to know our General Orders (11 of them) before we can walk guard duty and if we don't walk guard we don't go out on passes. I know 'em backwards and sideways but I just can't remember them front wards. I'm only kidding.

So Daddy got my car all fixed now, eh? Tell him to write and tell me what was wrong with it. Did he put new rings and rods bearings in it? Remember to keep the oil and oil filter changed, and then you can drive it till your heart's content. You break it in for me. Maybe I told you already, but I got my camera all right and I'm going to take some pictures the first chance I get. I'm running out of paper and am using a scrap to finish this letter. My next letter will be on new stationery. Tell Carol to be good and not to stay out so late. She should be in bed by 10:30 or 11 at the latest. Tell her to write too, I miss my sister. Be seeing you in November. I won't make it for deer season. I'll be a few weeks late. Till then, love, Son, Bill

—~—

Aug. 14, 1951, Journal Entry:

It got to be 110 today, and that was in the shade! Good God! After marching in this furnace, life for us guys rose from unbearable to horrible. We literally thought we were in hell. Twenty-one men passed out in line from sun stroke and were picked up by the medics. Two of them had gone into shock. Some of us, me included, were too exhausted to take another step, but we did. God knows how we did it. The sign for sun stroke is when you stop sweating. Well, I stopped sweating, but I was still standing and marching. Heard later that one of the guys died. Sure not going to tell my folks about that. Maybe I'll mention about the sun stroke, maybe.

—∾—

August 20, 1951, Sunday 9 p.m.

Dear Mother,

I wrote Carol a letter this morning and thought I'd better drop you a line, too. I got up at 8 o'clock today. On Sundays we don't have to get up early and that's the only day. I went to church and came back and washed my clothes. What I did was get in the shower and wash my fatigues. I'm getting along fine so far. I haven't had any trouble with any of the officers or Sergeants, yet. I'm going to keep it that-a-way, too.

I took some pictures today and will get them Thursday. I'll send some soon as I get them. By the way how much did that telephone call cost? As long as we are talking about money send me $10 the day you get this letter. We don't get paid till the end of the month. Most of my money was spent in getting my uniform fitted and cleaned. After we wear 'em once we have to get them cleaned. There are a million other things we have to buy too. The reason I want the $10 is because they say we are going to get a pass next week. If we pass our inspection. Seriously send me $10 soon by airmail. How much have I got at home, about 30 or 35 dollars, eh? My buddy and I went to two shows this afternoon, one of them was "Forces of Arms" the other was "A Place in the Sun". Both of them were really good shows.

Take care of my car for me. Change the oil at 2,000 miles all the time and try to use the same kind of oil. Daddy sell the '40 Ford yet? Send some pictures of the landscape and you in it, eh? I've got to be in bed in a few minutes so I'll cut this short. I'll write again soon. Miss all of you. Love and kisses. Your loving son, Willie p.s. That Suzie sent me five letters already and I've only sent one. Mary is writing regular too.

—∾—

Aug. 21, 1951

Dear Mother, Dad and all,

I have an hour before we fall out again for a little drill. It rained here a while ago for about an hour, then it quit and the sun is shinning again. I received both of your letters yesterday and was glad to get them. We went on the range again today and saw a fire demonstration on the howitzers. Dad, You probably know what they are don't you?

During the demonstration they showed us step by step what the Fire Direction Center teams has to do with it. They're the brains of the artillery. They sit way back and radio or telephone to the guns in the front line as to where to shoot. The Fire Direction Center guys get the information from men in the front lines. They're the men who look for enemy targets and we (the fire direction center guys) locate the targets on our maps and telephone to the guns and give them the range, deflection, wind, etc. We sit back and figure all this out by different methods much too complicated for me to explain at the present time. Our equipment consists of a slide rule, triangle and maps. I'm trying hard to pass the course because I like it.

We still haven't had a pass as yet. We're supposed to get one this weekend if we pass our inspection. Mom, you break my car in for me so when I get home I'll know it's all right. Drive it as much as you want, I don't care. Tell Daddy the carburetor needs cleaning. Ask him to clean it. How bad is the motor, and the clutch and transmission? I'd like to get home for deer hunting season in November. It's kind of hard to believe my kid sister; Carol is a senior in high school, already, eh? So now she's a big girl! Tell her to study hard in school this year.

Send me something that won't melt. It's hot here, you know. Chocolate chip cookies or something on that order. We have to fall out now, so I'll sign off. Write soon. Miss you lots, Love, Bill

p.s. What's the matter with Daddy's and Carol's arms?

—꩜—

Aug. 23, 1951

Dear Mother and all,

Got your letter today. In mine I'm enclosing pictures. They are pretty nice, eh? I'm just gonna scratch off a little note, the main purpose is to send you these prints. I figure you'd like to see them all about the guys at camp and the scenery!

I don't know what to write about except that I'm getting along pretty good. We went and shot our carbines again today. Naturally, I did well.

Tell me if you plan on coming down all the way or half way or at all to get me on my furlough. If you can't, Curly, that's my buddy, said one of his buddy's may come down here to bring us back. You could come down as far as Nashville, Tenn, or Louisville, Ky. I could get a lift that far.

We still haven't had a pass as yet. They say they'll give us one this weekend if we pass our Saturday morning inspection. I hope so. It's nice to hear that Grams came down to Pontiac, How does she like it? Tell her thanks for the cigs. How's my car running?

My pen is running out of ink. Write soon, Love, Bill

Aug. 26, 1951

Dear Mother and Everybody,

Well today is another Sunday. I just came back from church. We sure have got a nice priest here. Chaplan I should say. When he gives a sermon, it gets right inside you. He's a big Irishman.

It's just as hot here as it's always been. They say it'll be another month before it cools off. I received the ten bucks, but I had a heck of a time getting it cashed. After this send a money order. We didn't get our pass after all. They postponed it until Labor Day. They said we would get one for sure then, So I'll save it for then. The first thing I'll do when I get out on pass is to get a good meal at a restaurant. Then I'm going to find a beach somewhere and go swimming. How is the weather up there now? I suppose it's getting kind of cool for swimming eh? I'd like to be there and enjoy this cool weather. Is my car still running okay?

I'm sitting here in the barracks now and am listening to the radio. They're playing all the top tunes around the country. I heard one good one that you can buy. I think it's really pretty. It's Sammy Kaye's band with "Longing for You." Also the number one song is nice too. Ray Anthony and " I Love the Sunshine of Your Smile." My song, "Come Ona My House," is still up on the top. I told you it was going to be a hit. That Rosemary Clooney is good. Couple of the guys are standing around singing along with Rosemary. Guess they like that tune, too. I joined in too. One of the boys laughed his head off at all of us singing.

My buddy and I went to the show and saw "The Highwayman." That was really good show. It's all based on the poem, which I read in school, "The Highwayman." You probably read it too. There is one thing I wished I had learned more about and that is mathematics. Now, I know what schooling is all about. I know you kept telling me to study, but I wouldn't listen. Everything we are doing here in fire direction pertains to math. We've gone all the way from adding to trigonometry. They also are teaching us stuff in math that I have never heard of, deep stuff. There are a few guys here that never graduated from high school and a lot of them never got past the eighth grade. They really are having trouble.

I've been thinking for quite a while now about going to see the commander to see about volunteering for duty in Alaska. There are quite a few that I've hear of, that are being sent to Alaska. I'd give a million dollars if I could go there. I'm pretty sure Daddy would, too. What do you think of it? Remember now I haven't asked yet so don't tell everyone I'm going to Alaska. It would be better than Korea. I sure hope that "police action" over there stops soon.

In a while they will be coming around to the barracks looking for guys for detail. So I'll hurry it up a bit and get out of here. Confidentially, I don't like detail. None of the boys do. I got the box you sent me. All the chocolate chip cookies were broken. It got here in pretty good shape but there also were quite a few crumbs. Did you get those negatives yet? That other guy is my buddy, Curly. He's really a nice guy. If you come down here to get me on my furlough will it be all right for him to ride back with us, eh? He lives in Rochester. How are Carol and Bob getting along? I heard that Bob Logan and Thelma got married.

I've taken some other pictures of me in my fatigues and rifle. Haven't got 'em developed yet.

Curly and I are going to another show this afternoon. There's nothing else to do around here but go to the show. They do have good shows, though. When I get a pass I'm also going fishing. They've got a few lakes here. Wish I could get home for pheasant season. I may be there for deer season, but I can't say for sure. Write soon. Your ever loving son,

Bill

—~—

Aug. 28, 1951

Dear Mom and All,

I wrote Carol yesterday so I figure I'd better write you, too. We went out and practiced combat tactics today. There were men firing blank bullets at us from the hill and we had to crawl along the ground and hit the hill and capture it. It was kinda fun in a way. There also was an airplane that kept driving and strafing us during our maneuvers. That airplane flew within 50 feet of the ground many times. It was an exciting day.

After thinking about that leadership school for a few days, I've decided that I don't think I want to go. It's not a bad deal but we won't come home for another two months. If I pass I get to go to Officers' Training School and then you have to sign up for an extra two years. What do you and Daddy think? I think I'll just as soon try for an Alaska assignment or stay with my group. Most of the guys that signed up at first for leaderships school decided not to go either.

Well, have to rise at 2:30 a.m. cause I have K.P. I'll send some money when I get it. It'll be about a week before we get paid. Going to bed now.

Write soon, lots of love from your loving son, Bill

—~—

Aug. 29, 1951, Journal Entry:

I was seriously thinking of signing up for the leadership school. My Captain said I was "good officer material." Even the Sergeant said I had "the smarts." I don't know. Dad thinks I should forget it. I knew he'd say that. As for Mom, she goes along with him. What cha gonna do? Dad says, "Just get out as fast as you can, son." Maybe he's right. Do I want to be an officer? More grief? So I get out fast and work on the GM assembly line building trucks all my life, eh? No thank you. I plan to do something with my life, when and if I get out.

—~—

Aug. 30, 1951

Dear Mother, Dad and all,

It's too hot in the barracks to get to sleep so I'll drop you a line while I'm sitting out here on the porch trying to cool off. You go in there and lay down and the sheets are wet from sweat within a half hour. It should start cooling off about the last or middle of September.

There were 21 guys taken to the hospital the other day for sunstroke. We were at the rifle range all day. I felt weak all afternoon and while we were marching back I quit sweating, and got the chills, which is a bad sign. I made it to the barracks all right but I sure was sick. Now, I'm been enduring the heat fairly well. As long as I take my salt pills and drink lots of water, I'm all right. They give us lots of water now when we are out all day.

We had a big inspection today by Major General Tuffner, he's our post commander. He and his party inspected our barracks from top to bottom and inspected our own personal things like footlockers and clothes. Our barracks passed with an excellent rating.

We went out on the range again today and fired rocket launchers. They're about the same as bazookas. We were shooting at tanks 100 yards away and I got a direct hit. I guess I'm just naturally good at stuff like that eh? Ha. Ha.

We're going out tomorrow to fire rifle grenades. Then on Saturday we get a pass. I can hardly wait to get out of this dump. We get paid tomorrow and I'll send some money home. Bank it, eh? Did Daddy sell my '40 Ford? And if he did, for how much?

Say hello to Gram and all for me. Now have to get to bed. Write soon.

Love from your loving son, Willy

—~—

Sept. 2, 1951, Sunday, 1200 hr.

Dear Mom and all,

Well today is another Sunday with nothing to do so I decided to catch up on my letter writing. We had a pass yesterday and a bunch of us guys went to

Fort Smith. Boy it was a waste of time going to that town. It's quite a big town but it sure is "dumpy". There's nothing there except bars, lots of other GIs and some women hanging around the bars. When Curly saw them, he grinned, "See them gals? Wonder what they're doing here?" I knew what they were doing. But I wasn't having any of it, thank you.

We have to stay in camp today then we get another pass Monday. My buddy, Curly, and I are going to a few other towns around here to see what they're like.

In the evening we are going to go roller-skating. I can say one thing though about Fort Smith and that's that I filled myself up on malted milks and hamburgers while I was there. It sure felt good to order whatever I wanted.

Did you all have fun up North? I bet it's pretty cool up there now, eh? Fred finally wrote to me and told me of all the trouble he is having with his car. He says he's going to get another one. If I had some way of getting my car down here, I could keep it in camp. Then during the weekends when I get a pass I could drive it around town. I can't think of anyone who would drive it down here for me though.

I'm listening to the Hit Parade again. They have it on every Sunday from 9:30 to 10:30 p.m. There is a pretty song playing now. It's "Where Is Your House?" Another one that's playing now is "Longing, Longing."

Do you remember Beverly Hall from Lake Orion? I took her out a few times. Well, I'm writing to her.

How's everybody feeling? I'm OK. The Army hasn't got the best of me. I guess I told you that we've been shooting rifle grenades and bazookas and things like that there all week. There is a train load of trainees coming in now. Our barracks is just a block or two from the tracks. I sure do feel for them but I can't reach them. Well I guess I'll sign off now. Write soon.

Your loving sonny boy, Willy.

—∞—

Sept. 4, 1951, Journal Entry:

About my pass to Fort Smith. Well, we all piled in the busses and headed for that town. I'm telling you it was wall-to-wall bars and gals of all kinds. Curly and I went into a bar and had a couple of beers. In no time at all two gals latched onto us. I could tell they had been around the block a couple of times. The gal near Curly gave him a bear hug and a kiss, just like that! The one with me started rubbing my back, soft like. Say, we hadn't seen a woman since Basic began and those feeling were creeping up on me. The next thing I know, this gal was kissing me. And not just a friendly, "pleased to meet you kiss." This was getting too deep for me. I was remembering those films about sexual diseases the Army kept showing us. No way was I going to get the clap or anything else on my first pass. These women were what my Mom called "loose women." Fort Smith was too fast for me. Then why did we stay so long in that bar, eh? I glanced at the clock on the wall and it was almost time for the bus to pick us up. Where did the time go, eh? That gal was almost too much for me. "Not today, honey," I finally said to her, giving her a final kiss.

Then I grabbed Curly. No, I pulled Curly out of that hammer lock he was in with that gal and we ran out of the bar. Went to a soda fountain and had some burgers and malts. What cha gonna do? Next time we're going to find a nice quiet town to go on passes. Once back in camp, Curly and I pulled out a map of Camp Chaffee put a tack on the camp tied a string to it and circled around in a 50 mile radius. Then we marked the towns within that circle that sounded promising.

—w—

(Sept. 5, 1951, Korea, Battle of Bloody Ridge (Hill 983) U.S. 2nd ID and attached units sustain 326 KIA, 2,032 WIA, 414 MIA. Counted enemy dead total 1,389) 15th F.A. Bn. Sets a record by firing 14,425 rounds in 24 hours.)

—w—

Sept. 6, 1951

Dear Mom, All, Ollie and Brownie,

I'll scratch off a few lines just to let you know I received your most welcome letter today. It was the first letter I got in two days. For some reason everyone quit writing for a few days, but I suppose they'll start pouring in about the end of the week.

It seems as thought about everyone writes to you when you first go in and then after a little while they start forgetting about you.

We got out on the range and fired the machines guns. They fire some 10 to 15 rounds a second. It's a 50-caliber machine gun. We have to get up at 4 a.m. in order to have time to march out to the range. The September moon here at camp tonight has a big circle about it so I hope that mean a change in weather. Is sure has been hot down here. They say it's due to cool off soon though. So I hope the moon is telling the truth.

How much did that phone call cost last time? I'd like to call you again sometime soon. It'll be a good to hear your voices again. Name the time and try and get the gang over (Bob and Fred). I'm sending you some more negatives. How did you like the other pictures? These are even better (or worse). We're not drunk in these pictures, we were just fooling around. It sure was nice to get the OCSC (Oakland County Sportsmen's Club) magazine. Nice to see Daddy's pictures and Dick's Station. Getting late so will write more soon. Your loving son, Bill

—m—

Sept. 5, 1951, Journal Entry:

Man, the power in those machine guns, and the kick! Dad would love to handle one, that's for sure. Well, I'm learning all the basics of war, so that's what basic training is all about. They drill it into you, sometimes until you drop, and that's no bull shit. One of my buddies was out of line, smarting off to the Sarge and he landed on the ground doing 50 push ups. I'm not taking any chances. I'll do my push ups when its time, but I'm not asking for extras duty. No thank you.

—m—

Sept. 9, 1951

Dear Mother, Dad and Sister,

Since Wednesday, I received one letter and that was from you. The mail has been slow for some reason. Maybe it'll catch up to me soon, I hope.

Well, I'll come to the point of this letter right now. I'm financially embarrassed. These passes we've been getting have left us kinda broke. Curly and I went to about every town around here and we had to eat out and stuff such as that. You know how easy money slips through my fingers. I also have to buy shoe polish, send my uniform to the cleaners, buy cigs, soap, toothpaste, etc. Curly and I have been to just about every town around here and have decided where to go when we get another pass. We're going to a town called, Paris. The folks are nice and friendly there. Also, there are hardly any other soldiers there.

We get passes every weekend now. I've got to have clean uniforms and stuff like that so if you put two and two together, guess what you get? You're right. Ten dollars! That's my way of adding. I hope that $40 I sent you hasn't all drifted away. If you'll be so kind please send me ten bucks (money order). How much money have I got at home anyway?

We had a three-hour class on psychological warfare. It's all about how the enemy spreads propaganda in their various ways to wreck the soldier's moral. It was interesting. Also we learned how we do it to the enemy. Also learned to keep our yap shut. "Loose talk causes a needless loss. So keep your lips sealed," the captain said.

Boy, you should see how I make a bed now! It's all made just so and you can bounce a quarter on it. They teach us how to fight and also how to become good housekeepers. Everything has to be cleaned each morning including the latrine. I've had my turn at this job twice, now.

The Sergeant says, "All we want to see are ass holes and elbows. And if it doesn't move, pick it up. If it moves, salute it." They've got a million such sayings here. For example—"Stop feeling sorry for yourself. I'm not your mother." Or if you do something wrong the Sarge says—"If that happens again you'll do push ups." Believe me, it's not five or ten, but fifty (50) and your arms feel like they are about to drop off when you reach thirty. We also do double time marching because we are not marching to their satisfaction.

We just finished having a party about an hour ago, GI party that is! We had to scrub our barracks from top to bottom. I also cleaned and straightened my footlocker and shined my shoes and brass. They're so bright; they hurt my eyes when you look at them. Saturday afternoon is my washday; I wash my underwear and socks. I send my fatigues to the laundry (65 cents) and uniforms cost 70 cents to clean. See where my money goes?

Write soon and lots, Love Bill

Sept. 10, 1951, Journal Entry:

Well, Curly and I found a nice quiet town with really friendly people. It's Paris, Arkansas, just a sleepy old town. We found it on our last pass and liked it. So we started hitching a ride there whenever we get a pass. The second pass we got I spotted a theatre in the town square. There was a Clark Gable movie playing so I told Curly, who didn't want to see it, I'd meet him back in a couple of hours. I went up to the ticket booth and saw this cute gal, long brown hair, big brown eyes and a smile that lit up the booth. "What can I do for you soldier?" she asked in an Arkansas drawl. I could tell her just exactly what she could do for me, but hey, I just met this sweet thing, so I said, "One ticket, please, and by the way, what's your name?" She said, "That's 25 cents, and my name is on my tag, see? Anita."

To make a long story short, the Clark Gable movie was exciting and I was into it. I sat in the back row and was making myself comfortable by putting my legs over the seat in front of me. Sort of relaxing, and munching on my pop corn. Not a care in the world.

There weren't too many people in the show. Then out of the blue a bright flash light beamed in my eyes. "Soldier, take your feet off the seat. Were you born in a barn?"

The flash light blinded me for a second, but I sure recognized that Arkansas drawl. It was Anita. "Say, are you an usher too?" I asked. "Yep, sometimes," she said.

Later, after the movie, as I was walking through the lobby, I spotted Anita waving to a friend at the candy counter. "See you tomorrow," she said.

I walked along side her and mentioned that the Clark Gable movie was great. She agreed and said she had seen it a dozen times. We both laughed. That's when I asked her to join me for a malt at the soda fountain next door. She agreed. When we got out of the the-

atre there was Curly leaning on a telephone pole. I gave him the high sign and he scattered. I was alone with Anita. We walked to the soda fountain. What cha gonna do?

—✧—

Sept. 11, 1951

Dear Mom and all,

I guess I've told you we've been shooting machine guns haven't I? I did pretty good on them, but it sure does shake the heck out of me. Today we went out and they taught us how to drive Army trucks. There are quite a few guys here that can't even drive a car. There's a couple that have never sat behind the wheel of a car. It's a lot of fun.

On our passes, we've been going to a town Paris farther away from camp. The people seem a lot friendlier there for some reason.

I suppose it's because there's just a few soldiers that go anyplace else besides Fort Smith, which is swarming with soldiers on passes. I gave you the picture of Fort Smith and the bars in one of my earlier letters. Curly and I are staying clear of that dump. Paris is a much better town.

Did Daddy have a nice time up North? What was wrong with my car? Did Daddy have to put something new in it? I'm sure glad you were lucky enough not to wreck it then. Well, I'll sign off again for now. I'll see you in time for Thanksgiving dinner. Make it a good one. Write soon. Lot of Love, Bill

—✧—

Sept. 12, 1951, Journal Entry:

Most of the time when I go to Paris, I meet Anita in the show. She's usually working and I wait for her in the back row of the theatre. There isn't anyone sitting in the back rows except me. In fact, there aren't too many people in the theatre. So I sit there munching on popcorn until Anita gets off her shift. And then, of course, she joins me. It's make out time! She is a sweet gal. Nineteen years old, about 5' 3" or 5' 4" tall and maybe 112 lbs soaking wet. I'd love to see her in a bathing suit, soon. It's nice, sitting in the back row with my arm around my girl, sneaking a kiss or two, or three. Can't do much in the back row of a theatre, eh? But I sure try. So what was the movie about? Don't know and don't care. I think it was a western. All I care about is that I was with my gal, and I loved it.

—∾—

(Sept 13, Korea: Battle of Heartbreak Ridge (Hill 931) ID seizes Ridge. 597 KIA, 3064 WIA, 84 MIA. The 23rd Regt. alone takes 1,832 casualties)

—∾—

Sept. 15, 1951

Dear Mother, Dad and Sister,

Enclosed you'll find some papers that the Naval Reserve sent to camp. The letters say they want to promote me from Pvt. E-1 to Pvt. E-2 (because of the time I served in the Naval reserves). A big promotion eh? Also got my naval discharge. I wish that said Army instead of Navy.

(Bill joined the Naval Reserves right out of high school. He was drafted into the Army because he missed too many Naval Reserve meetings. He said he was busy dating and "forgot" about the meetings. He also said that while in the Naval Reserves he went on a Naval "tour of duty" on a ship near Florida.)

We could go out on pass today, but it's raining so we're going to stay around camp. Besides, I'm financially embarrassed again. I've got a quarter left so I'm going to the show this afternoon. Last night we went to town (Paris) and went to a dance. We had fun.

They have been teaching us a little about shooting the Howitzers. We will fool around with them most of next week. After that we will study FDC until our basic is over. I think I'll like Fire Direction. We've had some information already and it's nice. That's about all the news around here. I'm feeling O.K. I've had a little cold the last day or two because of the change in the weather. It's dropped down to 70 or 75 degrees and at night it goes down to 60. It will probably warm up again soon, darn it. I really enjoy the cool weather. There's not much to write about lately. But a letter each day is better than none, eh? Write soon. Love and stuff, Bill

p.s. Joke: The old lady was chasing the preacher around the church for quite some time when finally she caught him by the organ (Hammond organ, that is.)

—∞—

Sept. 15, 1951, Journal Entry:

I went to a dance with Anita. So much fun! Square dancing and slow dancing in an old barn outside of Paris, Arkansas! Real country. Curly latched onto a girl, a red head, at the dance and they seem to be doing fine. There was a good three piece band, and the fiddler was right on the ball. I didn't know much about square dancing, but Anita, who is an expert guided me through the steps. She is so sweet, and so tiny, a little doll. Haven't written home about her. Don't want to just yet. I'll just keep Anita all to myself for a while. It feels good holding her in my arms. Soooo gooood! I think the feeling is mutual, cause whenever I see that Arkansas gal, she's all smiles. Yipee!

—∞—

(Sept.15–19, Korea; Assault on Hill 749. U.S. Marines sustain 91 KIA, 714 WIA)

—∞—

Sept. 18, 1951

Dear Mom, Pop and Sis,

I received two of your letters Monday and also letters from Bob, Mary, Loretta and Beverly. I've gotta answer them one at a time as we are pretty busy again this week. The reason for this is because our platoon got more G.I.G's (Army abbreviation for not up to standard) during inspection than the other thirteen platoons. We weren't up to snuff, our lockers and bunks didn't quite pass. So that makes us the detail platoon for the week. But even though I'm in the platoon, I did NOT get any G.I.G.s since I've been here. I feel mighty proud of that, too. I'm writing this letter during our lunchtime.

I joined a bowling team here. We have five out of each platoon that bowl against each other every Monday night. We bowled last night for the first time and I didn't do too good 117, 90 and 107. Most of the other guys didn't do too well either. We didn't get finished until 1 a.m. and we got back about 1:30. We had to get up at 5:30 a.m. That left us about four hours of sleep. You can imagine how tired I am today. It was fun though.

We just got back from eating and we had some kind of stew. It was all right. The majority of the time they feed up very well. I'm surprised at the good food we get. But still I'd sooner be home. Last Sunday I went to the show here and saw "Texas Carnival" with Red Skelton and Esther Williams. You should see it when it comes to Pontiac, because it's really a Jim Dandy show. One of the best I've seen in a long time. You'll laugh yourself silly at Red Skelton.

I have to go to class again this afternoon. We are having classes on FDC. This Saturday we are graduating from our infantry basic. We have to march in a parade. I hope it isn't hot. After Saturday we'll be studying FDC straight through.

That sure is a pretty picture of Brownie. I wish I were home to take him bird hunting. Talking about birds, what kind of bird are you going to have for Thanksgiving? Also how is Ollie, my $5 bird?

Will you send me some more goodies such as you did before? They'd be appreciated. Send my ring (class ring) with them in the same box, eh. Is it O.K. to call you Sunday, Sept. 30 about 7or 8 o'clock? You name the time cause I can call anytime I want on Sunday. Wait a minute, on second thought I won't call then because about four of us guys are going to Nashville, Tenn, that weekend- maybe. We are planning on it. One guys lives near here and he's going to get his car ('48 Chevy). That is if we can get a weekend pass. We're going to try and pull a few strings. I'll call the Sunday before. That will be the 23rd. See if you can get a couple of the boys over and make sure Daddy and Carol are home too. Well, I think I'll sign off for now. This pencil is wearing down to nothing. Do you know of any of my buddies who has to leave for the Army yet? Like Jim or Little George or Fred? Write soon, Lots of love to all. Your loving son, Bill

P.S. I've been thinking of getting my teeth checked.

—

(Sept. 21, 1951, Korea: Operation Summit; A company of 228 Marines is lifted by 12 Sikorskys—in the first helicopter deployment of a combat unit.)

—w—

Sept. 21, 1951

Dear Mom and those others in Pontiac,

Carol wrote today and got a letter from you yesterday, so I figure it's about time for me to write back. Notice the green ink? I've got a pen that writes three different colors. It writes green. It writes red, and it writes blue. Pretty keen, eh? It cost 59 cents. Well, when you get this letter I'll have already talked to you so most of the stuff which I'm about to tell you, you will have heard. Tomorrow we march in the big parade. There are five batteries that are going to march in it. All the big brass will be there to watch it. We marched a practice run Thursday and did good.

For the past week they've been teaching us how to shoot the 105 howitzer. Also the nomenclature of it. Is that how it's spelled? We practiced the various positions that each cannoneer has during setting up the gun and firing it. There are several men to each gun, six cannoneers, a section chief and a gunner. The gunner sites the gun into a certain deflection. The section chief is over all the men. The six cannoneers each have different jobs all the way from setting fuse, cutting the charges, putting projectile and powder case together and loading it. The number one man sets the elevation and fires the piece. It works just about like an assembly line. The FDC (which I'm training for) is the one that sends down all this information. There are six guns in a battery. I could go on for three pages telling about that but then I wouldn't have anything to talk about when I come home.

We're all finished with our infantry basic as of Saturday. Then we have eight weeks of FDC schooling. During the past eight weeks they have taught us a little about everything. They taught us how to read every line and mark on out map and how to read a compass. We've learned how to shoot rifles and big guns. We've learned a little about unarmed defense, like taking a rifle or knife away from a man. But most of all we've been marching and marching. We've gone through the gas chamber and also out on some practice patrols. I didn't think a man could learn so much as I've learned during the past eight weeks.

But there is more to come cause we've got eight weeks of base study ahead of us. The next to the last week of our basic we go on bivouac. It'll be nice and cool and all the snakes will be holed up by then.

I've got to shower and shave soon. I've been showering every night since I've been here. It makes you feel a lot better. I've got to hit the hay cause it's almost eleven o'clock. The weather here has changed considerably during the last few weeks. Nights get down to 65 degrees and days about 85 degrees. It makes it a lot nicer sleeping. I'm going to see an Eddie Arnold show at Fort Smith on Wednesday. He will be there in person. He's one of my favorite country singers. I've seen some real back-in-the hills hillbillies in Fort Smith. Some of then actually look like they haven't been in a city, ever!

What's the matter with Carol? Can't she and Bob keep on friendly terms?

We get passes every week now. We have to be back Saturday night about midnight, but we are off again Sunday at 8:30 a.m. until 11 p.m. Pin Father down. I'd like a letter from him, too. Write soon, love and kisses and stuff, Willie.

—•—

> Sept. 22, 1951, Journal Entry:
>
> *We all went on a picnic. By we, I mean Anita, me, and Curly and his red head. Her name is Judy. The gals brought all the fixin'. Say, I'm starting to sound like an Arkansas guy, what with fixin' and hee haw! We found a nice spot by a lake and later we went swimming. A right perfect day! Anita looks great in a bathing suit. We played around in the water. She'd splash me and I'd splash her. Kids stuff? Sure it is, but who cares? Just playing around. Course Curly and Judy didn't pay any attention to us, they had their own games to play. Yes, I do believe that Anita is a find, and I'm glad I found her.*

—•—

Sept. 29, 1951

Dear Mom, Dad and Sis,

Today we had a full field inspection. That is we had to display all of our field equipment for the officers to look over. We also had another parade today and we're going to have another one next week. So far our Battery came out on top on the parade. In other words we marched the best. In a few more weeks we're going on Bivouac, I dread it. I think we'll have to be out there for two weeks. I'm doing fine in school. We had a screening test the other day and I passed because I'm not "screened out" as they say.

I received those pictures today and I sure did enjoy looking at them. It seemed to take me back home for a little while. What kind of a face is Pat making? He's funny!

Curly and I are going to town now for a little while. He's got a dollar, so that makes each of us 50 cents richer, you know what I mean?

Have you got your route planned yet? How far south are you coming, Nashville, Memphis or what? We are leaving here on November 17. I'm pretty sure about the date. I haven't got much paper so I'll cut this short because I have more letters to answer. We've been busy lately, as usual, but I'll try to write more often. Love to all, Bill

—∞—

Sept. 29, 1951, Journal Entry:

Curly and I hitch-hiked to Paris. An old guy in a beat up truck gave us a lift. He kept asking us if we had steady girls, cause he had two granddaughters. "Mighty fine gals," he said. We told him we were taken and he just laughed. He still took us all the way to Paris. Bless him. We only had a buck between us and our gals were waiting for us.

Well Anita and Judy took us roller skating. Another fun time. I didn't forget how to skate. Did enough of it in Pontiac when I was in high school. Once you learn how to skate, you never forget. Or is that about bike riding? Anyway, my sweet Anita had on a cute red skating skirt. She said she made it. All this beauty, and a seamstress, too. Now can she cook? After skating, the girls had packed a picnic lunch and we went to the park to eat. Later Curly and Judy went their way and Anita and I went our way. Had to get some hugging and kissing time in, right? We found a nice spot under a tree, no one around for miles and spent some time there, doing what comes naturally!

—∾—

(Oct. 3–9,1951, Korea, Operation Commando. To secure Line Jamestown, 3 U.S. Army divisions (1st Cav. 3rd, and 25th) participate. 405 KIA, 2,238 WIA (Vast majority of casualties are taken by the 1st Cav.)

—∾—

Oct. 4, 1951, Thursday, 9 p.m.

Dear Mother, Dad and Sis,

I've been busy, busy since payday getting all my patches sewn on and clothes cleaned and pressed and all stamped and stuff like that there. It seems like every night we've got something different to do. It's never ending around here. We have to clean our rifles every night. That's one thing I never did do at home. If they find any rust or dust on it, inside and out, we get 5 G.I.Gs for it. I haven't gotten any G.I.Gs since I've been here. There's only a couple of us guys in our barracks that haven't any. Going through basic without any G.I.Gs is rare around here. I hope I can make it.

I'm sitting outside on the porch now in my shorts. It's still hot here. It's hot enough so that I sweat during the day. There is a little breeze here now, that makes it nice sitting out here. During the day it gets about 90 degrees.

They're starting to give us speed marching now for an hour in the morning. It's mostly double time with our rifles. Other mornings we have our regular physical training, the Army dozen. Just to give you an idea of what we do each day, I'll review a day's schedule for you all. We rise at 5:45 a.m. and wash, dress, fix beds and sweep floors. At 6:30 a.m. we fall out for reveille. At 7 a.m. we have chow and at 8 a.m. we fall out again for our daily schedule. Our schedule now consists of FDC most of the time. Every once in a while they throw a few hours of communications at us. Our lunchtime is from noon to 1 p.m. then at 5 p.m. we get back and stand retreat. From 5:30 till 6:30 we eat. Then from then on it's supposed to be our time but most generally they find something for us to do.

The 14th and 15th week we go on bivouac. We start on the 22nd of October, I believe. I think they will tell us this weekend. A buddy and I were sitting out here talking for two hours about hunting experiences. He comes from Minn. We exchanged many a tall tale and had a very enjoyable time. He's a great hunter, too. Well, it's about 11 p.m. now so I'd better sign off again. Are you coming to get me and how far, and who's coming? You have my car all shined up for me, eh? How's Sis making out on her new job? A working gal now. Write soon, Love, Bill

—m—

Oct. 7, 1951, Journal Entry:

Well, I really blew it this time. I was supposed to meet Anita after she finished working at the show Saturday (yesterday) and—but I'd better start from the beginning. Got a pass but Curly didn't, so I decided to hitch-hike to Paris solo. Got a couple of rides and was in Paris early. It would be about four hours before Anita got off work, so I decided to go to the local bar and have a beer, you know just to kill some time. Some shift must have changed because the bar was full of men, laughing and drinking. When they saw me it was as if I was a movie star or something. Everyone wanted to buy the soldier a drink. So who was I to say no? After about five or six rounds I began to feel dizzy. See, I was so anxious to see Anita, I skipped lunch and raced out of camp to hitch a ride. Booze on an empty stomach is bad news.

Finally, I begged off. I was getting sick. I could feel my breakfast coming up and I didn't want to throw up in the bar, not in front of my new friends. So I ran out the door and ran all the way to the theatre. I didn't want to miss Anita, no way. I stood in front of the theatre, hugging the telephone pole and just as Anita stepped out of the door, I dashed for her, my arms outstretched, and threw up on her. (It must have been my breakfast, cause I saw bits of egg and bacon on her dress.) My, oh my, was she a sight! Mad as hell, she was, too. But finally she calmed down when she saw the shape I was in, and walked me back into the theatre.

We washed ourselves down best we could in the ladies' rest room. I mean tried to clean the vomit from her clothes and mine. But we didn't smell like roses. After that, she looked me straight in the eyes and said, "Billy, I think you'd better go back to camp. You are in no shape to go out on a date." And so I hitched a ride back to camp. The farmer that picked me up, took one smell of me and made me sit in the back of the truck with a couple of pigs he was taking to market.

—~—

Oct, 8 1951

Dear Mother and you all,

It's our lunchtime now. I've got a few minutes before I fall back out again. This morning we had two hours of FDC and the last two hours truck driving. We had to drive a course through the woods and up and down hill and dale and around trees. There were some guys driving who ran into trees. I have to laugh when I watch some of those guys drive. I made it through all right.

This afternoon we go back for five hours of FDC. We're learning how to plot our batteries (guns) and targets. Then determine from the chart the range, light deflection and stuff like that there. It's not too hard, once you get on to it. Here they teach us in a day what we would learn in four weeks of regular school. It's so fast, that half of the time I'm lost, like the rest of the guys. But I'm doing pretty good.

It's now Monday evening and I'm getting ready to go bowling. So far my average is 126. The first weeks it was 102 but it's rising slowly. Soon I'll be bowling 300—every game.

I hear Fred's got his physical exam coming up (finally). Have any of my other buddies gotten their papers yet? I hope none of them leave before I get home. There probably aren't many left anyway.

Today being Monday, I didn't get a single letter from anybody and I've answered all that I've gotten. Maybe tomorrow they will pour in. I hope. Boy I'm really going to miss the approaching pheasant season. Has Daddy had my dog, Brownie, out yet? How is he working? Pretty good probably, eh? Tell Daddy to save a few rabbits and deer for me. When I come home, I want to have something to shoot at, too. I've been thinking that maybe when I come home next month, I'd go out hunt deer in the lower.

You'll have my car cleaned up for me when I get home won't you? My pretty white sidewalls probably don't look so pretty now. How is it running? Is the new transmission and clutch all right? I hope it isn't like the other transmission.

How does Carol like her job? I noticed some of those pictures of Daddy in the OCSC magazine that he has been wearing my shirts again, eh! Just don't get them all worn out before I get home. And have then cleaned for me, too. Also my pants, jacket, and overcoat. Have you planned your route for coming down here yet? Write soon to let me know, and who is coming down. Curly is coming with me so have room for him.

We're going on bivouac the 22nd of October for ten days, so I don't' know how many letters I'll be able to write. Maybe I'll call some time in November or should I? Write soon. I have to hurry now. See you all either November 17th or 18th.

Love to all from your loving son, Willie

—w—

(October 13–22 , 1951, Korea: Operation Nomad and Polar. To secure Line later designated Missouri U.S. 265 KIA, 1.487 WIA)

—w—

October 17, 1951

Dear Mom, Dad and Sis,

I thought I'd better write right away and give you the dope. We had a troop information class yesterday and they told us this. Our furlough starts November 19 (Monday). They didn't tell us what our orders were or where we're going but we have ten days furlough time plus three days traveling time if we go overseas. But if we stay in the states we just get ten days, which includes the traveling pay. Otherwise we have to pay our own way. The six cents a mile is figured from Camp Chaffee to California and not from Chaffee, to home, to California. That will mean that we will get about $100 or more. Probably more.

There are some guys here trying to get 25 of us to charter a plane to Detroit. If they can get enough guys I think that Curly and I will go. It will take about seven hours to get home and cost about $50. If we get that traveling pay it will be worth it, I think. Don't you? And Curly and I are thinking about these guys who want people to drive out and make some money on the way. It would be better then spend a lot of money on a trip. But if we don't come up to Michigan on the chartered plane are you going to come down here and get me? I thought maybe by now you'd have a route planned. Just tell me how far you are coming, cause I don't know how far you want to drive. We'll be leaving here at 9 a.m. on a Monday, so if you do come you should plan on being at your destination by Monday night, whether it be Nashville, Louisville or Memphis or where ever, and you can wait for me at the Greyhound bus station. Or else leave word; saying you'll be right back, or whatever. I will figure out the time it takes me to get to a certain town (whichever one you choose). Then you be there about that time to take your little boy home.

Well, I guess that's about it with the exception of whether you want me to call a week or so before I leave on furlough. The reason might be to straighten something out that you don't understand about picking me up. You know what I mean?

I haven't much news to send forth. I'm going to school every day and am doing pretty good. We go on Bivouac the 22nd of October. Will be back about the 2nd of November. If I can't write while I'm there, I'll take notes so when I come back I can write and tell you what we did. Remember that I can receive mail.

Enclosed you will find $20. I didn't have a chance to get to the post office but I hope it reaches you all right. It's about all I have saved after I got my winter uniform all fixed up and many other things.

Well that's about all the time I have now. Lots of love and kisses to you all. Your loving son, William

---

October 19, 1951

Dear Mother, Father and Sis,

Got your letter a few days ago saying you wouldn't be able to come down here so I figured I'd better find another way to get home. There are some guys here taking names to charter a plane to Detroit and Curly and I signed up. We haven't got all the dope yet but so far I know it'll cost about $50 to Detroit. Therefore you can come to Detroit on a Monday evening. I'll let you know later what time our plane gets into Detroit. It won't take any longer than six hours to get there. So that means I'll be home for supper on Monday night, the 19th eh?

Our captain is making all the arrangement for us. Later he'll have all the schedules and prices on the bulletin board. So far what do you think of the idea? If I can manage to squeeze two weekends at home I'd like to spend four days up north, But if I can't I don't know whether I'd like to make a trip up north. They say we only get ten days, plus three days of traveling time. So if I went up north, I'd get to see Dad for a while since he won't get home from hunting until November 28 and I leave on the 29th, 30th, or 31st, one of those days. So I'd like to see him a couple of days.

It will cost $70 to come home by train and it will take three times as long. Also when I go to the West Coast it will take three or four days by train. So the captain has made arrangements for us to take a plane in Detroit after our furlough and fly us to the West Coast. So from Arkansas to Michigan, and Michigan to the West Coast it will cost me $130. We will get that much money for traveling time, so what can I lose? Besides there is a lot to gain in time saved. From Detroit to the West Coast it will cost $90 by train. So in the long run the plane will be cheaper by $30 or $40. I'll give you more details when I get them.

It's a hard trying to decide, cause I'd like to stay home, but also I'd like to see Dad up north. But if I only have a few days I don't think I'll go north. I'd like to see Dad, though. I can't explain the confusion my mind is in, trying to decide what to do.

In closing I have to say that the weather is nice. It's in the 80s. I don't believe they have a winter in Arkansas. Everything else here is fine. We can't send letters out when we're on bivouac so I'll write to you about our brief 10-day stay at bivouac.

Just heard we might get 15 days plus traveling time. If so will definitely go up north. I'll call you after I get my orders about the furlough time. It will be in the mail about the 16th, I guess. Bye for now.

Lots of Love, Bill

—ɯ—

Oct. 20, 1951, Journal Entry:

I'm all mixed up. Love does that to a guy. I'm leaving Arkansas soon, and I don't want to leave Anita. The other day was our last time together for a long while. I talked her into getting a hotel room so we could be together. Hey, there's only one hotel in town, and she was worried that folks would gossip. So, I told her, I'd get the room, and somehow she could sneak in, when no one was looking in the lobby. Well, she managed to sneak in and when she got into the room, I was all over her. Could not keep my hands off her. I could tell this was her first time and she was very nervous. Hell, I was nervous too. It felt so good to hold her, touch her, kiss her. We did spent a lot of time talking. No kidding. We were planning our future. We spent a lot of time kissing and touching. But in the end, we didn't do it. I didn't want it this way, in this flea bag hotel. I wanted it special for us. She agreed. We made a promise to be faithful to each other. We also promised to write as often as we could. This is serious stuff, eh? I still haven't told my folks much about Anita. They are always saying "no romantic ties" till I get home. So, I'd better not bust their illusion bubble. I did hint to Carol about Anita.

—w—

(October 23, 1951, Korea: BIGGEST AIR BATTLE OF WAR: "Black Tuesday" over Namsi. By weeks end, 3 B-29s are shot down and 4 crash-land, 55 KIA/MIA)

—w—

Oct 22, 1951

Dear Mother, Father and Sister,

Well we're on our first day of bivouac now and it's starting off rough. It hasn't rained but twice since I've been here but it sure is coming down now. I don't know, but every time we have to stay out it rains. I hate it!

We started out at 7 a.m. with an eighty-pound pack. And I'm not exaggerating a bit. We carry everything from our house to a toothbrush. When we got out a ways it was about 1 p.m. and we pitched our tent and started digging a foxhole. But we'll be on the move again, on Wednesday and Saturday. I suppose that is just to get us used to setting up and tearing down, over and over.

I received two of your letters today and the pheasant feather. I sure hope Daddy gets a couple more pheasants. That will be a delicious feast. The smell of that feather make me homesick.

As for that chartered plane to Detroit, it's all set. And I've decided to buy a ticket that takes me from here to Detroit and then picks me up and takes me to my next destination. That way I'll have my full furlough time plus a few extra days that they give us for traveling time. The trip will cost $150, and we'll get $140 traveling pay. That's the best rate I'll find anywhere and the least traveling time. I don't know what my orders are, but if I take the plane home it will be only six hours. So, I'll be eating pheasant at 7 p.m. Monday night. So you'd better be in Detroit on time. I'll let you know for sure about the exact time, when I find out.

Tell Carol not to spend all her money. Save a little for me, eh? Is she going North with us? I'm running out of paper, so I'll say so long for now. Love, Bill

On Bivouac

October 28, 1951, Sunday

Dear Mom, Daddy and Carol,

We even have a day off out here on bivouac so it'll give me time to write a letter or two. It turned out to be a pretty nice day today compared with the last week we spent out here. The sun is shinning and the sky has nary a cloud. But last week it rained constantly. We spent a miserable week. I'll back track a week and fill you in on the high spots.

Sunday we packed our gear. This consisted of a cargo pack that held our sleeping bag and blanket. Also in our field pack we had to carry all our other necessary things. Then, neatly rolled over the top of these two packs we carried our tent and two additional blankets. The whole thing weighed 75 pounds.

Monday morning at 7 a.m. we set up our tents, etc. and did a few necessary bivouac things. On Tuesday we started early on our journey with our 75-lb. burden and staggered six miles to our first bivouac area. Here we unloaded and set up our tents again and got ready for a three-day stay. The first day we had an all-day problem that lasted from 7 a.m. until midnight.

Wednesday we had a class in FDC in the morning and later we moved tents. Thursday and Friday we did a bit of everything including moving tents. Did I mention that all this time it rained? I swear we pitched our tents right smack in the middle of the Arkansas River. We hiked in a foot of mud. Enough mud to build a house. Rain came down in sheets and buckets, etc.

Saturday, yes we packed again and moved our tents to a different area. We will stay here for the remainder of the time. The good Captain let us go in Saturday night to take a shower. It sure did feel good after a week of mud and mud. Next week we go through the infiltration course and shoot the howitzers and stuff like that.

Only twenty more days until I get to Pontiac. I'll know the score when I get back to camp. Then I'll write you and tell you when the charter plane lands in Detroit. I think it will be Monday night about five or six o'clock. Drive my car down. Has Daddy fixed the brakes? I've decided not to go up North to see Daddy and go deer hunting. Of course, I don't care if I go up North or not. I'll see Daddy when he gets down to Pontiac. I figure I'll get 14 days furlough. Besides there are so many things to do at home and not enough time.

Well, it's getting dark out here now so I'll sign off for now. I'll write you when I get back to camp. Tell Carol to have my gas tank full for me. (ha. ha.) Write soon,

Lots of love and kisses, Bill

—∾—

(Korea: November 12–30, 1951: OFFENSIVE OPERATIONS CEASE. 8th Army begins "active defense" in a rare pitched air battle, 31 F-86s take on 50 MIGs escorting 28 enemy bombers: 12 enemy planes are shot down.)

—∾—

Nov. 15, 1951, Thursday

Dear Mom, Dad and Sister,

We're taking tests and processing out this week. By the time you get this I'll have already called you so don't forget to call the airport and find out when the chartered plane from Camp Chaffee, Ark. is due to arrive. The captain can't tell us for sure. So you'll have to call. I do know that we leave here the 19th of November (Monday) at 1:30 in the afternoon. The plane is scheduled to land in Michigan around 7 p.m. but that's just a guess.

Love, Bill

p.s. It's been pretty warm here—85 degrees.

—ɱ—

Nov. 21, 1951

PFC. Sal Amati, of Chicago, Illinois, was discharged after serving in Korea. Before his discharge, the American soldiers were retreating. "It was a see-saw situation, retreat and advance," said Amati. "I remember when a bridge from Seoul to Yung Dung Po blew up just as we crossed it. It seems a Communist, who had posed as a South Korean had wired it and after we crossed, a large group of South Koreans were crossing and that's when it exploded. A terrible sight. We barely escaped."

Amati said, "When we were in the Army they warned us that only half of us would come back from Korea. I was one of the lucky ones."

—ɱ—

Seattle, Washington
December 13, 1951

Dear Mom, Dad and Sis,

I'd better drop you another letter before I leave the States (sounds funny, eh!). We're shipping out this coming Saturday, which is two days from now. As I told you it's supposed to be Yokohama, Japan. We haven't done a thing here but get our clothes and field equipment and a few shots. We sleep and eat and go out on passes to the big town of Seattle. It really is big, too, bigger than Detroit. I get lost every time I go there. I bet I've seen about 100 shows already. Another soldier and I went to a dance last night. I danced a few slow dances with the local gals.

Yesterday we moved down to what used to be a naval base. The Army took it over for embarkation purposes. I can't think of anything else to write about. The temperature is around 65 degrees. Surprising nice weather. The only place I saw any snow was in the Dakotas. When I come back (and I hope soon) I'm going hunting in the Rockies. They sure are nice.

I sure hated to leave the old homestead. Oh, by the way—Question—Is Carol still going with Bob or not? (ha ha) Write soon, Love and kisses, miss ya all, Willie

—ɱ—

Dec 13, 1951, Journal Entry:

I can't understand Carol and Bob. They're always battling it out and making up. Is that love? She's only 18 and she can't make up her mind. I think she's too young. Better she concentrate on school and see what happens when she graduates. Can't understand Mom and Dad putting up with her antics, and yet here I am a man and they are trying to tell me what to do with my love life. I saw the look on their faces when I told them about Anita. Why do they want me to wait until I get home to make up my mind? Beats me. I think I've already made up my mind. Maybe they think I won't come home? No, don't go there. I am coming home!

—ᴍ—

On the ship, U.S.S. General R.L. Howze
December 24, 1951—Christmas Eve, 8 p.m.

Dear Mom, Dad and Carol,

Well this Christmas Eve surely isn't being spent the same as previous ones. All night long, I've been thinking of you all decorating the tree and remembering how Carol and I used to fight and argue over who was going to put the ornaments on the tree. How many did you break this year before you got them all on the tree? I guess this is a "blue Christmas" for a lot of people though, eh!

The weather we're having sure doesn't help any with the holiday. It's been really warm for the past few days. About 80 degrees. Summer weather. Although when we started out it was quite cool. All day Sunday we sat idle in the bay while they had to fix the motor. Something broke down during the night. Some say it was a burnt out main bearing and some say it was a universal joint. What it really was I don't suppose we'll ever find out. Then the next day we ran into a storm that lasted for about three days. I suppose it was the same storm that reached the states a few days later. I heard it was pretty bad. We get a newspaper here once a day that gives us the highlights of the news.

There wasn't a man on this ship that wasn't sick during that storm. It just took a few days and most everybody is feeling as good as new again. We all got our sea legs. I can walk a pretty straight line now even though the ship does rock quite a bit. During that storm the waves were coming over the bow of the ship. I bet that the waves were 20 feet high. It was really rough. There's one thing for sure though and that's that I'd like to be out of this tub. The voyage isn't too pleasant. We're below deck most of the time. And when we do get on deck all we see is water, water and more water.

We're supposed to cross the International Date Line Tuesday or Wednesday. Some of the sick guys will miss it. As of tonight we are seven hours behind Pontiac, Michigan, time. Santa has made his trip there already. We've still got a few hours. All of us are supposed to get a Christmas present of some sort tomorrow. I'll tell you what I got when I write some more tomorrow.

Even though I won't be able to mail this letter until I get to Japan, it's nice to write to you anyway. It sorta makes me feel less lonely. I sure do miss being home, especially tonight and tomorrow. To tell the truth, I've been home a hundred times already (in my mind) since I've been on this tub. We're supposed to have a real good dinner for us tomorrow. Turkey, with all the trimmings, dressing, yum, yum! I guess I'll quit for today and write more tomorrow. I'm going to see about having some money taken out of my check each month to send home. About 50 bucks so I'll have a nice goose egg when I get home.

Miss you all, Love, Bill

On the ship, U.S.S. General R.L. Howze
Christmas Day, 1951

Dear Mom, Dad and Carol,

We rose in time to eat breakfast at 8 a.m. They started serving dinner at 2 p.m. and our department didn't eat until 6:30 p.m. The meal was good and instead of naming the stuff we had to eat I'll just send along a little menu that they gave us. We had everything that was on it. When I got away from the table I was just about as full as I was after my Thanksgiving dinner. They let us have as much as we wanted.

The weather started getting a little bad again Christmas night and it made it sorta rough on a few guys. The ship started tossing and bobbing about like I mentioned before, but not quite so bad this time. A lot of the guys got rid of their Christmas supper. The rough water didn't bother me any this time. I didn't get sick.

All of us got Christmas boxes. Most of them were donated by the Red Cross from different parts of the country. I was talking to a lot of guys and I found out many of the boxes came from Michigan. I saw that one box had come from an individual from Iron Mountain, Michigan. I don't remember what the name was. My box came from the Red Cross in North Dakota. I got about the same as the others, a checkers game, deck of cards, candy, gum, a 25-cent pocket size book, and stationery. It was nice. While I think of it, you can send me every now and then, or more often, a box of cookies, candy, gum, etc. You don't have to wait for me to ask for them. Is Carol still going with Bob?

We are supposed to dock in Yokohama the 31st at noon. Boy, I can hardly wait to get off this tub. I haven't felt right since I've been on it. I'll sign off for now. Lots of Love, Bill

—~—

Dec. 25, 1951, Journal Entry:

What hell we experienced on this tub. We were below deck all the time. The storm swept the decks and if we even tried to get on deck, we'd have been thrown into the Pacific. And as for below deck, it smelled like vomit, piss and farts. We would wash the best we could, but some guys were either throwing up or farting. There was no exception, every last one of us did it. Not the comforts of home. More like a pig pen. I did my share of up-chucking but finally got my "sea legs" as the old timers said. Thank God we are in Japan!

Babysan with bouquet welcomes soldiers
JAPAN

JAPAN

Japan

The Army frowned on soldiers fraternizing with Japanese women. They did not take disciplinary action as they did during World War II, but they still discouraged GIs from becoming too friendly with Japanese women. When Bill was in Japan on R & R or during training he wrote about how attractive the Japanese women were especially when they wore their beautiful multicolored satin and silk kimonos.

Since basic training at Camp Chaffee, the soldiers were repeatedly shown films about the sexual diseases that were transmitted by prostitutes who were found near Army camps. That's one of the reasons Bill did not want to go to Fort Smith when he got another pass. "Too many loose women," he would say. "And I didn't want to get the clap, or whatever they were dishing out."

And of course, Bill's parents in many subtle ways reminded him that Japanese and Korean women were off limits. When Bill was home on furlough before he left for overseas, he had a few talks with his parents about women. He mentioned his Arkansas gal, Anita, and that he had been seeing her every time he got a pass. When he left Camp Chaffee, they had an "understanding" between them. His parents tried to discourage that relationship. They wanted their son to come home to Michigan "without any ties" and when the time came for marriage, he was to find a girl from Pontiac.

Japan, Asia

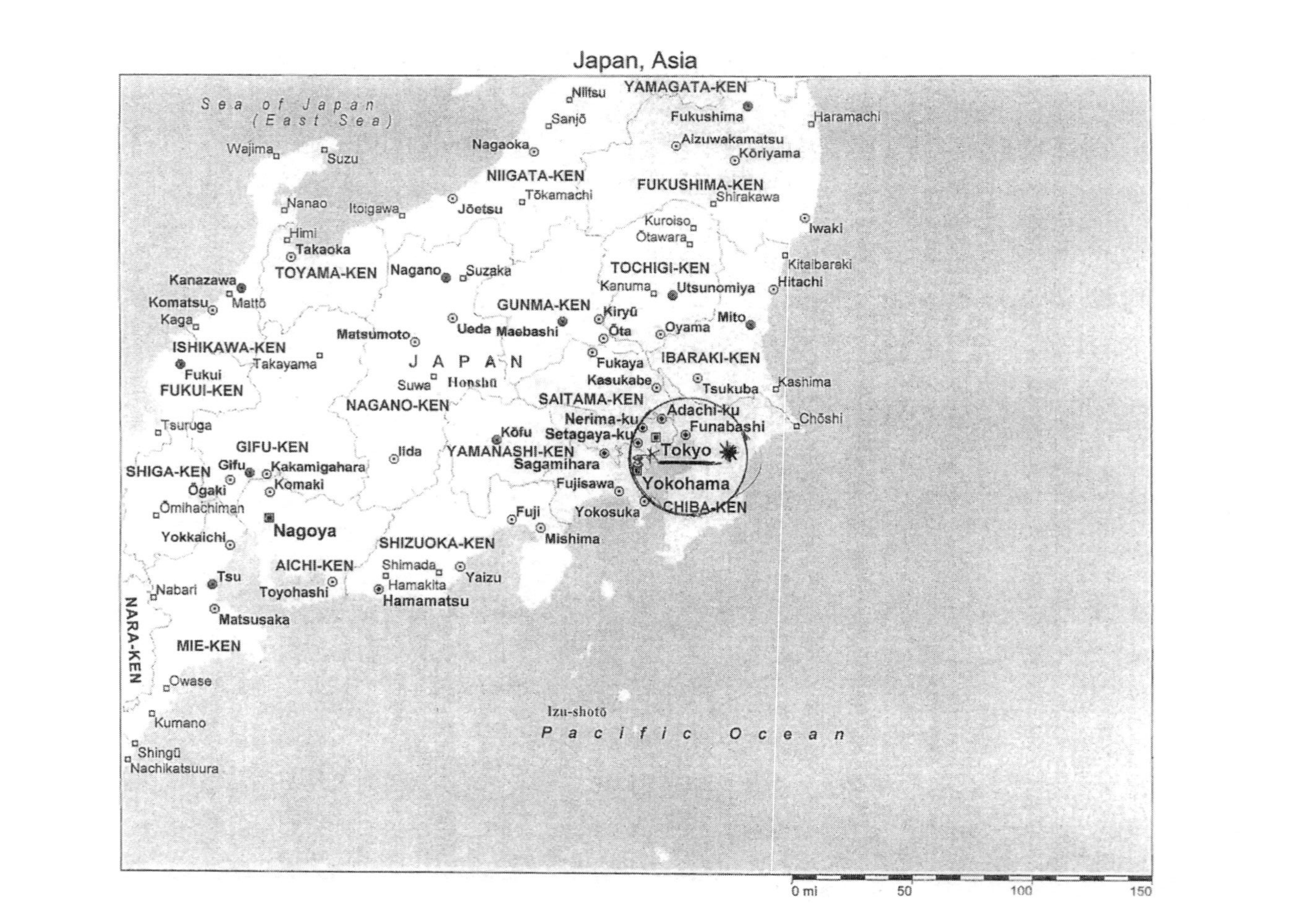
Sea of Japan
(East Sea)
Niitsu
YAMAGATA-KEN
Sanjō
Fukushima
Haramachi
Wajima
Suzu
Nagaoka
Aizuwakamatsu
Kōriyama
NIIGATA-KEN
FUKUSHIMA-KEN
Nanao
Itoigawa
Jōetsu
Tōkamachi
Shirakawa
Kuroiso
Ōtawara
Iwaki
Himi
Takaoka
TOYAMA-KEN
Nagano
Suzaka
TOCHIGI-KEN
Kitaibaraki
Kanazawa
Kanuma
Utsunomiya
Hitachi
Komatsu
Mattō
GUNMA-KEN
Kiryū
Kaga
Ueda
Maebashi
Ōta
Oyama
Mito
Matsumoto
ISHIKAWA-KEN
Takayama
IBARAKI-KEN
Fukui
JAPAN
Fukaya
FUKUI-KEN
Suwa
Honshū
Kasukabe
Tsukuba
Kashima
NAGANO-KEN
SAITAMA-KEN
Adachi-ku
Tsuruga
Nerima-ku
Funabashi
Chōshi
Kōfu
Setagaya-ku
GIFU-KEN
Iida
YAMANASHI-KEN
Tokyo
SHIGA-KEN
Gifu
Kakamigahara
Sagamihara
Ōgaki
Komaki
Fujisawa
Yokohama
Ōmihachiman
Fuji
Yokosuka
CHIBA-KEN
Nagoya
Yokkaichi
SHIZUOKA-KEN
Mishima
AICHI-KEN
Shimada
Yaizu
Tsu
Hamakita
Nabari
Toyohashi
Hamamatsu
Matsusaka
NARA-KEN
MIE-KEN
Owase
Izu-shotō
Kumano
Pacific Ocean
Shingū
Nachikatsuura
0 mi
50
100
150

Bill in rickshaw

Bill in front of Japanese temple

Japanese temple

Japan

United States Army stationery
January 2, 1952, Wednesday

Dear Mammy, Pappy, Carol, Ollie and Brownie,

I arrived safe and sound Tuesday morning in the land of the Orient. We never saw land till the time we left Seattle and arrived in Japan. Although we got here in the morning, it took me till 2 p.m. before I got off the ship. We went by the numbers, which we got back at Ft. Lawton, and mine was near the end. When I left the ship with my barracks' bag, we boarded a train that took us to Camp Drake, which is twenty some miles from Yokohama. Before we got off the ship we stood on deck and watched them unload. They've got Japanese working on the docks. They sure are strong people. One of many interesting things about them is their height. The average height of the Japanese man is 5′2″. I only saw one who was almost as tall as me, 5′10″. Their features are also alike. When we came out on the train we traveled through a lot of railroad stations and electric trolley stops. The tracks run through the main part of every town.

It's really fascinating the way the women dress. I only saw a couple of men in their native Oriental costumes, but a large majority of the women still dress in kimonos. Colorful? You bet! They look like beautiful walking Christmas trees! Really beautiful! I also saw a few streets of some towns as we passed by and they sure are lit up with neon signs. If it weren't for that you'd think you were in another century, 100 years ago. The people seem real friendly, too. Although a lot of Japan is Americanized it's still pretty Oriental. About their houses, there is just one floor, and most of them just have two rooms. There is a big fire pot in the middle for heat. The people don't sit on chairs, they sit on the floor, and they always take their sandals off before going into the house. They wear wooden sandals with small black nails on the bottom. They are about two inches thick. A lot of them wear socks that look like my loafer white socks.

I'm aiming to get one of those robes, or whatever they call them for you. Pictures you see of the women in their robes aren't exaggerated a bit. They really look nice.

We're processing here for about three days then we ship out for somewhere. They have issued us winter clothes and rifles. I'm going to mechanics school in Tokyo for the next seven weeks, starting Monday, Jan. 15. I got out of the Korea deal so far. I know you all will feel as good as I do about it. Did you get the slippers? They gave us this gold emblem United States Army stationery on the ship. Give everyone at home my address. I'll write more later, Love, Bill

—∾—

January 2, 1952, Journal Entry:

Boy, those Japanese women are beautiful! All decked out in their silk kimonos, they look like Christmas trees! After 15 days at sea, I can't keep my eyes off of them, they're like a breath of fresh air, graceful and gorgeous. Hands off, the Army says. Anyway, I'm taken. There is an Arkansas gal that has my heart. I can look can't I, eh?

—∾—

(January, 1952 in KOREA: At one point, a war within a war broke out in the U.N. Prison Camps. The flashpoint was KOJE ISLAND, a fortress off the southern tip of Korea where 100,000 Communists were held in compounds ringed with barbed wire. Some prisoners had renounced Communism and intended to defect after the war, while the Communists organized ranks to keep comrades in line. In this nasty place, gangs of prisoners could sentence a man to death. During a rock fight in late December, 1951, 14 prisoners died and 24 were wounded.)

—∾—

Jan. 7, 1952, Tokyo, Japan, 5:30 Monday

Dear Mom, Dad, and Carol,

Well, today we started school. It turned out to be a pretty interesting day. I'll go further into it later in the letter. I'll begin about when I left off before, if I can remember.

When we reached Camp Drake we started processing right away. We got there at 8:00 in the evening and started right then and got all our records checked and straightened out. We finally hit the sack at midnight. Then before you could say Jack Robinson, they had us up again at 3 a.m. We went to the theater and saw some movies about the hazards of Korea, such as the cold weather, frostbite, and trench foot. It made me sick watching the film on trench foot. Then some guys came out on the stage and showed us six different coats and sweaters and three pairs of pants you have to wear all at the same time in order to keep warm. When you get them all on, topped with your white snow parka, you look just like Frosty the snowman. Ho. Ho. Ho.

The stuff will really keep a person warm during the cold months I hear from men of experience. Then we went over and drew all kinds of clothes and field equipment and a MI rifle. After carrying our burden back to the barracks our day was finally over.

The next day we were up at 3 a.m. again and cleaned the barracks. Then we fell outside after morning chow to receive our orders. They called out a slew of men for shipment to Korea. All this time I had my fingers crossed. Lucky my name wasn't called. Then they called off the men for local shipment. Here I uncrossed my fingers. It worked. I was chosen to go to school in Tokyo. When I left, Curly still hadn't got his orders, so I don't know as yet whether he is going to Korea or going to stay here in Japan. I hope he stays here. Korea ain't fer da boids.

At the present time, 5:45 Monday night, I am listening to the radio. It's the Bob Crosby program, which is normally on at 9:30 Sunday night back in the States. Seems funny to set our watch ahead all the way out here and still we are about a day behind. We crossed the date line but I still don't see how it's possible, but we did.

Well, anyway we were chosen to go to this school and we arrived here in Tokyo, Saturday afternoon. On Saturday we didn't do much. Sunday morning I got up at 10 a.m. and went to church. They've got a pretty nice church here also a nice priest. Sunday all day long it snowed. Then today the sun was shining and there is mud and slush everywhere. Just about like the winters in good old Pontiac. Sunday I wandered all over the post trying to find something to do. I finally came back and wrote some letters and went to bed. Oh yeah, there's another Bill, he's my buddy and came from Camp Chaffee with me.

Now for Monday. We ate breakfast and went to school. By the way, the chow here is excellent! Likewise the mess hall. Well, anyway our first day they took us all around the whole camp on a tour. The camp is where we learn, and repair everything concerning track vehicles. They take for instance a battered old tank that's been in combat and repair it from the bottom up.

We went through all these little shops and watched them working. Incidentally these mechanics are mostly Japanese. The soldiers just supervise. After our schooling is finished, we will most likely be sent somewhere else. They took a tank out on the track and demonstrated for us. Some of these newer model tanks are equipped with a new type of transmission called the "cross-drive transmission" With this they can spin around on a dime at a complete stand still. I saw the transmission and it's twice as big as a Cadillac motor and has a million and one gears in it. They can almost make those tanks talk. It's a wonder the way these Japanese build up these battered up old tanks. Then send them back to Korea when they finish them.

Well, that's about enough for today, I guess. Write soon. Love, Bill

p.s. I've got a different address.

—w—

> January 8, 1952, Journal Entry:
>
> *What a screw up! I spent most of my basic learning all about FDC and when they ship me to Japan, they put me in mechanics school. That's the Army for you. Whatcha gonna do? Also learning hand-to-hand combat. Going for the eyes, breaking thumbs, kicking the groin area (ouch), and surprise them by spitting on them in the face.*

—w—

Jan. 12, 1952, Saturday, Tokyo, Japan,

Dear Dad,

Seeing I received a letter from Dad today and no one else, I will write only to him. But, of course, the rest of you may read it if you want. First of all, I want to thank Pop for writing the letter. It's the first letter I got from home all week long. I got one other letter Thursday from Anita, in Arkansas. It was 28 days getting here. It had four different addresses on it and fifteen postmarks. But it's better late than never, especially over here. It sure makes a person, meaning me, feel a heck of a lot better when he gets a letter.

Well, we've completed one week of school so far. They gave us three examinations already. The first one I got 80% on the second and third I got 100% on 'em. Pretty good! During the last week we tore down and put back together two motors. The Continental and the Studebaker. The Continental goes in the M46 tank and the Studebaker goes in the Weasel I guess. I do know about the M46 tank though. You should see what a monster of a power plant that is. It's not too awfully complicated though. It's an air-cooled engine that develops 800 h.p. (V 12). It's got separate barrels for each of the pistons and valves. It's also got two carburetors, four magneto's, they look like distributors to me, two overhead cones and two spark plugs for each cylinder. They're going to teach us everything here from changing a plug to driving them. All in seven weeks, too.

A little about the weather now. It snowed once here and rained twice. The remainder of the time it's been quite nice. It gets up to about 50 degrees sometimes but the nights get pretty cold, 20 degrees the lowest. I haven't had a chance to get to Tokyo yet for the simple reason that I am financially embarrassed. We haven't had a payday since October. That's two months and they said not to expect any mulla until the last of January. I got a fly $50 in Seattle but I say it really did fly. Did I tell you that the Army is sending home $50 a month for me, starting next month. I made out an allotment.

Curly and I finally got broke up at Camp Drake. I sure hated for him to go oneway and me another after all this time. He felt the same way, too. I haven't heard where he went. He's going to write me soon as he can. I only knew one guy when I came here to Tokyo but it sure didn't take long to get acquainted here. We've got a bunch of nice guys here.

There's one thing I'd like to make clear right now and that's these Japanese women over here. You've probably heard about 'em. They're not good medicine. The Capitan preached to us about 'em for quite a spell and he told off many a soldier, if you know what I mean. I'm staying strictly away from them. I'm coming home the way I came here. The women are not the least bit backward. I just thought I'd mention it.

Other than that, the place is pretty nice. I remember when mother told me about her young days when she had to wear those long black socks. Well, now I know what they look like. Most of the girls here wear those silly looking black long socks. This place is still living back in the days of the 1920s. You have to laugh at some of these things they wear. Another strange thing is their fertilizer. They got what we call "honey buckets" that they carry around in a cart most generally pulled by an ox. They go from place to place collecting this and then dry it and use it for fertilizer. During the summer they say you can hardly stand the smell on account of the heat. I've seen quite a few "honey buckets" along the road already.

The transportation here is mostly bicycles. They can carry some of the biggest loads on them that I have ever seen.

We've got a company commander here that has strictly "hen house" ways. By that I mean chicken shit. We've scrubbed the barracks four times last week and waxed the floors two times. I've heard of GI-ing the place once a week but not four times. And I never heard of waxing the floors. We can barely stand up around here anymore. Our bunks and footlockers have to be exactly in line or we have to GI and wax the floors again. They have Japanese around here that'll do everything for us, even make our beds, but the C.O. won't let us students hire them. They'll do it for $10 a month. They work very cheap here. That about 3600 yen. We can ride the train the full length of Japan for $50 in U.S. money. Cheap! Write soon, Lots of Love, I miss you all, Bill

—ɯ—

Jan. 16, 1952, Tokyo

Dear Mom, Dad and Carol,

Well I'll scratch off a few lines to you to let you know I received your most welcome letter. It took ten days to get here but better late than never. Letters sure are slow getting here. You should be getting mine by now.

I got a letter from Curly today and he is going to a specialist school too. He didn't say what it was, but by the sound of his letter I guess he is doing pretty fair for himself. I sure miss him. As for myself, I'm doing good too. School is coming along fine. The weather is going right along. It's been like spring the last few days, but you can never trust it for long. It might snow tomorrow, you can never tell about it. I've not been feeling on top of the world the last few days or I should say four or five. A cold hit me and hit hard. I could hardly talk and my nose and eyes would water. Also I had a splitting headache. I feel a lot better now though.

As you probably guessed by now, we got paid. Boy that money sure found home about the right time cause I was badly bent. One more buck and I was broke. I made about $139 rocks. I kept the 39 and am sending home a money order for $100 which you'll find enclosed. Write soon and tell me if you got it.

I was hoping those pictures you took at Christmas would have turned out. I surely wanted some of them. They would have been nice to see.

I hope Father made out on his rabbit trip. He should have gotten at least one during the two days. Or did he come back "smelleth of strong drink and the truth not in him."

New Year's Eve we spent on the ship. We didn't get off till the morning of the 2nd (a hilarious holiday). The lights are going out in a few minutes so I'll sign off for now. Write soon and often. Lots of love. Bill.

—※—

(In KOREA: Prison conditions; An irony emerged over prison camp conditions. The United Nations camps were open to inspection by the International Red Cross. But the communists refused outside inspectors while charges surfaced about torture, beatings, brainwashing, filthy conditions and ill treatment at the communists' camps.)

—※—

January 21, 1952, Tokyo, Japan

Dear Mom, Dad and Carol, Before I forget to say anything about it the next time you send a box please enclose a couple bottles of "antihistamine". They work pretty good on me when I have a cold and a cold over here is common, especially for me. I get some lulus, when I get a cold here.

I just got a letter from Grama today. She answered my letter right away, too. Grama didn't quite understand about the clothes the people wear over here, I guess. She thinks they dress like they do on Samoa, hardly no clothes on at all. Where does she think I am? In Hawaii with the Hula gals? She mentioned a couple of songs that Arthur Godfrey sings. I think the titles are pretty cute, "I warm so easy so dance me loose," and "It shines so bright the moon." Have you heard them? We get a few radio programs here but mostly they play old songs—like "Peg of My Heart".

I went to Tokyo on Sunday and found it to be pretty big and interesting, but I don't know where to start telling you about it. I wrote Anita (in Arkansas) about it and it took me an hour and I still didn't say much. It's hard to explain. Next Sunday I'm going to take some pictures of Tokyo.

Did you get the $100? When next payday comes I'm going to Tokyo again and buy some stuff to send home. Stuff like a robe or pajamas, or dishes. They really have some beautiful chinaware here. And at a reasonable price, too. It's surprising how low prices are here. I bought a cigarette lighter and they wanted 350 yen, which is less than $1. I bargained down to 250 yen, cause that is what they expect us to do. Never pay the first price. This lighter is like a man's Ronson but I think it's better. It's got engraved leather on it, in color. Really pretty.

So far in school, we tore down and put together every kind of motor that goes in these tanks (radials, V-type and in line). The best one yet though is the V-12 Continental. Next week we start on trouble shooting then we will learn about overhauling a tank and then how to drive them.

I'll close now . I sure miss you all, Love, Bill

—ˢᵃ—

Jan. 22, 1952, Tokyo

Dear Mom, Dad and Carol,

Everything over here is going all right with me. The weather has been real nice and all conditions are ideal. School is coming along good, too. I'm studying all about tanks. Every kind of tank and everything about them. Also other track vehicles. Today we saw a lot of movies on the different types of transmissions they use. They sure are complicated, but not too hard for me. Here, back in the company they are getting pretty strict. There is a rumor that they are cleaning out a field and using it for a drill field for us. Guess they think we need some practice in marching or something. They belly ache about everything we do around here. They will almost court marital a person for having a wrinkle in his bed. You've got to be told when to breathe around here.

But I've haven't any gripes coming because I got out of going to Korea, anyway. I'll take their crap for sixteen more months if I can stay in Tokyo, Japan, instead of Korea.

Too bad the Japanese slippers didn't fit, but I guess they'll make a better decoration than something to wear. By the way, I'd like to pick up a little something for you but I can't think of anything. Have you any suggestions?

The country (Japan) is very densely populated so there isn't much room for scenery. Mt. Fuji is about 60 or 70 miles from here. That's about the prettiest site I've seen yet. That's the one with the big active volcano. I hope it doesn't start bubbling or shooting fireballs while I'm around. Earthquakes are common here but I haven't heard one yet.

Like I told Carol when I sent home some pictures, they show the landscape better than I can describe it.

The weather is warm. And the grass is brown. I'm getting sleepy. So I better lay down.

Keep the letters coming,

Love, Bill

January 23, 1952, Journal Entry:

They're strict about every screwy thing. It's a pain in the ass. More drill and marching than in Basic. This Army is pissing me off, but whatcha gonna do? The mechanics' school is not bad. I'm learning a lot of new things. Those Japanese mechanics are like robots. Been at it for some time, so they know what they're doing. Of course, I can't understand a word they say. They are always smiling and bowing. Can't believe we were fighting them not too long ago, and now we're friends, and fighting the North Koreans and Joe Chink.

Japan, January 22, 1952

Dear Carol,

I done received your letter today. Yes, my "beautiful sister" you'd better start writing a little more often. One letter in two months since I've been gone isn't exactly an avid writer. You better stop your running around for a night once in a while and write to your brother. By the sound of your letter you sure must have Bob turning in circles. He's running all over creation trying to keep track of you.

I saw some beautiful kimonos down in Tokyo last Sunday. When payday comes around I'll buy one for you. They sure are beautiful. Would you like pajamas or one of those kimonos, and what size do you wear? Write soon to tell me. I'd like to send mother something too. They have some beautiful china dishes and tea sets and stuff like that. Or shall I send her a robe too?

So you're going to be a senior pretty soon, eh? My little sister is sure growing up fast. I'll miss being there to watch you graduate.

I wouldn't advise you to come to Japan or anything like that. It's not that nice. Hawaii would be better. I would have liked to see it myself. That's a pretty neat picture of you. I was trying to think of whether that was one that I picked or not out of the proofs you sent me.

Write real soon. I enjoy hearing from you all. Lots of love, from your dear brother, Bill

—~—

January 26, 1952, Tokyo, Japan

Dear Mom, Dad and Carol,

Well here goes, I'll start answering a few of your questions now.

Buddies—They are from all over the United States. From California to New York and Louisiana to Minnesota. I sure was surprised to find a Finlander here too. He's all Fin (not half, like me). He lives somewhere around Marquette, Michigan. His name is Aino Alto (real Fin, eh?)

There are a lot of guys from Minnesota, Wisconsin, also got some Texans and some "hillbillies". I didn't exactly know what people were talking about when they said that they heard a lot of Bull Shit—. But I sure do know it now. They can sling it faster than I can understand it. I've only got one buddy that came here with me from Camp Chaffee. That's Bill Barrett from Grand Rapids, Minn.

About that two bucks that Grama sent. Tell her not to send me money. Candy is good or something like that.

I don't hear too much new music. Mostly tunes that used to be popular in the States.

I sure hope that Daddy makes General Foreman. It'll be a good deal.

Every morning we get our milk and cereal, fruit juice and eggs. They have substantial meals here. Write, write. Lots of love, Bill

—~—

January 27, 1952, Tokyo, Japan

Dear Mom, Dad and Carol,

I think I told you that I was going to go to Tokyo today, but the Captain didn't like the way out barracks looked for the Saturday morning inspection so he pulled all our passes.

I was going to buy some things down there today with what little money I have. But I guess I'll have to wait till next weekend and I hope we get paid through the end of the month so I can send home some stuff. I haven't received that box you sent me as of yet but I imagine I'll get it sometime this week.

We're going out tomorrow and learn how to drive the M-46 tanks. They are big bruisers. I've driven the M-5 tractors and the weasels already but those M-46 are going to be something else. Then the rest of the week and part of the next week we're going to be trouble shooting. They mess 'em up for us so there is something wrong and we're supposed to find out what it is and repair them. Next week I'm going on sick call to have my teeth checked and fixed, if needed.

That's about it for now. I'll write later. Write soon, Lots of love, Bill

—~—

Feb. 1, 1952

Dear Mom, Dad and Sister,

They had us marching after hours a couple of nights. The reason is beyond me. I guess they thought we weren't good and rough enough soldiers to suit them or something. At the end, we were teetering on the brink of exhaustion. On occasion this madness seeps down to us, so whatcha-gonna-do?

Monday and Tuesday we went out and learned how to drive tanks. They're real easy to drive. I had quite a bit of fun during my turn. The rest of the week we've been troubleshooting and learning the essentials in tuning up the motors. That's about all that school consists of at the moment.

The weather here sure has changed in the past few days, too. Three days ago the sun was shining and it was really warm and now it's been snowing and raining. I barely know what to expect next. I was planning on going out Sunday and take some pictures but if it doesn't clear up, I'm sunk. I was going to buy some things to send home too but with the paycheck I got it's not possible. They proudly handed me a $10 bill for my month's wages. I believe my allotment started this month, but I'm going to Finances to see what happened to the rest of my pay.

I still haven't got that box yet. It's about time for lights out so I'll close for now and write more later. There was one letter for me from mail call. It was from my little "hillbilly gal," Anita, from Arkansas. She's keeping quite a correspondence up. Guess she loves me. Write soon, love, Bill

—~—

Feb. 2, 1952, Journal Entry:

This marching at night is full of crap. And with a full pack! What gives? I sure don't know. They don't think we do enough marching during the day, and double time at that? Well, at least it's not like Camp Chaffee where we were marching in 110 degrees guys passing out from heat stroke. Thank God for small favors.

—~—

2/3/52 6:00 p.m., Saturday, Japan

Dear Mom, Dad and Carol,

I've been spending the last few days in the barracks. Today has been a pretty miserable one. It's been half raining and half snowing and half something else all day long. I had planned on taking pictures of some scenic spots in the land of the Rising Sun but the weather got the best of my plans.

I wrote a letter to Anita last night and finished it about eight. As I said before she is a loyal letter writer, and her letters are interesting. I guess I'm stuck on that Arkansas gal.

I hit the sack right after that and never set my feet on the floor till 9:30 a.m. Sunday morning. I wished that I could have stayed in bed longer but I had to get up and shower and get ready for church. I'm going to communion again, after a long time. I'm getting strict with myself. After church I ate a fairly good dinner (steak). Then a few of us guys took in an afternoon movie, "Painting the Clouds with Sunshine." I thought it was pretty good.

My financial state is "bent" but I'll be darned if I'll ask for money. It's home now and that's where it will stay. Good idea, eh?

School, as I've said is fine. I learn a little more each day. Pretty soon I'll be an expert tank mechanic, as they say, "We learn to fix about everything on these tanks except the radio.

I wish I were home instead of here. I'm getting that trout fishing fever and I sure get lonesome as all get out. I'll write soon. Love Bill

---

Feb 5, 1952, Tuesday, 6 p.m.

Dear Mom, Dad and Sis,

I received a letter from my little pal "Anita." I guess I should break down and write her a letter cause I can't get her out of my mind. Maybe it's love. Oh well, that's life, I guess.

Well, I think that should answer all your questions, that is if you can read my writing. Also I hope you can follow the pages okay. When you write letters why don't you fill up all the pages. I got a big fat letter today (I thought) but there were three blank pages in it. No gripes though, it was a letter and that's what I like to receive.

School is the same. Thursday we are going down for blood donations. The ones who give a pint of blood get the rest of the afternoon off. We start at 1 p.m. so naturally I can't pass up an afternoon off. I've never given blood. Well anyway, I'm going to give it.

About the guys here. Louisiana is a good chap, also Irish. We sit on the beds here lots of time and just shoot the breeze, really Bull Shit back and forth and before long we're rollin on the floor. That kid (Irish) really strikes me funny. I get a kick out of him. Bill is a heck of a guy too, he also is from Minn. And so is Irish.

Before I get out of here, I'm going to try to take some interesting pictures of Japan. Some guys who were out already, say it is really beautiful country. I don't doubt their word. But I want to see it for myself.

I've got a book on Japan and I'll write you a little about it. "The home islands add up to about the size of Montana. Yet there are 82,000,000 people living here." Less than 20 percent of the land is suitable for farming (and they use every bit of it). The rest is mountains and woods. The people are very artistic. Life here moves at a much slower pace than ours. They have two major religions—Buddhism and Shinto. That's all I know.

Oh yes, the Japanese are very polite. They bow to everyone. They will do about anything for you. The Japanese who live in cities dress mostly in western clothes. While the rest dress in those long flowing loose fittings garments. Very colorful, too. The houses consist of one room made of flimsy paper or wood. Their main foods are fish, rice and vegetables. Downtown you see the fish laying right out in the open with flies all over them and people come and buy it. Some of that stuff I would be afraid to feed a dying fox.

One thing I want to see is Mt. Fuji. It's on the Island of Honshu. The so called sacred mountain is 12,365 feet high and its snow capped peak is visible from Tokyo which is 100 miles away. It's really beautiful. The Japanese have a proverb. "He who climbs Mt. Fuji in a life time is a fool, he who climbs it twice is a bigger fool."

There are quite a few earthquakes and typhoons here. Although I have not as yet witnessed one, I'd like to in a way, to have a grand stand seat during an earthquake! Seems like it would be an exciting experience. (but I don't want the earthquake to be too big!)

Tokyo's weather may be compared to what the climate would be in Washington D.C. so I can't prove it for a fact. I took that weather statement out of the book, so I trust it's right.

One thing I've been told that struck me as quite interesting was that the Japanese used the knife, fork and spoon even before we were a country, but they discarded them for the chopsticks. They really know how to use the chop stick, so what can I say?

The three most important things that impress you about the people are: 1. They are small in stature, 2. There are so many of them, and 3. They are formal and polite. In spite of their size, they are very tough and hardy people. I see them carry such heavy loads on their backs. Even a horse or mule couldn't carry what they lug around. And you should see some of the things they pull on their bicycles. It's unbelievable. They pull big old trailers full of stuff.

Their houses have no foundations, they sit directly on the ground. Something like a small beat-up barn. They sleep, eat and entertain on the floor of the house. They have straw mats that serve the purpose of rugs. About the only type of furniture they have is a table about a foot high. They sleep on thin mattresses.

Sure miss ya all. Write soon. And again I say I'm getting your letters O.K. Lots of love, Bill

(In late 1951, General Dwight D. Eisenhower, a military hero, started dropping hints that he was available to run for president. In 1952 the Republicans nominated General Eisenhower as their candidate for president. Politicians of both parties had tempted him with the presidential nomination since his triumph in the European campaign, and Truman often said in 1948 that he would step aside for the general.

Also about that time, Corp. Max Guernsey, Army 31st Regiment, of St. Joseph, Michigan, was wounded in the head in Chosen. "When we were in Inchon, fighting, the Chinese came over the mountains like flies," Guernsey said. He sustained a head injury (life threatening) which required a plate put in his head. The operation was done at Percy Jones Army Hospital. To this day, Guernsey can not remember how he was injured. He carries a duplicate plastic plate with holes in it and a tag explaining that the holes in the plate are for the skin to grow around it. He earned the Purple Heart.)

Feb.7 1952, 8 p.m.

Dear Mom, Dad and Sis,

During the day, the highlight was the blood donations drive. I gave a pint. It was voluntary. I didn't like it, and I was kinda scared. The only reason I did it was because we got the whole afternoon off and I came back and fell into a dead slumber. I slept from two to six. I've been sleepy and weak all afternoon. I guess I'll pep up in a day or two.

We're not doing too much in school, now. Just standing around or listening to lectures on the nomenclature of the tanks. We're going to graduate from here the 23rd of this month. We get diplomas and I'll send it home to you. Did I leave my Basic Training diploma home?

I'm trying to listen to the radio and write this letter at the same time and I'm finding it quite difficult. It's a murder mystery and ever time somebody gets killed a cat meows. Fantastic and stupid!

I went to the show last night and saw "The Day the Earth Stood Still." I sure like that kind of picture. It was very interesting. I'd give my right arm if I could be a scientist. Experimenting with atomic power and rockets in space and other planets is exactly what I'd love to do. It always happens that you finally know what you want to do and it is too late.

The water on the post is contaminated for some reason so they got purified water in bags for us to drink. It sure tastes funny.

The weekend is coming up soon and once again I'm going to try and take some pictures. I haven't got much money so when I get back in Japan again in four months I'll have it and then I can buy some stuff and send home. Till then you have to be content with the slippers. Lights out. Will write again later. Lots of love, Bill.

—~—

Feb. 9, 1952

Dear Mom, Dad and Sis,

Yesterday I received the box you sent the 19th of January. Everything was in good order. Half of the guys in the barracks helped me eat the cookies and the other things. Strange how a box from home attracts everyone within a radius of a mile. I still got the candy though. Another thing that you could send me is the Pontiac newspaper. You could send me one a week. Quite a few guys are getting their hometown newspaper and it seems pretty good to read old state-side news.

The weather here turned for the worst the last couple of days. The night before last it snowed four inches but already it's all melted. It's turned warm again and I hear it's due to rain Sunday. We just had mail call and I received one letter from Mama and one from my dear little sister. I will write her a letter tonight.

You're doing more walking and working at home than I am over here. Walking clear to Packers! I haven't walked more than a block at the most since I got back from Furlough, with the exception of going to town and I ride the train or trolley, which ever. The school we go to is about a mile or so from here and we ride trucks to and fro.

I got my income tax return but they made a mistake on it and I'll have to get it fixed before I send it home. They say I made $900 when I really only made about $400. a slight mistake of five digits.

Well that's about it for now. Write soon. Lots of love, Bill

—∾—

February 9, 1952

Dear Sis,

I received your letter today and I'll bet you thought you were getting a big fat one in return, hey? I fooled ya though. I meant to enclose this in mother's letter but I forgot. So much for that.

Well I'm glad things have been 'hep' for you back there. I sure am learning a lot about motors. But then sometimes I get a pass. That's when I get out into town (Tokyo) and I can't understand or read a darn thing, it's all Japanese to me. I just stand around with a stupid look on my face and try to figure it out. The first time I went to Tokyo I got lost and asked some Japanese which way to go. I should have known better because the only thing I could get out of them was #%$ (#%*)&. Don't ask me what it means. I finally asked another soldier. My poor back is just about broken from bowing to these Japanese around here. Instead of just a plain "Hello" they bow and bow and bow, and naturally I have to be polite and bow back.

I'm at the present time broke so I'll just have to wait before I get back to Tokyo (about four months) so I can buy some stuff to send home, that is if I go to Korea. Personally between you and me, I hope I don't.

So you're stealing my ole line now eh? "Just riding around" in the car. Now you know just how easy it is to 'just ride around' till umpteen o'clock. Only I did it over and over not just once in a while. Furthermore, I don't want my sister on the black list or whatever you call it. So watch yourself when you're riding around. Take it slow. What the heck am I blabbering about anyway? I forget that I'm talking to a Senior in high school!

Besides saluting and taking pictures I've been a—er. I———hmmmm—nothing I guess.

You sure are giving Bob the run around. He must be nuts or he likes you a lot. You ought to read some of the letters I've been getting from Anita (my Arkansas gal). She wants to marry me now. She said she'd wait for me to come back. I said it may be ten years and she said she'd wait anyhow. Love, ah love! How long will that last? I expect the end any time. But I may be surprised.

Your loving brother, Bill

p.s. you asked me to write
and so it'll be in two
golden words: Remember Me.

Feb. 13, 1952

Dear Mom, Dad and Sis,

With what little "muxit" I had left I bought a little jewelry box and a lighter which I'll try to send.

We're not doing too much in school now. We're timing all these tanks and tractors. After we pull out and replace the distributors and time it, we get to take a spin. I've driven everything from a weasel to a M46. We do all our work outside the building and it's really nice working outside. It gets to about 50 degrees during the day most of the time. We go to school from 8 a.m. to 5 p.m. with an hour off for dinner. The food isn't bad at all. It won't be long before we'll be moving on. On the 21st to be precise. I guess maybe I told you that already.

This is a mighty short letter but I can't think of anything to write about so I'll sign off. Love to hear from you all soon. Lots of love, Bill.

—≈—

Feb. 15, 1952

Dear Mom, Dad and Sis,

What a miserable day today has been. It started off good then it started to rain and now it's changed. More than likely it will be hot tomorrow. We are getting ready for the final tests. Then we receive our diplomas.

By the way did you ever receive that International Date Line certificate I sent a while back? You didn't say. In a while now we are going to start G.I'ing (cleaning) the place. I'll probably finish this letter afterwards.

We had a fire drill here the other night and we had to have all the beds and lockers out of here in double time. Boy, did we scramble!. In other words, we were falling all over each other in the rush. What a job. This barn we're living in will burn to a crisp inside of fifteen minutes or less. A fire trap!

I dreamed last night I was on the Au Sable fishing and hunting. I was wishing I never woke up. I've been reading too much Out Door Life and stuff like that there. Well, I finished G.I'ing but no mail call yet. So I'll sign and seal this letter now. Write soon. A letter is always welcome. Love and that there stuff, Bill.

—≈—

Feb. 16, 1952, Saturday night

Dear Mom, Dad and Sis,

Well here it is Saturday night again and I'm not even going out. The main reason is that I haven't any money left. If you keep taking my money out of the bank, I won't have any left at home either. The car is costing me more money just sitting there than if it were on the go, I think.

I'm listening to Moon Mullans sing, "Sail my ship alone." That music really sounds good here, good hillbilly stuff.

Even though the insurance company where Carol works moved close, I bet she's still late. My buddy here, Allan Barron, said he didn't get up enough nerve to write Carol. Guess he's scared of being refused. He's really a nice guy but pretty bashful.

We had one final test today. Really a rough one and I got 84 percent. There were only a few guys that went over 90. I figured I did okay. The next week we just have to clean tanks inside and out. We're now officially finished with the course. Enclosed are some pictures. Write more later. Write soon. Lots of love, Bill.

—w—

Feb. 18, 1952, 7 p.m.

Dear Mom, Dad and Carol,

I got a letter from Curly today. He sends his mail free now. In other words he's in Korea in the 101st Signal Battalion. He says it's not too bad there. He is forty miles below the lines or two miles north of Chechon. I'm going to look him up if I'm anywhere near him. Send me Jack Salter's address just in case I get as far as Seoul. Well, in three more days we "Hank Snow" this place. We're going to pull a "clevus" on this coming Thursday at 2:00. Thursday morning we graduate and receive our diplomas. We have to dress up in "Class A" uniforms and go before the General to receive them.

In school now, we're cleaning the tanks up for the next cycle that comes in. We're washing them down with good old soap and water. Some of the ones we've finished look like they just got off the assembly line. Nice and shiny. We also saw some movies on the electric brakes and air brakes. Quite fascinating the way they work. We were going to see them the first thing in the morning but the projector went to pots. Then they brought us back in the classroom just before noon to attempt to show us the film again, but this time the sound failed. By now everyone was thoroughly disgusted and so they continued working on it all afternoon and finally got it working about 4 p.m. We were cleaning tanks in the meantime. We finally saw it with only one interruption—the film broke. Finally we saw the whole film Sunday, after dinner I went down to the Service Club with another guy and stayed there all day. That was the cheapest way I could spend the day. Less than no money to my name. I have a U.S. dollar, but I'm saving it to spend stateside. We played ping-pong, I won two games and my buddy won one. What an exciting day!

Later on in the evening the Japanese put on a demonstration for us. They had six Japanese in the center of the floor showing us guys Judo. They showed us step by step how it's done, then they do it to show the effectiveness of it. They got some treacherous holds and flips. I'd hate for one of them to get mad at me. They are as fast as lightning. The Japanese specialize in Judo. They are little but tough. After that we went home and to bed. Well that's about it for this time. Lots of love, Bill.

—~—

(During the first few months of 1952, the Truman administrations expectation was that the North Korean government, for some undefined reason, would accept any negotiated settlement the UN might achieve. President Truman indeed wished a settlement before his term of office ended for the Korean War was not an event he wished to hand over to Eisenhower.)

—~—

Feb. 20, 1952

Dear Mom, Dad and Carol,

I received that income tax form. They made a mistake in my earnings and when I went to see about it they told me to hold it until I go to my next base. I may be a little late in getting it back but I don't care. I wait for my money-let them wait for their money.

All told I got eight letters and three Valentines, and a very nice one from my Arkansas gal. Guess, she really loves me!

The weather here has been snowing lately. It's started to melt already though. They've changed our schedule for leaving here to Camp Drake three times already. As far as I know now we are leaving Friday morning. I wish this thing would hurry and get over with so I could get home.

Write soon, Love Bill.

—~—

Japan—Army Service Club Stationery
Feb. 21, 1952—To Whom it May Concern:

"Amo/ida natsu/kashi Ano Tenu Waltz Kayaimo nagarekuru Wakafrita Ana/koyo imawa iguko Yobedo Kairanal, Sariuishi Yume. Ano Tenn. Waltz Eatsukashi ainouta omakagi shinonek. Kajoimo Utan Ano Tenn Waltz."

That is the Tennessee Waltz in Japanese! This is the way the words sound. They write in sign language but you couldn't read that, so here's the next best thing.

We just got back from getting our diplomas and we have the rest of the afternoon off so I'll drop you a short note for the purpose of enclosing the diploma I received. The highest the Army gives in grades now is Satisfactory, so we all got it, of course. There should have been an exception and given me an Excellent, eh? We had to listen to a few B.S. speeches before we got our diplomas. Anyway, I made it. Now I'm on the down hill skid. Just run out of things to say. I'm feeling good, the weather is nice. I'll write again when I reach my destination. It'll be three, four or five days. Write soon, Love, Bill

Army Service Club Stationery

February 25, 1952

Dear Mom, Dad and Carol,

Well I'm on my way now. We left school Friday morning at ten in trucks and went as far as Camp Drake. The trucks and us departed from Camp Drake and within an hour we were on a train heading for Sasebo, a southern part of Japan, somewhere. The train ride was bad, all 32 hours of it, although we did see some beautiful country along the way. The next evening we were in Sasebo and we took a little boat ride to Camp Mower (about twenty minutes). Here we stayed until three today.

During our brief stay they loaded us down with clothes of all sizes, shapes and forms. I'm still having one heck of a time handling it all. But it's good and all that stuff. We slept in 15 tents. They had bunks and a stove in each one, so that was pretty nice of them, considering there's a war on.

Along about Monday afternoon they trucked us to the ocean side. Then we boarded a Japanese luxury liner and proceeded to our destination. At the present we are now on our way. There are no such things as beds in Japan, also on the ship. We slept on the floor on straw mats. Real George, eh? We ate C rations. I can't name a good point about the whole flawed situation. I'll finish this when I reach Puchon.

I'm in Puchon now waiting orders. It wasn't a bad trip now that I think back. I got a bit seasick though. We are now sleeping in Quonset huts. Not bad, and not good. I'll mail this when I get my new address.

Lots of Love, Bill.

KOREA

March, 1952–February 24, 1953

Korea

March, 1952–February 24, 1953

About killing. Bill learned to kill long distance as a member of the Fire Direction Center (FDC) in Korea. First he received instructions at Camp Chaffee, Arkansas, and later further training in Korea. As a member of the team, quartered in a tent, Bill and the other men on the team, plotted on charts, where the enemy was, after receiving information from ground runners and helicopters flying overhead enemy territory.

Then the information was relayed by telephone to the front line where U.S. and United Nations soldiers fired on the enemy with their Howitzers. The Fire Direction Center was usually a few miles behind the front line. Bill's FDC team was located on the western side of Korea, north of Seoul and close to Panmunjom, where the peace talks were being held.

Frustration? You bet! Bill was a member of a long distance firing team and the front line infantrymen resented FDC guys because they "didn't take the heat". Maybe that's why Bill welcomed driving his Captain to the front line because then he could observe the damage the FDC did, and also see first hand the "Hell" fields of Korea.

Fear? Damn right! "Bloody fear," as Bill would reminisce. Fear that years later gave him nightmares and caused him to wake up many a night in a cold sweat (now known as post traumatic stress disorder.).

—ɯ—

Kyonggi-do, South Korea, Asia

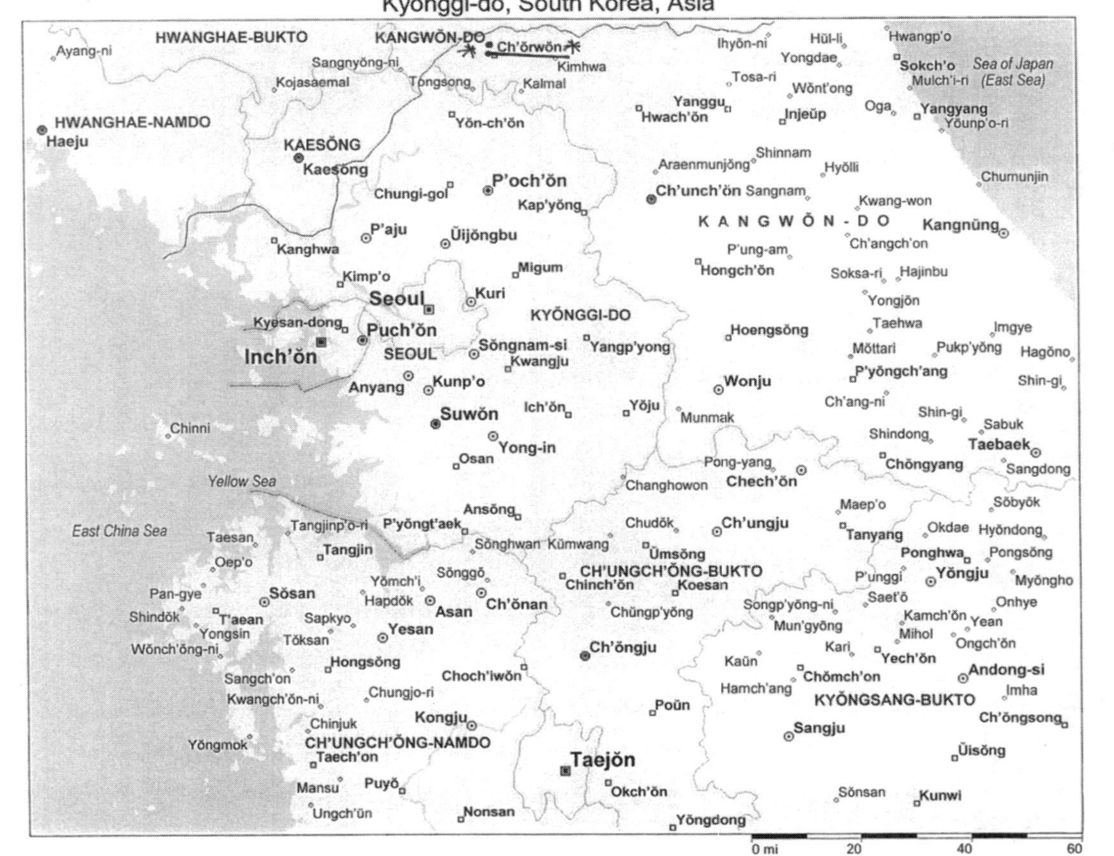

Bill (left) at Fire Direction Center

FDC men at work

Pete Ginapolis at FDC

Soldier on phone at FDC

Prison compound

General Ridgeway cutting bridge tape

Plane crash

Engineers building bridge

Bill digging bunker

Bill (right) and two buddies

Market place in Korea

Mamasan begging from soldier

Gust Anton giving jacket to Korean boy

Bill (left) and buddies

Devastated hut where Korean family lived

Korean selling soup on street in Seoul

USO show

After bombing in Seoul

140th Tank Battalion tank

Paul Balasick with tank

Marine Cpl. Duane E. Dewey and President Eisenhower
– Medal of Honor –

Korean children begging at camp

Korean boy carrying load of straw

Freedom Village site

March 2, 1952, Journal Entry:

I'll never understand this Army if I live to be 100! Why was I taking a mechanic's course in Tokyo? Why? And then when I got to Korea, they assigned me to the Fire Direction Center, Artillery Headquarters. Not that I don't want to be in FDC. That's what I trained for at Camp Chaffee. That's what they said I was good at, no not good, great! I was the best man on the team there. Not that I'm bragging, or anything.

—◦◦—

Army Service Clubs Stationery
March 2, 1952, 3:30 p.m.

Dear Mom, Dad and Carol,

We are out of the danger zone here, so that should solve one of your worries. Listen on the radio or TV for the 150th FDC team and how good they are and that's us. Did I tell you they put me back in Fire Direction Center after all that mechanics training in Tokyo? Well, I'm also getting four points a month. I like that. I'd just as soon be home though. Later on I'm going to see about going on a little hunting expedition. Shoot me some tiger. Only kidding. The shooting I'm going to be doing is aimed at those Commies.

I need some paper, stationery that is, and envelopes, cause it's hard to come by over here. We have everything else though. Free cigarettes, gum, candy, toilet articles, etc. and we can even send our mail Free!

I'm writing this in the FDC tent. We've got electric lights, two hot stoves, too. The only thing I'm missing are my slippers. It's pretty nice today. The sun is shining brightly and melting what snow was on the ground. The nights are pretty chilly though. We've had one fire mission all day so far. In between fire missions we review our maps, check our equipment, read, write or talk. The old guys tell us we will get a lot of action during the full moon, that when Joe Chink gets an itchy finger and all hell breaks loose.

I'm learning the computer. I'm going to try real hard because I think I have a good deal here as far as the Army is concerned. It's a lot cleaner up here than in lower Korea, especially around Pusan. The further up you go the nicer it is. This is as far as I want to go though. I'm about five miles from the front now so any farther I'll be in the infantry.

Well that's about it for now. Write soon.

Lots of love, Your son, Bill

New address: Name, serial number
Hq. Batt. 159th F.A.Bn.
A.P.O. 301 % Post Master
San Francisco, Calif. U.S.A.

—w—

March 3, 1952, 2:30 p.m.

Dear Mom, Dad and Sister Carol,

I'm working now and it's slow during the night so I sit here check charts, read and write letters. (Not much shooting cause we don't want to shoot and make a mistake in the dark. That makes sense, right?) I also got letters from Suzie and Anita.

Suzie writes a stupid letter. It's all questions, no news or anything. She never seems to run out of questions. Stupid questions. Like she was wondering if I'm in California since my address is S.F. California. I wrote her a letter. She doesn't give my letters a chance to get to the states. In one letter she asked if I was a soldier! I give up! I'll be going insane with her letters.

On the other hand, Anita, my Arkansas gal, writes like she has brains in her head. No nit wit stuff in her letters. She tells me what's going on and even mentions some of the friends I know back in Camp Chaffee. Good sensible, happy letters! The more she writes, the better I like it. She is some gal!

I hear rumors that we will be getting three points starting the first of April, instead of the four we are getting now. I hope it isn't true but it probably will be. That means a few more months to do over here in this hole.

> *(Discharge from the Army was determined by the point system. A soldier had to earn 40 points. Usually they received three or four points a month, depending on where they were stationed.)*

What is this about Daddy having homework now? Is it because of his promotion? You and Carol both sitting around the kitchen table helping him? What kind of homework does he have to do? Send me a few questions and I'll help him.

I wonder what's the matter with Ollie, my boid? Maybe he's just homesick for me. Don't let him hurt himself when that silly boid falls to the floor. Did you clip his wings? That may be the problem. I suppose I should tell you that I'm feeling okay. No ailments or nothing like that there. I'm just getting mighty sleepy at the present time. Be glad when 8:00 a.m. rolls around so I can hit the sack for the day. These occasional 12-hour shifts get to me. I'm going down to take a shower this afternoon.

I'm trying to think of a humorous incident to write to you, but I can't . Maybe tomorrow, till then,

Love, Bill

—m—

March, 1952: Cpl. Ted Anbuhl, of Mobile, Alabama, survived three battles, Iron Bull, Heartbreak Hill and Pork Chop Hill, before his discharge on October 17, 1952. In the Army, he was a crane operator and helped build the Freedom Gate Bridge above the 38th parallel. That's the bridge where prisoners walked to freedom during the big exchange.

The memory that sticks in Anbuhl's mind is when he was on top of a hill one day and watched as Napalm spilled from the sky and burned out everything (enemy supplies and ammunition) in sight. "Just horrible!" Anbuhl said.

—m—

March 4, 1952, 6 p.m.

Dear Mom, Pop and Sis,

Right now, I'll tell you a bit of our living quarters. First, we live in 15-men tents that have small oil stoves located at either end. In other words, two stoves to keep the place nice and warm throughout the night. We also have a wooden floor. They provide us with cots to sleep on. We sleep in sleeping bags. I know that the guys on the front line calls this cushy, but as the Captain keeps telling us we need our sleep because we are the brains of the Artillery and we direct the fire, so what-cha-gonna-do?

The FDC is located about 25 yards from where we sleep. It's also the same size and also has two stoves in it to keep us warm. Instead of bunks or cots in the FDC tent we have tables, chairs, boards, telephones, maps, and eleventy seven other things.

Our mess hall is also the same size. In other words the whole bloody outfit looks the same. Then scattered everywhere are the battery's 155 Howitzers. There are six guns to every battery. Our position is located in a valley. Anyway there are mountains on all sides of us.

I guess I told you about our free rations. We get toilet articles, cigarettes and stuff like that there. As I said earlier, most of the time we work eight hour shifts and I worked last night from midnight till eight this morning and slept all day except for chow time. Every other midnight shift we get off cause there's nothing doing at night. Usually there are seven guys here during the day, but at night there are only three of us.

Write soon, Your loving son, Willie

Army Service Clubs Stationery
March 7, 1952

Dear Mom, Pop and Carol,

I saw Betty Hutton, the movie star, today. It was pretty exciting for me to see a real live movie star. She put on a pretty good show for all us guys too. There were almost 3,000 men in the audience here. It took place outdoors. There was Betty Hutton, the Sky Larks (singers), and Johnny Kento, an accordionist. Betty sang some songs from her new movie, "Annie Get Your Gun." The songs were "Somebody Loves Me" and "Annie Get Your Gun." She also sang some more songs, too. The Sky Larks sang quite a few songs also. That Betty Hutton is just as crazy and lively as she in on the screen. The show lasted about one and a half hours.

Enough of that. The weather here is pretty nice, warm during the day and cool at night. No snow. My work here at FDC is coming along just fine. Although we are not firing too many missions, it's not monotonous. We can always sit and listen to calls coming in over the radio or go outside and watch the mountains. Every once in a while we get a few magazines in here to read, but

I spend most of my spare time writing letters. We rise and shine between six and seven. We just make sure we get to work on time. About once a week my turn comes around to pull guard duty. We pull it for a straight four hours then we're off again till our next turn. That's all the work I do around here, other than FDC. I'm in FDC right now writing this letter.

That's about it for now. Write soon, Love, Willy

—w—

(Beginning in February, 1952, UN guards began a screening of POWs to determine which wished to be repatriated. As Ridgway had anticipated, the vast majority did not want to return to either China or North Korea. Then the screening teams reached Compound 62, which housed 5,600 inmates, and which was under firm control. When U.S. guards moved into the compound on the morning of February 18, 1952, they were attacked by some 1,000 to 1,500 Koreans wielding crude but deadly weapons-steel tipped poles, knives, flails, clubs, even a hand-fashioned firearm or two. The U.N. troops opened fire, killing 55 POWs outright, and wounding another 140. The U.N. lost one man and 38 wounded. Days later the Communists put the incident into the form of world propaganda, calling it a massacre.)

—w—

Army Service Clubs Stationery
March 9, 1952, Sunday 6:30 p.m.

Dear Mom, Dad and Carol,

I'm starting to get a little peeved now cause I haven't gotten a letter from anybody since the 20th of February. I sent my address to Tokyo again and told them to hurry up and send my mail. It gets pretty lonely without any mail around this place. I hope mine is coming through to you all right.

I did have a little fun this afternoon before I came to work. Today I work from 4 till midnight. Anyway they were looking for a work detail to clean machine guns. We were lucky to hear about it before time. Then the fun began. You see in order for the Sarge to get us boys to work, he had to catch us first. To avoid detail, we boys play hide-and seek. It's an Army game, the old timers taught us. So I ran fast like a rabbit and took my clothes off and jumped into the sleeping bag. The Sarge came inside our tent and looked around and just as he was about to leave, somebody laughed and then the Sergeant stayed in there and tried to find out who it was, and before long we were all giggling so he got ALL of us to clean the guns. It was funny when the Sarge walked in. That's about the only way we have of amusing ourselves here. Just like a bunch of kids. When we're not working in FDC we're working trying to get out of detail.

"Come on soldier, don't give me any sweat," the Sarge would roar.

Yes, we have movies here once in a while. The last one I saw was "Calvary Scout" which was fair, but the one before "Too Young to Kiss," I didn't like the way that one ended. It seems Van Johnson always gets the girl and I didn't want him to this time.

We had a pretty good meal tonight corn, spuds, steak, coffee, applesauce, bread and jam. I've been in this Army for nine months and I still can't drink the coffee. They have powdered milk sometimes in the morning and that stuff tastes like icky-sticky-goo. Their cocoa isn't bad. The Army gets some of the finest meats and other food but once those cooks get a hold of it, that's all, it ain't good no mo!

I'll make like a door now and close and save a little for another letter. Write soon. I'm going pheasant hunting my next day off. I can dream can't I?

Lots of love, Miss ya all lots. Willie

—~—

March 14, 1952

Dear Mom, Dad and Carol,

I'm in the FDC tent now and there's a lull so that will give me ample time to scratch off a few lines. I'll be skipping from subject to subject cause I'm answering questions and making statements while I'm reading your letters. I also got letters from my Arkansas girl and Grama. A whole pile of them.

You'd better watch yourself on this hiking business Mom, or before long you will be qualified and be entering a cross country track meet. You should be used to a lot of walking now so why don't you try double timing to town. Ha.ha.

Nice to hear Bob and Carol are all right again. It won't be long till they'll be on the outs. I can't understand those two. Is it love, or is it hate? Now as for my little Arkansas gal, I think it's love, and I can't remember every having any disagreements with her. I certainly didn't have any battles like Bob and Carol seem to have. What's wrong with them?

There sure must be a marriage epidemic going on around there by the sound of it. Believe it or not I also am getting pretty serious with my gal in Arkansas. She practically has the wedding date set. I've got intentions of marrying her, too. Like I said, the marriage epidemic is spreading. Your little boy is growing up. I'll be 22 in a few more months and still waiting for his father's permission to drink his first bottle of beer.

I'm glad to hear that my $5 boid is feeling better. Keep 'em chirping till I get home. That brought up the subject of money. Precisely how much money have I got stashed away? Give me an up to date account of it. I'm inquisitive.

It seems like you had a lot of fun with the TV while the sound was out. I can see you all jumping around and laughing, making up your own dialogue, especially Daddy. I bet he created all the plots, and they were about hunting, of course.

Flash! Have you sent me a box of stationery and envelopes? Hurry, I'm out. I'm borrowing. This is my last envelope.

We went through a few dry missions here in FDC today. The purpose is to acquaint us with the proper procedures. First we contact the firing Battery by phone and say "Fire mission" then follow up by giving the commands in proper sequences. They are starting to do things very military like around here. You'd think we were in the Army or something.

Flash! I'll do my shopping on "R and R" and send ya all some souvenirs like the kimono, china and stuff like that. Write soon, Your loving son, Willie

---

March 16, 1952, 6 p.m.

Dear Mom, Dad and Sister Carol, I'm glad you liked the pictures I sent. Who in the world do you think took those pictures besides me? Or was it an Army photographer who walks along side me and snaps when I give the order? Nope, I don't' hire people to take pictures for me.

About the money, I trust ya all but hate to be hearing all the time that you're paying a little here and there for this and that with my money. My bank roll won't grow that-a-way.

Speaking of Ash Wednesday I was on the train that day between Tokyo and Sasebo. For Lent I gave up driving a '52 Cadillac. You know the one I mean, that silver Caddie, with the leather seats. Hate to do it, but whatcha-gonna-do? If I give up anything to eat I'd starve. You say the day was nice there with a temperature of 39 degrees, eh? Right now it's up to 67 degrees here, nice and warm.

I'll cut this short cause I have to work all night. So I'll get some sleep now. I'll write more tomorrow. Love, Willie.

—~—

March 19, 1952, Wed. 7:30 p.m.

Dear Mom, Dad and Sis,

It rained all last night while I was on guard and what a sight for sore eyes was I. My uniform is still hanging out to dry. My rifle was muddy and starting to get rusty and what a job I had cleaning it. It took me about two hours. It is finally back in shooting order.

Because of guard last night, I didn't have a chance to answer your letters. As for guard, we walk and watch, watch and walk, always on the alert, always with our gun ready. Also today I received the box with the stationery and cookies. I think that's what it was, or something. What exactly was in the box? When it got to me it was torn up a bit. What I found in the box were cookies, three licorices, a tablet, two packs of envelopes, book and a part of the Pontiac newspaper. I was suspicious because I thought the box was opened and inspected. It took more than a week to get here, though. Good timing. I needed the envelopes. Thank you.

It cleared up a little today but the temperature dropped quite a bit. It was 65 yesterday and today it's 35. Quite a dip! It's good that my 50 bucks allotment came through. Sometimes they're slow about that but they were prompt this time. I get paid at the end of the month and they say they'll give me all my back pay. They owe me for two months. I'm going to send home as much as I can of it. I use my money here to pay these Koreans to wash my clothes. The Korean kids come around and take the clothes to wash. I guess their mothers wash them. You should see these poor kids, they are dressed in rags. I give them food whenever I see them. About once a month a mobile PX comes around here and I might buy something.

Have you got that income tax straightened out yet? I was over to personnel and they told me to send it all home the way it was and let them worry about it. Not you, they meant the income tax guys, back there. I guess they don't like to fool around with income tax stuff here.

Speaking of you getting heartburn, I really got it. It might even be ulcers. Lately it seems as though everything I eat gives me heartburn. It starts in my stomach and burns all the way up to my yap. A lot of times it really hurts. I'm going to see about it, too, soon.

I went on sick call the other morning and had my teeth looked over. The dentist looked real good and lo and behold there wasn't nothing wrong with them. It made me happy to not have them drill in them. Good teeth, eh!

I was showing Carol's photo over here to Vaughan, a buddy, and he thinks she's it! He voted her the one he most like to complete a fire mission with. The rest of them voted her Queen of FDC. My sister is up there with Marilyn Monroe, or something. Pretty soon we'll be pinning her photo on the wall. Vaughan is a heck of a nice guy. Comes from Mississippi. Tell Carol to expect a letter from him. He's really a nice guy. Better quit now. Write soon, Lots of Love, Bill

—ʍ—

March 20, 1952

Dear Mom, Pop, Sis,

One more day and it's spring. Ah, beautiful spring. I'm getting the fever. Sure wish I was back home tearing up the roads now, but it's only a matter of months now before I'll be home. Approximately eight months to be precise.

Daddy, that rear spring on my car is NOT broken. I had it lowered three inches and it's always been standing over to one side ever since I had it. You could put the other shackles back out in order to raise it back up to its normal position. I had it looking like that hot rod style. I hope you get a least $800 for it.

I got a nice letter from my Arkansas girl today too. She sure is writing regular. She likes me quite a bit (says she loves me) and I believe the feeling is mutual. Might take that trip down to Arkansas when I get back. I know what you are thinking about waiting. But if I can fight in a war, I can make up my own mind when it comes to marriage. I'm a man, right? Enough said on that subject for now.

When I go on R & R I'll send Carol her birthday present. Now I'll just wish her a happy birthday.

We have shower facilities here, and Koreans do our laundry. I don't need any shampoo. I'm trying to get the scoop on hunting and fishing here now. As far as I know we can go hunting but we first must get permission from the captain. There's boo-coo pheasants around here. Every morning I hear them cackling. Really sounds good. They seem to be bigger out here. We've got 12-gauge pumps here for our use and also plenty of shells. I'll get the scoop on fishing as soon as possible. I hope there's a lot of trout here cause if there is, that's where I'll spend my free time, if any.

If possible please send me a tour book of Michigan. I got the guys out here talked into Michigan as a good state to live in. I'm with a bunch of hillbillies from way down Mississippi and there about. That tour book will show them a real state, better that I can tell them. Also I'd like it for my personal use.

More questions answered—Chunchon is the nearest town here. About six miles or less north. Panmunjom is closer still. We're along the 38th parallel. That's about all for now. Write soon, Love, Bill.

—w—

March 22, 1952

Dear Mom, Dad and Carol,

I'm working the night shift at FDC tonight after I get my chart work done (and it's done), I decided to catch up on some of my letter writing.

Now I borrowed a guy's pen to write. I'll have to have one of the guys get me a pen when they go on R & R soon. It's much better than writing with a pencil.

I finished off the last of the cookies about an hour ago, then I started on the crumbs. You can send some more anytime. They are sure welcome. The mail comes in bunches, I guess. I'm sitting here by the stove writing this letter and it sure feels good. It's chilly out tonight. I had to pull guard the night before last and it rained cats and dogs. What a sight I looked like when I came back. Soaked to the skin. The Army ain't quite as lenient as home life. Here, we're like the mailman, no matter what the weather—we work.

There is a rumor that we'll be moving back several miles in a few weeks. That suits me fine just so it's back and not forward. I don't know what their plan is all about. All I know is we won't be living in these big square tents. I don't like that idea very much. A pup tent seems a bit too small for me. That's the Army for you though.

I read in the paper where all draftees will now be discharged from the Army in 21 months instead of 24. It sounds good to me. I wish they'd started shortening our time over here to about six months too. Soon as 8 o'clock comes I'm hitting the sack and not getting up till 4 when I have to go to work again. I'm getting sleepy.

Send me Jack Selberg's address as soon as possible cause we're starting to go on three-day passes once in a great while and I may have a chance to look him up. We go to Seoul for a three-day rest period.

I believe I told you about the recreation we have here. Anyway we play softball, volleyball and stuff like that here. We also have movies every other night. The other night I saw "Anne of the Indies". A pretty good movie. All about a woman who was a captain of a pirate ship. Pretty fantastic but exciting. We do all these things to cut down the stress level. Anyway that's what the Captain told us. Too much stress and then we can't concentrate on the targets. We don't want that to happen, do we?

Yesterday I was picked for detail with two others. We dug flag pole holes, three feet across and six feet deep. What a hectic job. Worked digging flag pole holes most of the day. My aching back! I didn't know we had that many flags.

I bet I saw 25 pheasants on the hill by our tent yesterday morning. I'm aching to go out and shoot them birds. Too many mines, and those birds aren't worth getting my head blown off. I'll write tomorrow again, Write soon, Love, Bill

—~—

(President Truman had decided not to run for re-election and gradually shared his secret with other Democrats. He also thought that Adlai E. Stevenson, governor of Illinois, was the best all around candidate. However, Stevenson was still vacillating when on March 29, Truman made a surprise statement at the annual Jefferson-Jackson Day Dinner that he would not run again.)

—~—

March 22, 1952

Dear Mom, Dad and Carol,

Received a letter today from Curly. We are keeping in touch on a regular basis. There is only one thing I regret and that is he is only getting two points a month. I'd like for him to get home the same time I am. But what-cha-gonna-do.

You sure are giving that old pen of mine a good working over. I wish I had me a pen cause I'm getting sick and tired of writing with this pencil. When I get paid I'll buy me one at the P.X. when it comes around.

I guess Pat, Carol's girlfriend, sure did turn Dad for a loop, eh? I kinda figured she smoked. I guess Daddy thought Carol was in the habit too, but I don't believe we should worry about that, cause I don't think Carol smokes. She'd better not. I don't smoke too much here. I go through a pack of cigarettes in about two days. I don't think that's too bad, do you?

That antelope hunting deal sounds fascinating. If I were home Daddy and I would make that trip. I'd love to do something like that.

I'll write again, tomorrow, Love, Bill

—~—

March 22,1952, 8:30 p.m. (typed letter)

Dear Sis,

Surprise? I was going to put an exclamation mark after surprise, but there isn't any on this typewriter, or else I can't find it so I'm using a question mark. The reason I'm typing this is unknown to me. My finger is worn to the bone already and I just got started. It's taken me twenty minutes to get this far. I can't find the keys I want for love nor money. Think I'd do real good in a speed test?

I've made a few typing mistakes but whatcha-gonna-do. The situation here is a moot topic so I won't go into that.

My Arkansas gal is getting pretty serious. She wants to marry me, loves me, and all that stuff. It looks pretty serious now, but I'm just wondering what it will be like when I get back to the states. By then she may have forgotten me but then again I may take that trip to Arkansas and go ahead with our plans.

How are you and Bob at the present? Are you or aren't you going steady? That is the question. Neither one of you will give in so it looks like you both are going around in circles. Like I say, what-cha-gonna-do. Best I get to bed now and rest my tired finger.

Write soon, Your loving brother, Bill

—∞—

> March 22, 1952, Journal Entry:
>
> *Anita! What am I going to do? She is constantly on my mind. Damn this war! But if it wasn't for this war, I would have never met her. Now, she's driving me crazy.*

—∞—

March 24, 1952

Dear Mom, Dad and Sis,

I got Carol's letter. She sure makes me laugh, she's so silly, I mean.

So Daddy's starting that stuff again. What I mean is throwing all your shoes out so he can count them. Your letters sure do sound like you have a lot of fun at home. I'd like to be home laughing with you all. Won't be long now though. I told the boys here that Carol was going to send some cookies that she herself baked and they can hardly wait for them to arrive so they can test her cooking.

I don't know if Vaughn will write her (you know the boy I told you about in my last letter). He is bashful so what-cha-gonna do?

It snowed like mad until about midnight. Then it turned cold and it's still cold now. Last night of all nights we went on a practice move. We left at two in the morning with bag and baggage plus tents and the whole works including FDC equipment. We went about 10 miles from here and set up our stuff. What a job to set up one of those big squad tents when it's pitch dark. Especially out in the snow and cold. I had on shoe pacs, with two pairs of socks, and cap and gloves. Bet you think I'll say I was still cold. Yes!. As a matter of fact I buttoned the top of my winter underwear. Brrrrrr!

I sure hope the boys in Washington get my income tax straightened out. I don't believe I have to pay any more money do I? Unless it's from my earning from G.M.T.

They had an article in the Stars and Stripes that said that if we don't get our income tax paid by June 16th at the latest, they will start adding a few percent interest on it and increasing it as the months go on. So I think we had better get it straightened out before the deadline. I haven't got money to throw away as the expression goes.

I got to Mass on Wednesday. Since the boxes with goodies you send cost so much, you don't have to send them so often. Just whenever you want. They are always welcomed though. Oh yes, before I forget we got back from our overnight the next day at one in the morning. That would be today. I have work to do now. Will write again, tomorrow. Love, Willie.

March 26, 1952 8 a.m.

Dear Mom, Dad and Carol,

I worked all night last night and in a half hour I'm getting relieved and I'm going to bed. I am so tired, I can't see straight, and certainly can't write.

I got a box that you sent on February 6th. The cookies were, shall we say, old! My candy, gum and cold tablets were all right though. The boxes you air mail get here in 10 days, but the parcel post takes about a month.

Whenever I get off work at 4 in the afternoon, the other guys and I play softball. Last night I played outfield and did more running than I have in the last three months. It done me good, though. I might mention that the FDC team won. Well I'll quit now and go sleepy by and finish this tonight.

While I'm thinking about it, I'll write it down. I woke up in the middle of the morning and remembered about my "dog tags". I lost mine but I'm having a new pair made, but that will take about three months. But we have to have them to go on a three day rest or when we go on R&R. I just remembered that I left a pair of them at home. They are in a little paper envelope including a chain. Please send them to me as soon as possible. The last time I saw them they were in a tray on the buffet. They are probably around there, somewhere. Do you know what they look like? If you send them in a box, make sure they are secure in the box, (tape or something) so that if the box tears, they won't fall out.

The other thing I thought of was my car. When you clean it all out, including the glove box, save all the stuff and put it in a box upstairs for me. I will want all that stuff. Thank you.

I received a letter from Daddy tonight. So you got that good map of Korea eh? Can you find my position now? You should, from the towns I mentioned in my letters. I'm located on the 39th parallel.

I saw a movie tonight and one of the shorts was about the icebreakers on the Great Lakes. It showed the straits of Mackinaw and a few others. Brought back memories.

That gun sounds like quite a thing. If it's not better than the one you have, best you get an Army one. That's it for now. Going to bed. Write soon, Bill.

—~—

(About this time, General Eisenhower saw deep dissatisfaction throughout the country over President Truman's handling of the Korean War. Eisenhower had the idea he could win the GOP nomination simply by issuing a statement. Other GOP members disagreed. Winning the nomination over Senator Robert A. Taft, of Ohio, would be considerably more difficult than winning the election. So Eisenhower was counseled by GOP regulars to keep quiet about his thoughts on the handling of the Korean War.)

—~—

March 27, 1952

Dear Mom, Dad and Sister Carol,

Received a box from you today. It was the box with film and razor blades that you sent March 17th. And it got here in good shape. How did you happen to think about sending those nuts? I love them! I've eaten most of them already. I still haven't got a newspaper from home with the exception of those enclosed in the boxes. It's good to read those newspapers even though they are almost two weeks old.

I went to the movie tonight and saw "Callaway went That-a-Way" with Howard Keel. I liked it. What magazines we are getting here all seem to advertise "The Greatest Show on Earth". That must be quite a show. I'll be glad when it gets here. We usually get them pretty late.

Well, I'll cut this letter short cause I'm sleepy. I had two hours sleep last night cause I had guard. It's 10:00 p.m. now and it's six o'clock over in Michigan. I'm going to bed and you're getting up. Seems funny, eh?

Write soon. Love Willie.

—~—

Pvt. First Class Louis Arent, of Benton Harbor, Michigan, was discharged in 1952 after serving both in Korea and Germany. He was an ambulance driver as part of the Eighth Army's 121st medical combat unit, stationed in Inchon, Korea. On one occasion when he was driving a truck loaded with soldiers, medical supplies and ammunition, he hit a land mine. All he remembers was that he woke up in a Tokyo hospital in a full body cast from his neck to his toes. He also remembers a VIP general paying him a visit. The visitor was smoking a corn cob pipe and wore a garrison cap low over his forehead. It was General Douglas MacArthur. Arent was the lone survivor in the truck he drove with thirteen soldiers. The General pinned a combat medal on his cast. Arent suffered a broken back and several fractures. He was paralyzed for thirty-one days.

—~—

March 28, 1952

Dear Mom, Dad and Sister Carol,

I took one roll of film today of the scenery and stuff like that there. There are two guys going to R & R Tuesday so I'll send the film along with them to have them developed. I'm going to take some pictures of the guys around here that I work with also and send them home. You can enter them in my "Travel Album". While I think of it, when I go on R & R I'm going to get an album and send it home. They got some pretty ones in Japan. I'll send Carol her kimono, too. I think robe is easier to spell.

I've been thinking rather strongly of getting a fly rod in Japan. You can get them at a good price, so I believe I'll get me a good one.

I looked on the map and I couldn't find Karangro on it. Is that town in Korea?

We've got a radio in the tent and for the past week every night I've heard "Cry" and the flip side. I like it. I haven't heard any of those new melodies you mentioned. I'd like to hear the "Blue Tango." Sounds like it's nice and hep! I'll stop now and save some more for tomorrow. Love, Bill

—~—

March 30, 1952, night time

Dear Mom, Dad and Sister Carol,

I was sweating today, the first time since Camp Chaffee. It was really hot! About 2 p.m. I went for a walk to the showers. I stayed there for a while soaking up the water. It really felt good. After that I went back to work at 4 p.m. Not much action tonight. Guess it's too hot for Joe Chink too.

If I'm lucky enough I may go out hunting pheasants, I found out that as long as we clean them, the cook will cook it for us. I'm going to have me a feast soon as I get permission to shoot a pheasant. There are a million pheasants around here.

I learned a new word today. These people around here are awful fastidious. Get me, eh! Fastidious! This will be a short note for now. Gotta work. I'll write again tomorrow.

Lots of love and kisses, Bill.

—ꟿ—

April 1, 1952, 2:20 a.m.

Dear Mom, Dad and Sister Carol,

I'm starting out another night to work but we had two guys go on "R & R." from my shift this week so that leaves only three left on this shift and we will be doing a little extra work for the next week. But it will soon be my turn to go on "R & R."

I don't know if I told you how we work here but I will anyway. There are two eight- hour shifts. One starts at 8 a.m. and works through to 4 p.m., then the next shift comes on at 4 p.m. and works till midnight. Only two men work the midnight shift, instead of the regular five men. So we have to work every other night shift, that's when our turn comes around. It doesn't make it too bad.

We've got a "time on target" to fire tonight at 04:45, so I'll have to put forth some special effort. A "time on target" means that about every gun in or around this section is going to fire on a certain point at a specified time. We have to figure the time of flight of the projectile and compensate for that too. Say the time of flight was 53 seconds, well we'll have to fire 53 seconds before four forty five in order for the projectile to hit the target at exactly 04:45. Each firing battery does that so you can imagine what the target will look like about five seconds past 04:45.

While I'm on the subject more or less, could you give me the price of that 30.06 slide action. It seems to be a nice weapon. It probably costs a lot. I'm just thinking of buying it, not directly, just thinking about it.

The Eagle pooped last night. He left me a nice tidy sum. To be a little more specific it was $167.00. I'm going to keep $20 for myself and send the rest home. Twenty bucks is a lot of money over here. I give five dollars to the wash boy who does my clothes. Then I keep the rest for PX when it comes around twice a month. What money is left may be set aside for whatever may arise. Can't make a money order until the 10th of the month so I won't be able to send home the roll until then. If I could send money home like that every month besides my $50 allotment, I'd have a nice roll of green backs waiting for me eh! Most of that money is back pay. Next month I doubt whether I get as much as $50.

No movies last night, so I went to bed early. I sleep with my wallet now. I found out one thing and that's don't trust your buddies as far as money is concerned. They'd snatch the $167 just as fast as I'd lay it down and turn my back, then again, maybe not. You never know, and I'm not taking chances. It pays to be safe. I'd trust any of the guys in the tent with my life, but still you have to be cautious.

I ordered a new pair of combat boots. I'm still wearing the ones I went through Basic. They're getting a bit ragged around the edges. New ones don't cost me, so what can I lose?

I acquired an air mattress the other night and am using it on my bed, now. Those air mattresses are really nice to sleep on. Then I think of those poor bastards in the infantry who are sleeping who knows where, if at all. I shouldn't complain and I should thank God I'm sleeping in a tent and not out in the field.

I'm running a little short of words now, so I best be saying so long. I'll write later. You write, soon. Lots of love, Bill

—ʍ—

April 2, 1952

Dear Mom, Dad and Carol,

It's not that I'm worried about my bank account. I just wanted to know how much I had. I hope it climbs up pretty fast. I got all excited about the jelly beans then later on you say you ain't gonna send them. I almost flipped. I want my Jelly Beans! You know how much I like them, love them, I mean.

I inquired about Jack Selberg's location and I know approximately where it is, I think. Those questions that Daddy asked me, I believe I've answered them all in that little diagram I sent. We've got a lieutenant here that's a sportsman and I was talking to him about that 30.06 pump. I mentioned that you got one. We had a good discussion about it. He's a S-3 in FDC here. One of those 90-day wonders. He's only 23 years old. Good Joe though.

Don't worry about me and that girl from Arkansas. It may not last the full time I spend in Korea. I'm still thinking about her, but as I said don't worry. I'm a big boy, or should say a man and can make up my own mind. You should worry about Carol and Bob for a change.

Just a skoska list about over here. Day after tomorrow I'm going down the road to visit the 107th Ordinance. I heard they're all National Guard from Pontiac, 95% of them worked at G.M.& T. I may know some of them. Well that's about all for now. Write soon, Your loving son, Bill.

—m—

April 2, 1952

Dear Mom, Dad and Carol,

In each letter so far I've asked for something it seems, so I can't let this letter go by without asking for something. This time it's a pen. The one I'm using now is a borrowed pen. I haven't had one since I've been here and I hate to write in pencil and it isn't nice to be borrowing all the time. Don't send an expensive one but send one that is pretty good. Take my money to pay for it if you want but I want and need a pen!

I think I know what I'm doing (** about Anita) but as you say I have a long time to think it over. Both my girl, Anita, and I have been thinking it over. We've admitted that it may be different when I get back home but we are going to wait and find out. Maybe we are just silly kids in love but what-cha-gonna do. That love is sure a powerful thing! Even long distance.

So it's $175.10 in the old bank account, eh! That seems about right. I want to see that number climb right up. I'm sending home over $100 soon as I get a money order made out. That will bring it up quite a bit.

We don't see films of any TV shows over here as yet. We may sometime though. Lot of love, Willie.

—m—

April 5, 1952, 1:00 morning

Dear Mom, Dad and Carol,

Well here it is once again early in the morning and I'm working a littler oftener now because a couple of guys have gone on R & R. it won't be quite so bad after they come back. I had an unusual day. I was nominated on April 4 to drive a jeep for one of the officers. I was supposed to drive only in my spare time but they went and called in and took me off work and put me driving that officer all over. The FDC. did not think I would be gone all the time so they are going to take me off driving the officer around and just leave me with FDC work. I guess they figure that one job at a time is enough. As a matter of fact, I do too. And for a measly 3 dollars a day I think two jobs is too much.

Tomorrow is the day we start moving our tent 2 or 3 hundred yards next to the mountain side. What a job it's going to be. We have to build a floor for the FDC tent also skeleton walls. We've got more than enough lumber for it. Be good when the jobs done. I'm so sleepy now that I'm darn near falling off the chair. My eye lids are so heavy. I have the privilege of sleeping in tomorrow morning but I imagine I'll be working on the tent until afternoon.

I sure hate carrying this money around. I've got too much to lose. There will be about $130 in the mail after the 10th. I can get a money order then.

Are Bob and Carol still "Phetooee"? Is it love, or do they just like to argue? It seems that is all they do. He and Pat seem to have a better time anyway. What-cha-gonna do? I heard Johnny Ray sing "Cigarettes to Song." Pretty good. I'll write later—more—lots of love, Bill.

April 5, 1952, 9 p.m.

Dear Mom, Dad and Carol, A thousand pardons!!!!!!!. Meant to wish my sis, Carol a Happy Birthday before but it plum slipped my mind. It's a few days late now but Happy Birthday Carol. She'll be catching up to me pretty soon. Not long ago I was eighteen.

It's good to hear that you finally got a letter saying where I am. Every letter you all seemed to get more impatient, but now you finally know my location.

I don't know for sure now whether we will move out of our squad tents and into pup tents. I hope we don't. We turned in one of our stoves the other day. Everybody has only one stove in their tent. Right now I'm sitting by the stove in FDC trying to keep warm. It still gets cool here at night but warm during the day. That 107th Ord. is just a little ways from us. I intend to go down there. Did Daddy know any of the guys that got interviewed?

It's surprising but there isn't much mud over here. It's solid ground. Yes, I'm a one-finger typist. Yes, Fred is in Korea. His present position is East of me and about 25 or 50 miles from the front line. I get mail from him often.

Another new thing is about our movies. We changed from seeing them in the mess tent to outdoors. All we're missing is popcorn. Well that's about all for tonight. I'll write more tomorrow. The letter I wrote yesterday I was half asleep. I don't know how it turned out. Love, Bill.

—ꟺ—

April 7, 1952, Nite time, 1800 hr.

Dear Mom, Dad and Sister Carol,

I came off work at 0800 and slept. I dreamed like mad this afternoon. I dreamed I came home. You were the only one home and it was a different house, cause I remember I fell down the stairs and landed in the living room and I remember putting on some clean fatigues and going out somewhere in Daddy's car. It was all very dumb.

We just got three more new guys in today. Iowa, Chicago, and Ohio. Nobody from Michigan yet. We're getting some Yankees anyway. They were all Rebels when I came. I got the radio on now and they just finished playing "Cry." I slide all over the floor when I hear it. I really like it. Have you ever heard "Let Old Mother Nature Have her Way"? It's really a corker.

We are going to live in pup tents after all and I don't like that one bit. I acquired an air mattress, did I tell you? It makes nice sleeping now. I noticed we are having chicken for chow tomorrow. I hope it's good. Today we had some sort of hash stuff. The nights have really been nice lately. Nice full moon that light the area up like it's day light. I'm getting spring fever.

Three more days and I'll get a money order to send you. I don't like carrying all this money around. It'll make my bank book look better. I'm sending home as much money as I can. Lots of love, Bill

p.s. Our mail just came in an I got a letter from ya all and an Easter card. That was a very nice card. Thank you lots. I too wish I was home to get all dolled up in my Easter suit. But here I'll put on my clean pair of fatigues and shine my boots real nice. That will have to do. I have no necktie to wear to church though. What-cha-gonna do? Didn't get a card from my Anita. Well, maybe tomorrow.

When your Easter card got to me that little wheel in the back was turned to grandson.

You don't think I'm your grandson?

—ꟺ—

April 7, 1952

Dear Mom, Dad and Carol,

We've got mine fields all over this area and it seems that's where the pheasants stay. It's nice to hear them cackle. It makes me homesick. There must be a thousand of them around here. They're safe.

Well, I've just about got this night shift whipped. I only have about two more hours to pull. Nothing at all happened tonight so I was lucky enough to grab a few hours sleep. Hit the sack at 1800 hours last night so I'm not too tried. For the past few days we've been working on our tent. We've got the floor all laid down in it now. All we have to do now is up the 2×8's up along the sides and throw the tent over the works and the job will be almost done. The worst part of the job is moving all of the equipment over there and getting it all set up. Then we'll move over sleeping quarters next to the FDC tent. Our sleeping quarters' tent is going to be right next to the movie site. It will be nice.

It's just starting to get light outside now. Looks to be another nice day. This hour of the morning it's real quiet around here and all I can hear is the scratch of this borrowed pen on paper and the pheasants over the hillside.

I'm out of words so soon. Will write more tonight. Lot of love, Bill

—ɯ—

April 8, 1952, 2030

Dear Mom, Dad and Carol,

I just got back from taking a shower about 15 minutes ago. We had to go about three miles by truck to get there. These roads really are dusty. I could almost go right back and take another shower, after eating that dust all the way back. It feels good anyway while you're standing under water.

All day long today we've been moving the FDC tent and all the equipment. That took the whole day, too. We got it all set up and now it looks pretty good. I have a few pictures that I forgot to enclose in the last letter so I'll just put then in here. I don't have to go to work tonight. My night off. I go again at 4:00 p.m. tomorrow afternoon. I plan on getting a little sleep. I'm writing this letter by candlelight so I hope you can read it O.K. I can't think of a darn thing to write about. I guess it's because I'm a might tired from working all day.

To give you an idea of what driving conditions are like around here: The trucks and jeeps drive in 4 wheel drive most of the time. When going up hills they gear it right down to the lowest gear they got and just barely make it. Some roads here I swear are almost vertical. Really steep! I'll write more tomorrow.

Lots of love, Bill

Enclosed in April 8, 1952 letter

This poem was passed around by the guys.

Memories of Korea

Beneath the Manchurian border Korea is the spot
Where we are doomed to fight a war in the land that God forgot,
Down with the gooks and rice paddies
Down where a man gets blue.
Right in the middle of nowhere
8000 miles from you.
You sweat, you freeze, you shiver,
It's more than a man can stand
Bullets around us are flying
But we just don't give a damn
For we are soldiers of artillery
Fighting to earn our pay
Protecting the millionaires
For a measly two fifty a day.
Few people know we're living
Few people give a damn
Hoping we're not forgotten
We belong to Uncle Sam.
Staying with our memories
Thinking about our pals,
Hoping that while we're away
They don't steal our gals.
Then when we reach the great blue yonder
St. Peter will surely yell,
"Just send those boys to heaven,
They've spent their time in hell."
Soon when the war is over

We'll go back to the U.S.A.
The people around us will gather
And to them we'll surely say,
"I wish I was back in Korea
back there where every thing is swell
away across the ocean,
I wish I was there, like hell
For the time we've spent in the Army
Is the time of our lives we've missed
So boys if the draft don't get you
For God's sake don't enlist. . . . . . .

—~—

April 9, 1952, 2100 hr.

Dear Mom, Dad and Carol,

We had a horrible accident in the battery. It was a young boy, a Korean. One of the ones working K.P. After he finished work, he picked up some left-over food to take home. He walked out in the field and stepped on a mine. The first time I saw him they already had him back at the medics. My stomach still does not feel right. Poor kid. The back of his head was blown off. The rest of him was covered with a blanket. I saw that Korean kid take his last breath. Damn, why do those things happen? He was just an innocent kid. His face was gone. A helicopter came here after him and took him. I'll never forget that boy! War stinksl! Take care of yourselves, Love you all, Billy

—~—

April 9, 1952, Journal Entry:

Why do these things happen? I'm still shaking. I saw that poor Korean boy with the back of his head blown off. God! He was just a kid, working on KP. Just a kid and then he was dead, gone! His poor folks. The kid just wanted to help his folks, earn some money and bring some food home. These Korean people are starving. These kids are dressed in rags. What are we doing here? The place is surrounded with mines. I know one thing for sure, I'm cured of ever going pheasant hunting (not that they'll let me). Those pheasants can cackle all they want, for all I care. What am I talking about? Pheasant hunting and a kid is dead. I'm really losing it.

Well, we moved our FDC tent again. The next thing we do is move our sleeping quarters. If it's not one thing it's another around here. Never a leisure moment. What-cha-gonna-do? The Captain says we move often to elude any attacks from the Communists. Since the FDC is a strategic part of the Artillery, the north Koreans are super anxious to locate our headquarters and bomb it. That's something I'm not writing about to my letters home. They have enough to worry about. If I wrote all this stuff to Mom and Daddy, I'd scare them all to hell.

—∾—

April 10, 1952

Dear Mom, Pop and Carol,

I rose and shone at 0600 this morning. Sometimes I think I'm damn lucky to be sleeping on a cot, in a tent, with a stove nearby. Those poor infantry men on the front lines have it rough, and sleep anywhere they can, if they get any sleep at all. I should stop complaining about lack of sleep and the food that's dished out here. At least it's not C-rations.

After breakfast, I went back to fix up my bunk a little bit. Directly I was slapped on a detail. I had to clean a 50 caliber machine gun. I just finished and whamo another detail. I helped terrace a mountain side for our outdoor movies. We dug bleachers out of the mountain. What a job! We finished with that about 1200 then we ate chow. Seems strange but I wasn't bothered again until 1600 when I had to go to work. Was it ever hot today. It got up to 79 degrees. I actually was sweating. By the looks of it, I bet we really are going to have a hot one this summer. It won't be too long now before we'll be taking our baths in the creek.

I'm sending home $140 (money order) in a few days.

Write soon, Love Bill

—∾—

April 10, 1952

Dear Mom, Dad and Carol,

As I said before I'll try to get a letter off every day (this is my second letter today). I'll make it more or less as a diary of my time over here. I won't write about the dull stuff, and will try to concentrate on the exciting things.

Enclosed is my money order which totals one hundred and forty dollars. That'll shove the ole bank book figures up a little, hey? Wish I could send home 100 to 200 dollars every month but it'll probably never happen. I just struck a high pay check this month.

When R & R comes along I'll have to have a little spending money for that. My turn will come up in about two months. I'll send Carol her Kimona then. A skosha bit about the weather now. It's been nice and warm. You know what skosha means? It's the opposite of tak-a-san. It's Korean. "Little bit" is skosha and tak-a-san is "lots".

We've got a movie showing tonight, "The Barefoot Mail Man." I couldn't seem to get interested in it so I'm writing this letter. We're well on our way now of fixing our tent. We're finished with the FDC, that is moving and setting it up. We just started making a floor for our quarters tent. We laid logs down and are nailing board over it and it may serve the purpose well enough. By tomorrow or the next day we should be just about ready to move the tent over the floor then follow with our beds.

I'm on guard tonight. I get it about once every week. It's a full moon tonight anyhow so it's pretty light outside.

Till tomorrow. Goodnight. Write soon,

Love, Willie.

—~—

April 11, 1952, 1900

Dear Mom, Dad and Carol,

I'm trying to write enough so you will have a smile on your face everyday. Last night while I was walking guard I notice that the moon had a big circle around it. That usually means a change in the weather and I'll be darn if it didn't change. After all these nice warm sunny days we've been having it has finally rained. It's raining pitch forks at that.

About the snow. I haven't seen snow this year with the exception of twice in Japan and once in Arkansas. During the month of June and July we'll get a lot of rain. I've been told that that's the monsoon season. I'm sure glad I'm not in the infantry soaking up the rain.

So you still don't know where I'm at, eh? Maybe this will help a little bit. You say you know where Char'won is? Well I'm in that vicinity. Can't tell you much more.

In regard to all those clothes I mentioned that I had on during that practice move. I was merely jesting. It hasn't been that cold here during my tour. By the sound of father's letter, I guess spring must be there. I guess you'll have to cut the grass and stuff like that without my assistance this year. I'll miss mumbling to myself all the while I'm doing it.

So you'd like to know about the fighting here. We see the jets fly over here and raise hell with the Chinks on the line but that's about it. Haven't had a round of fire land within three miles of here. They have to keep this place secure, don't forget we at FDC are the "Brains" of the Artillery.

About once every three days one of our reconnaissance planes lands on the road out here and that usually gets most everybody out to watch it. It's usually a Piper Cub.

I wish I could take more pictures of the area and personnel around here, meaning the property and what for. . . . That's Army talk. I can't get away from it. You know how it is, being I've served faithfully now for nine months.

Sure wish I were home so you could possibly squeeze me in on that trip to Canada. You're not going to take your new rifle, are you? Have you test fired it on the range yet? Bet she's got quite a kick, eh? This sportsmen lieutenant here brought over a sports magazine which featured an article on that particular weapon. It must really be a honey. I found out that a M-I cartridge round will fit in them.

We haven't got any new Army tanks over here. I think maybe they are going to try a few out later. They are sending them all to Europe, I guess. We're still using all World War II stuff, guns, trucks and stuff like that. This police action here doesn't even make the headlines so they figure we don't need the equipment.

We got our tent (quarters) just about finished now. We've completed the floor in it. Now we have to pitch the tent over it. We got it made in the shade, eh? Floor for the tent and all. Now if they'd only dispense with guard duty from the FDC, we'd be all set. I leave at 2200 tonight and it's nearing that hour now. So I'll cut short this letter.

Almost forgot to tell you we had a U.S.O. show today. Eva Brown was the star it was pretty corny. She's somewhat of a contortionist, I guess, and a comedian. Did you ever hear of her? Till tomorrow, Lots of love, Bill.

—∞—

(April 12, 1952: During the Korean War, Corporal Duane Edgar Dewey, South Haven, Michigan, of the 2nd Battalion, 5th Marines, was the first person to receive the Congressional Medal of Honor in Michigan. He earned the nation's highest award for heroism on April 12, 1952. Although already wounded, he smothered an exploding enemy grenade with his own body to save the lives of his comrades.)

—∞—

April 13, 1952

Dear Mom, Dad This is Easter Sunday, so I went to church. Usually we have mass on Friday here in the Battery but today they had it in a different battalion that is located about five miles from here. That was quite a jaunt over there especially in the back of a truck over these (paved highways). What did I say? I must be delirious. Anyway we made it to and from church fine. I also went to communion. I have fulfilled my Easter duty.

We stopped on the way and watched the engineers repair a bridge that was washed out during the big rain last night. They say the river went up three and a half feet over night. It really poured.

One of the guys told us about a terrible tragedy that happened the other day by the bridge. He saw a young Korean mother in the water with her baby. She drowned the infant and then plunged into the river and the fierce current took her before anyone had a chance to rescue her. Her body and the baby's body were found later by some soldiers. When we talked to some of the Korean villagers, we found out that she had been raped by a North Korean and became an outcast in her village. Her family shunned her. The poor girl didn't know what to do, so she ended it. See? The innocent suffer during a war. Damn it!

I'll cut it short now, so I can hit the sack, so tired. I'll write again tomorrow. Lots of love, Willie.

—m—

April 13, 1952, 0100 hr.

Dear Mom, Dad and Carol,

Well so far one hour of Easter has passed. I sure ain't got the holiday spirit. It doesn't seem like Easter. I received a letter from you last night also one from Curly. He's also as lonesome as I am. Already we are making plans on what we're going to do when we get home. I wish he'd get close enough so I could look him up.

It stopped raining yesterday before noon and the sun tried to shine. Although it didn't rain the rest of the day, it was kind of dismal. We saw a movie in the evening in our outdoor theater. I really enjoyed it. It was "Distant Dreams" with Gary Cooper. A very thrilling Everglades adventure.

All day long yesterday we worked on our tent and finally got it finished. We tore down the tent and loaded it on trucks along with the cots and trucked 'em over and had it all set up within two hours. Right now we haven't got but three steps to take between our tent and FDC. I'll have to do a bit of roadwork for exercise.

The "Easter Parade" song is playing on the radio now. Memories, ah sweet memories. Remember when we got all dressed up for church? I even wore a suit, a tie and a hat. And then coming home and sitting down to a delicious ham dinner with all the trimmings. Those were the days. Sure miss them. Will write again tomorrow. Till then, Love, Bill

—m—

April 15, 1952

Dear Mom, Dad and Carol, It was a rush, rush day at FDC. We had too many missions to fire today and there was no let up. It makes calculations just that much more difficult. We must have got a lot of gooks. It was a mass assault on Joe Chinks! Tremendous casualties for them! What a day! The weather didn't help the matter either. It started out real windy this morning and lasted until two in the afternoon. It rained and hailed and once it even snowed just a skosha bit. The clouds broke about once every hour to let the sun peep through for a minute before it went hiding again.

We had to rework our tent and the FDC tent cause they both darn near blew down during the wind storm. This is the first break I've had since eight this morning. The time really goes fast when I'm busy. The faster it goes, the better I like it.

I don't know what to say about the article you sent me about rotation. It seems like every day you hear something different. If they keep on with the same point system—three a month—I figure I'll be home by January anyway. Can't say for sure with the way they keep changing it.

I'll write again tomorrow and each and every day till I return. Love to all, Your son, Willie.

—ₘ—

April 16, 1952, 2030

Dear Mom, Dad and Carol

You mentioned about the coffee we get here. Well, I turn down the stuff myself. Don't like the taste of it. We get cocoa here quite often and once in a while they stir up some juices for us, but nix on the coffee.

So Carol really likes her G.E. radio. I sure would like to have one of them when I get home. I always forget to turn that silly radio off and I think one like Carol's will do the trick.

About that deal of me working the night shift. There are two of us on and one can sleep while the other works. We take turns like that there. There is also an officer on duty but he also sleeps all night (well maybe some times.) there's hardly ever any missions to be fired during the night. If there are any, they are unobserved missions.

The day after tomorrow we will be moving. We will go about 45 miles west or southwest or somewhere in that direction. I'll tell you about where we are after

I get there and get orientated. Can't give you the exact position. We're trading places with the 999th F.A. Battalion. Don't worry it's not any more dangerous. So far this battalion has moved about every two months or so. We have to keep moving, don't want Joe Chink to find us. But I think I'll be getting a little closer to where Curly is. We just found out today about the move after we built floors for the tents and moved everything in again. (Now they tell us.) I wore myself out this afternoon. What a workout! Same address, no change.

Love, Willie.

(Presidential Executive Order 10345 (April 17, 1952) extends enlistments involuntarily for nine months.)

April 17, 1952

Dear Mom, Dad and Carol,

Well I started the day off right this morning by getting up at 7:10. When I was awake at 6 a.m., I told the guys I wasn't going to eat breakfast this morning, I though a few extra winks would do me good. When I finally arose to greet the hectic day, I immediately started working. We worked till noon loading all our equipment on the truck. We got her all loaded now and ready to move out at 6:30 tomorrow morning. I got a little of the low down today. The new FDC location is in a frame building. They say it is nice and warm. Tomorrow I'll be able to tell you all about it.

Now here at the old FDC, all we got left is three chairs, one firing chart and a couple of phones. This place really looks bare. I wish I were leaving to make it more so. I wish I was on my way home to see you all and Anita.

I've got a sneaking suspicion that I'm going to drive our 6 × 6 over to our new area. I don't care one way or another. They're gonna pick me cause I'm the only one can drive the thing and keep it on these road, or whatever they call them. That would be a long hard pull driving one of them things 45 miles especially over these roads. The roads look like they've been digging for gold and never did fill up the holes.

It rained this morning and although the sun is out now, it never dried up the place. That's about all for now. Lots of love, Bill

—∞—

April 19, '52

Dear Mom, Dad and Carol,

We've been so darn busy that I haven't had a chance to think. We moved to our new position the other day and the whole thing here sure is in a heck of a mess, yet. We left our old position at 8 a.m. Friday Guess what? I didn't drive. Someone else drove and I wasn't too sure about his driving. He was one of the guys that drove into a tree a while back. I, along with eight other guys, rode on the back of our 6 × 6 all 45 miles of the trip. They tell me we went through some pretty scenery but I wouldn't know. I covered myself up with a blanket and curled up and slept all the way here. Wasn't taking any chances with the driver and his passion for driving into trees. (joke). As it is, I'm getting so I can sleep anywhere, any place now, even on these canyon-holed roads.

Now our FDC section is set up in a frame building. It's a fairly decent place. It's a good roof over our heads. It's one of these Korean structures if you know what I mean, basic building.

It rained like pitchforks today. This morning it even snowed a little. The tops of the mountains have snow on them, now. The rain has ceased tonight and it is very muddy now. Sloppiest mess I ever seen around here. Sucks the boots right off your feet. I can't tell you where I'm located now, cause I don't know myself. I do know we are 35 miles from Seoul and Panmunjom (peace talks) is west of here, many miles. We're just east of a big river, a few miles. On your map you can see where it splits and comes together again. We're southeast of there somewhere. About 15 miles behind the lines. We're supporting the Marine division.

Glad to hear that I have another allotment check there again. I guess that's right so far, I mean, the two checks. You should receive one for April then that'll make three. I hope that $140 got there O.K. I haven't heard anything from you about it yet.

So Fred is in Georgia, now eh? I wonder what he's in, the infantry or what. From what I hear the infantry isn't too good, so I hope he gets a better deal. That would be nice to receive a cake from you all for my birthday. A few guys here have gotten cakes from home in pretty good condition. Well that's it. Write soon, Love, Bill.

—~—

April 20, '52, 2100

Dear Mom, Dad, Carol,

I got up at 6:30 this morning and found it had stopped raining but was it ever foggy. Like pea soup I guess you'd say. By ten o'clock it has all cleared up and lo and behold before our eyes was a clear sky.

We're still trying to get this FDC set up properly. We're having trouble now getting proper communications. Can't shoot straight without it. Who knows what we'll hit. In another week we expect to have the situation well in hand, I hope.

Ten more days to go and I get paid again. I hope to get a lot of money again. But they'll probably start paying me 10 dollars a month again. I hope not. More money they pay me, more money I send home. So more money in the bank. That all folks, lots of love, Bill.

—~—

(April 21, 1952 : Cruiser St. Paul, while engaged in a gunfire support mission off Kojo, N.K. loses 30 men killed in a powder fire.)

—~—

April 22, '52

Dear Mom, Dad, and Carol,

I made a slight error in my location the last time I wrote. You know where Munsan is on the map. Well, I'm 4 miles east of there. That should plot my position fairly well. We've got a lot of restricted zones around here where we can't fire on account of the peace talks. We, ourselves, are just outside the area where the enemy can't fire. A reasonably safe area I guess. Our firing batteries are quite a distance from us too. Our nearest one is 12 miles from here.

(Corporal Gordon Wilson, of Stevensville, Michigan, was a member of the Artillery 196, one of the firing batteries FDC was directing fire. Wilson's duties included making sure the track was ready. The track was the prime mover of the how-

itzers and the team of men who operated it were on the track. Wilson recounts an incident in the dead of winter when the track was icy. "One time we lost the howitzer and all the men involved. It was icy and snowing and the track ran over a mountain. Every man was lost, all dead. We got a tank to retrieve the track, but it was too late for the men.")

I worked all day yesterday now I'm on the night shift again. I just diagnosed my own ailments and decided it was ulcers. I will hang up my doctor's shingle, soon. But probably the wrong kind of food no doubt. What I need is home cooking.

So the time has come when you can put up my car for sale eh? We should get the money out of it if it's cleaned up pretty good. It still runs o.k. doesn't it? Carol said it makes a lot of noise. I wonder if a new muffler would increase the selling price any. Probably won't make much difference.

I heard all them songs by Johnny Ray that Carol mentioned. I love 'em all. What a crooner he is. I'll write Carol in a few days. Love to all, Willie.

—∾—

April 22, 1952, 2000 hr.

Dear Mom, Dad, Carol,

At one o'clock I was nominated for detail. (Couldn't run fast enough, ha.) We were assigned to find some white sand to beautify the area around the captain's tent. Say, there's a war on, isn't there? I guess they want it to look like Palm Beach. Anyway, I got the front seat in the truck and we then proceeded on our journey to collect white grains of sand. It was a very interesting assignment.

We must have put about 58 miles on the truck during the afternoon. And guess what? Nary a grain of white sand. Or any color for the matter. Although it was a great scenic journey. The territory around here is very beautiful this time of year. You can see patches of green here and there where it isn't all shelled out. If you take a closer look, you can see trees scattered throughout the area. Sorry to report that many of the trees are burned-out stumps now. It's sad.

One thing I saw that brought tears to my eyes. Korean women walking barefoot with their crying babies strapped to their backs. Kids, maybe six, seven or eight, years old wearing too large cast-off Army fatigues clinging to each other. Saw one child, a little boy, with only one arm. All of them were walking, some with packs on their backs. This is a police action? I'd like to see some of those congressmen here seeing all this, I'd sure like to see them.

The wind around the mountains is fierce. It will blow you away if you're not careful.

On one level road here, if you want to call it level, the truck and jeeps usually have to go in four-wheel drive. Many times we have to gear then right down. I also noticed the primitive way the natives till the soil. It's a slow process but how they manage to get their back forty plowed before the snow falls is beyond me. By the looks of their living standard here I don't believe they do. I thought the Japanese lived in poorly made houses, but you should see what these people live in. At first glance you think it was a deserted chicken coop, only the chicken coops in the States are made better.

I also saw five pheasants on the tour; four of them were beautiful shots. They were all cocks and brilliantly colored. Even more so it seemed, than those in the states. We don't see many jets lately. Although there are lots of helicopters flying around here, thick as flies on a hot summer Michigan night. They use them for transporting supplies instead of the trucks. It's more efficient considering the roads here.

We don't have a decent shower system set up yet. The Marine division is only about ½ mile from here so we're using their showers. Once I get into the shower, I hate to get out. That water feels sooo good. I've often wondered what it would be like to take a bath in a tub and sleep in a soft bed with clean sheets and blankets. And eat out of a plate instead of a mess kit. I'm used to it now, though. When I come home I'll probably line up at the stove with my mess kit in hand. Can't break the habit. The Army sure changes a person. It makes me realize what I left behind and what life is really all about. God bless America!

Write soon, Love to all, Your loving son, Bill.

—~—

April 24, '52, Thursday

Dear Mom, Dad and Carol,

Two guys came back from R & R today with my film. Enclosed you'll find pictures and all the negatives. I kept a few pictures out to send to other people.

That's a good photo of one of our helicopters. As a matter of fact, all the pictures came out good.

Big news-special news flash, flash! Li'l Abner got married! That's big news isn't it? Ha! Anyway, it's big news in Arkansas. That's what my gal in Arkansas, says. I know, don't get serious. No hillbilly belles, Koreans or Japanese for daughter-in-laws. Only kidding.

But Anita says she loves me and wants to marry me. How can I resist that? We shall see. That gal is getting to me. I keep thinking about her all the time. You can't tell me to wait. I'm a man, now. What about Carol and Bob? She's only eighteen and tangled up with Bob. They fight and argue and then in your next letter you tell me they are still going steady. What gives?

Well enough of that stuff. I went out in the truck today to look for more white sand. I drove for twelve miles. We went to the Big River (the biggest one here but I don't know the name of the silly thing.) Anyway all along the shores of the river is a great beach, someo-someo. It's like Port Huron, a beach on both sides of the river. So we finally found some sand, and white at that. We loaded the truck and came back and made paths with it. It's starting to look like a beach around here, with all that sand. What a place! Some of those streams around here look promising. There's some beautiful fish here. I sure would like to slip my waders in there and do a bit of fishing. I know I could catch a few big ones.

There's a good movie on tonight, "Hurricane Island". But I won't be able to see it, cause I'm working. Maybe, tomorrow. In a few minutes I'm going to get a haircut. So I'll cut it short. (That's a joke.) Write soon, Your loving son, Willie.

P.S. You'd better send me a $50 money order just in case I need it for R & R. If I don't I'll send it back. I promise. I may not get enough money this payday.

—w—

April 25, 1952

Dear Mom, Dad and Carol,

I worked most of the day. That is until 4 p.m. In the morning I worked on our stove in here trying to get it to produce some heat. I ended up overhauling the carburetor and with my mechanical ability was finally able to get it to work.

Later we went down in a jeep (to take a shower) and almost didn't make it back , the clutch was gone and we had to push the jeep up the hills all the way back. This was a perilous journey, and we shuddered along inch by inch, pushing, pushing. I felt like taking another shower after that experience. That jeep reminds me of my Chevy. There was always something wrong with it.

We had a battlefield promotion here today. One of the soldiers here made it to Lieutenant. We had a big ceremony, stood at attention and had to salute and all that stuff. Really fastidious, if I do say so.

There was a helicopter circling around us the other day. What a sight! It stood suspended in midair, dove down, circled around again, sideways, every which way. It was spraying something around the area. They say it was insect repellant.

Excuse me for hurrying through this letter, but it's getting late and I must hit the sack. I'm dead tired. Will write more carefully tomorrow. Lot of love, Willie.

The American Red Cross Stationery

April 26, 1952, 1900 hr.

Dear Mom, Dad and Sis, What an exciting time we had in the battery last night. I was the life of the party, but didn't know it at the time. I had a nightmare, and dreamed someone was killing me.

I let out some of those blood-curdling screams (like I did when I was home on furlough, remember?) I woke up everybody in the four tents around and three guards ran into the tent to see what was happening.

During the episode, the guards were hitting me trying to wake me up. That made it all the more realistic. So in my sleep, I started hitting them back, trying to escape. They were going to kill me! That's what I thought. Finally they woke me up. I was all tied up in knots in my sleeping bag, sweating and chilled at the same time. That was two in the morning. So I went to the FDC tent and sat up all night. I couldn't sleep. It makes me shiver, even thinking about it now. The guys were real nice to me and understanding That really helped a lot.

Now to answer some of your questions.

Yes, we have a few Koreans around here and you should see them. The majority of them are kids, three years old to ten. All you ever hear them say is "Chop-chop" (means eat). I give them apples and candy all the time. Tonight I gave a little girl two cans of chocolate milk. She was really cute. She thanked me for fifteen minutes. They appreciate anything you give them. I feel sorry for them. I guess I've got a soft spot in my heart or something. They'll never forget you either. They dress in rags or anything they can get. You see these kids wearing discarded fatigues that are 20 sizes too big for them. Looks funny but that's all they have, I guess.

If people in the States could see with their own eyes they would learn to really appreciate what they have in the good old U.S.A. I hope Sis takes heed to that. The kids here would be in millionaire' heaven if they had 1/10 of what she has.

The next day, I went on detail. As the Sarge rounded up us boys, he handed us barbed wire, nails, hammers and all sorts of good stuff. I strung barbed wire all afternoon. What a job that is. I was on detail for three hours and strung wire about ½ mile. When the crew got to the other end we sat down and talked about old times back in the states and wishing we were home. Some of us even started singing some of those old songs. I guess we're nuts, or home sick or something.

That's all for now. Love from son, Bill

—∾—

April 27, 1952

Dear Mom, Dad and Carol,

I got the box today with the cookies and the pen. I should say brownies. It's Carol cooking, ain't it? Very good I must say. Those boxes are quite skosha, aren't they?

I'm writing with the new pen you sent me too. It's a nice pen. Better than borrowing all the time.

About the 20th of May you probably can expect fishing equipment in the corners of the house. Right? Just checking. I know Daddy is itching to try out his reels. So, nothing has changed at home, eh? Yes, it has. I'm not there. But be sure to reserve a corner for me next year.

Nothing happened since yesterday worth talking about. Just the every day procedure. Sameo-sameo-grind. Did I tell you I'll be going on R & R the last of May. You have to have $50 before you can go so I hope to get a pretty good paycheck this month. If I don't you best have some money ready for me. I'll be writing home for it pronto. It'll kill me to draw it out of the bank.

The income tax of mine sure is making a tour of the world. I may get home in time to straighten it out myself, the rate they are going. I hope Daddy gets more than 6 for my car. Try $750 cause then you might get $700 out of it.

DaaaaaDats it Ma, Son, William

April 28, '52

Dear Mom, Dad & Carol,

We had the articles of war read to us today. It's compulsory I guess to read them to the troops at least once each year. We sit there for three hours and listen to that stuff. I can't understand half of it. I think only Einstein can understand the words they use. I looked around at the guys and you might say we have the "league of nations " here, there's my friend the Greek from Chicago, Pete Ginapolis, the Finn from Minnesota, a scattering of Kentucky hillbillies, a Swede from Mississippi (no kidding), others from Detroit, New York, Las Vegas, Seattle, and me from good ole Pontiac, all dressed up in fatigues and Army boots.

I sure hope Father wins the power mower in that drawing. It'll be as much a relief to me as it will be to him. I sure hated the sight of that short-handled grass cutter we had. That's the poorest lawn mower I ever seen.

So that smelt run is on again, eh? You mean to tell me everybody else is getting smelt and daddy came home empty handed. I wonder where he tried dipping smelt. He's getting like Carol. "He cometh home smelt of strong drink and the truth not in him." Gram laughs every time she hears that. Well that's about all the B.S. for now. Til tomorrow, Love, Willie.

April 28, '52, Monday

Dear Mother, Dad, Carol, It's 3:00 in the morning now and I'm working the night shift. I'm not too sleepy to write for some reason. Maybe it's because I hit the sack at 6:00 and had six hours sleep before I came to work.

I went to church yesterday morning. We have church Sunday morning in the Marine division now. The Marines are only a mile from us. They've got a nice little place set up over there for their church. When I got back from church I went to work and stayed till 4:00. We didn't fire a shot at all yesterday. Sure was a quiet day. Before church call we had a formation and they said today being Sunday there won't be any details." Also you guys can lay around on your fannies all day for all I care." Oh, we all cheered over that. Good Deal. Good Deal! But when I got back from church what did I see but 85% of the men on details. They were digging holes and picking up rocks all over the place.

I got out of that one. What pranks we do pull. We had a softball game in the afternoon between HQ Battery and Service Battery. Service won the game 11 to 5. What a defeat, eh? There was a Major umpiring the game and consequently nobody argued with him. If a sergeant as much as dared speak back to the umpire he'd probably be a corporal tomorrow. That's the way it works. Well soon as I get off this shift I'm sleeping and never getting up till 4:00 p.m. The writing paper and envelopes are getting low. Send me my knife sharpening stone. I think it was in my glove compartment. Love Bill.

—~—

April 29, 1952

Dear Mom, Dad and Carol,

After breakfast we immediately started working on our tent. They rounded us all up. The Army is strict about getting the job done fast and there was a lot of ground to cover. We put a floor in it. It wasn't such a hard job because we had a floor from our old area and brought it over in four sections. So all we had to do is slap 'em together and pound a few nails and presto a keen job well done. It makes it a lot nicer than just having the plain old ground as a floor. Plans include putting electric light in all the tents too. That'll really make it nice, but I still won't hate to leave. They can't make it too good here.

We got a big empty field in the middle of our area and the grader was here today and graded it all down level for us and it really makes a jim dandy ball diamond. The movie is set up out there during the evenings too an it gives us'uns a lot of room now. This area here is a lot better that the other one.

I went to take me a shower again today. A shower a day around here isn't too much. No sense in looking like a pig just cause you're away from home, I guess.

We got a big inspection of the area tomorrow and we've been getting it fixed up for the last few days. It looks pretty nice now. As I said, the Army is a stickler about cleanliness. So the rakes, shovels, brooms come out and everyone is scrambling around picking up and scrubbing anything that doesn't move. It's a lot cleaner around here than you'd think it'd be. We have police call (means clean up) every morning. Till tomorrow, Love, Bill

—~—

April 30, 1952, 2130

Dear Mom, Dad and Carol Ann,

Been on the go all day. I think I told you about our big inspection. The mops, brushes and brooms came out and we scrubbed dirt and grime from every surface in the tent. There was a lot of ground to cover. I worked my tail off. That was this morning. This afternoon more work. Get this now. I sat myself in a 6x6 all afternoon and drove around and around and back around. I was dragging two big timbers behind and the purpose was to get it level. Going around in circles for three or four hours at two miles an hour, you either have to be very alert or else. That's my hectic day in brief.

Oh yes, I almost forgot. This morning I went out and washed the truck. Well, I was going to wash it but it so happened that I had a few packs of cigarettes in my possession and two Korean boys done the job for me and got the cigs for it. I believe they'd wash trucks all day long for a carton of cigs.

This afternoon a helicopter came here and landed in our ball park. It brought our money. You know, today is payday. I got exactly $48.00 this month. I guess it's best you send me $50 so I can go on R & R. I'd hate to miss out on that. Before that helicopter left, the pilot put on a show for us. He took that thing up and did everything but turn upside down in it.

He was spinning around like a top and going up and down like a yo-yo. Them things can do about anything except talk. They say you really have to know the pilot's business in order to fly one of them.

Enough blabber for now. Got the page filled anyhow. Write soon, love ya, Bill.

—ꟺ—

May 1, 1952

Dear Mom, Dad & Carol,

Happy Birthday Dad. I tried to locate a card for you but there were none to be found. They had a few Mother's Day cards here but no Daddy cards. So to wish you a happy birthday is the best I can do.

We had a record high today of 83 degrees. I hope it doesn't rain to spoil all the nice weather. But it probably will. This weather over here is changeable as Pontiac's weather. You don't know what's what from one day to the next.

We got a new major in FDC the other day. Anyway, today he had us rearrange the whole set-up in here. The Major is a tense but composed kind of guy. He wants everything in order, and he's getting it. Within several hours of rearranging and cleaning, the FDC looks like a mother-in-law went thru here and straightened up the place and later checked it out with her white glove. Everything is to a tee. It works out a lot better this way, I must say. We at least know where everything is now. Before we had to hunt for a half-hour for a pencil. Now we just look for fifteen minutes.

The Major was satisfied with our work and he said, "Don't forget the stakes are high in FDC and we've got to know where everything is, and get to it in a second!"

To unwind, late this afternoon I played ball and during the process I got my arms and face all sunburned. You'd be surprised how much better you feel after you get a bit of sun soaked in you. I feel half-human.

Well, as I always say, what-cha-gonna-do? I can't think of a darn thing to say tonight, so will sign off for now.

Write soon, Love, Bill

—ꟺ—

This is May 2, 1952, 1:30 P.M.

Dear Mom, Dad and Carol,

Yesterday some of us guys went on detail a short distance from here. I drove the truck and we passed a river. There was a large old frame building across the river. "What's that?" I asked one of the old timers. He said it was an ice house. "So that's where they keep their ice for martinis?" I said. You know me with the jokes.

He was kind of serious this old timer when he said. "Nope, that's where they keep the bodies of our dead soldiers. Keep them until they are sent out."

Well, that blew me away. I had nothing to say for a few miles.

(This part was written when we got back and I got your letter.)

I guess ya-all didn't make that deal about getting that 50 Chevy, eh? Well, I guess it's all just as well cause you probably wouldn't have made out much better anyhow. Are you gonna get a 4-door Chevy this time too? Why don't you get a nice two-tone. Blue, with purple wheels to set it off. Also when I get home I'll put a set of green mud flaps on it and a couple spotlights and maybe even four yellow boids to stick on the window. Curtains on the side windows would really set it off in Number One shape. Oh yes, I almost forgot the Hollywood muffler. Doesn't that sound just dilly? You'll probably be driving my car instead.

Later today, to dodge some more detail, I took a truck out and washed it. There's an old saying in the Army, "When there is work detail, scramble!" No kidding, I heard it from the old guys. But the funny thing is, they find you where ever you are hiding. As for the truck washing, I found a Korean boy who did it. Wash the truck for two packs of cigs, also got my shoes shined. Good deal! They'll do almost anything for you for almost nothing. I feel sorry for those kids, but there isn't much I can do, except give them food, and cigs.

I don't know of anymore things to say. Your loving son, "Willie"

—m—

May 4, 1952

Dear Mom, Dad and Carol,

Got a letter from my Arkansas gal. That's the first one I got from her in six days. Maybe it was because I neglected to write her. I sorta wrote her a strong letter about her not writing too often and I guess she got the impression somehow that I was giving her the cold shoulder. I guess she's afraid she's gonna lose me. I got her where I want her now. So much for that. Ah sweet mystery of life! These lucky women, I just can't understand why they have to fall all over me. Do I sound too conceited?

Well it sounds like so far nobody wants to buy my car. They don't know a bargain when they see it do they? I hope I can get something out of it, at least $650. I bet those new Chevy are ready eh? The upholstery is the same as the color of the car? Real keen. I'm thinking that I want a new Chevy when I come home if they don't cost too much, or else I could buy a good used '52 model. Belaire if possible. High ideas, eh? I may as well dream.

Well that's about all I can think of now. I bet you are getting ready to go into town, aren't you? It seems as though you never miss a day, do you Mom? Write soon, Lots of love, loving son, Willie.

—∾—

May 4, 1952

Dear Mom, Dad and Carol,

I got the pictures, thanks. Very nice. I sure did get lonesome looking at that car of mine. Or I should say my second home cause I practically lived in that Ford. Received the O.C.S.C. magazine too. That really would be some thing if you could win that trip, hey? You know where I'd go don't you? It wouldn't be South America that's for sure. I'd go along with Dad to Alaska. You know, hunting and fishing and all that stuff.

I worked last night so I slept all morning so I can't tell you what happened this A.M. this P.M. though, I went to see a ball game in Service Battery. We were leading 12 to 6 in the 7th inning then we broke a bat. The only bat we had, too. So that was the end of the game. I got back just in time to go to work at 4:00. Today was sameo, sameo, just like the past few days. Nice and warm.

I'm praying that they cut the points or something so I can get out of here. I need 40 points to get out as of today. If they cut the points, better for me. But it might be just a rumor. All these officers run around here and seem just as lost as the enlisted men. They don't know what's going on. I'll be glad when I can say good bye to this Army. Well I get off at 10:00 tonight so I only have

45 minutes to go. We got another radio. The guy that owned the first radio went home on rotation, and his radio with him. That good ole hillbilly music peps me up. "Corn Fed Arkansas Gal" is playing right now. Have you heard it?

I keep thinking of Anita, when I hear that tune.

Well till tomorrow, your loving son, Bill.

—~—

May 6, 1952, 2030

Dear Mom, Dad

I shot out of bed this morning by the sound of a machine gun. It scared the hell out of me. See, I didn't have to go to work until 4 p.m. so I tried to catch up on some sleep. When I heard the machine gun fire I thought those gooks were in our tent. Who knows? So it was panic time in the tent for me. In that moment of panic, I bargained with God.

Then I discovered that we were just test firing the machine guns. What a relief! They test them to find out which don't fire.

So I got the detail to clean the one that didn't fire. See what I told you about detail? We get detail all the time. I spent all afternoon cleaning that darn gun, got all sunburned in the process. But I did fix that gun and now it fires.

It's been so darn hot here lately that all I want to do is go swimming. But there's no place to go. Even if we could it isn't safe. One of the men in a different battery went swimming yesterday and today he is in the hospital with some kind of fever. I'm really trying to be as careful as I can cause there is boocoo fevers and diseases you can catch here. If I stick to the beaten path, I'll be all right.

Last night I had guard duty and what a beautiful night it was for pulling guard duty. The night was just about as bright as day. The moon really put out the wattage, a bright show.

I didn't mind guard that night.

We get out clothes washed for 1000 Won here, now. The Koreans do it for us. Cheap eh? (6000 Won equal $1.00) So that's a little more than 16 cents. I'm enclosing a Won for a souvenir.

May. 4 - '52

Dear Mom, Dad & Carol.

Rec'd two letters from ya all today also got one from my Arkansas gal. That's the first I got from here in 6 days. Maybe it was - I neglected to write to her. I sorta wrote a strong letter about her not writting to [illegible] and I guess she got the impression somehow I was giving her - the cold shoulder. I guess she's afraid she's gonna loose me. I got her w[illegible] I want her now. So much for that. A sweet mystery of life - these lucky women. I can't understand why they have to fuel all over Do I sound too conceited. ha he ha.

Well It sounds like so far no body won't buy my car hey. They don't know a bargain w[hen] they see it do they. I hope I can get some thin[g] out of it tho' at least $650. I bet those new c[ars] are really it eh. upholstery same - same as th[e] color of the car. Real Keen. I'm thinking stro[ngly] that I want a new Chevie when I come home if they don't cost too much. Or else I could by a used '52 model. Belaire if possible. High eh. I may as well dream.

What a ... [illegible]

to-day. I romped around out side most of the day & I got myself quite a sunburn. That's what I wanted and that's what I got. I was actually sweating today cause it was so hot. As I said it was a beautiful day today. If they were all like this I wouldn't be half as bad. I [illegible] a pretty good price you got for that old wreck of a garage. More than I thought you'd get. Put a little money in our garage & it'll be set. Doors on the thing would help a lot.

I couldn't figure out my self who the heck John Thomas Lee was. (Jack Lee)

I've been thinking that maybe Ollie is just plain lonesome for me. He knows who bought [illegible] and he wants me back. Well that's about [illegible] I can think of now. I'll bet you get on your way to town. You are going again you. It seems as though you never miss a day.

Write soon – Lots of Love –

Lovin Son "Willie"

P.S. Did I tell you I got a letter from Gram yesterday. I guess she likes for me to write to her. I write pretty often.

Well only a few more weeks till "R & R". I can hardly wait It's a relief to get away for a while. I'm listening to news on the radio now. Who will win the election? Who?

So I'll write again tomorrow, Love, Bill

—ꟿ—

May 7, 1952

Dear Mom, Dad and Carol,

I'm writing this a little early today. I was sitting here in FDC studying those pictures you sent with a magnifying glass. I noticed that Father is wearing my moccasins. Also our car has quite a big dent in the bumper. When did this happen? Carol's got a new coat, hat, gloves, dress and maybe shoes. She sure is all dolled up. That's a pretty coat she is wearing. When are you going to clean that back porch? Every time I see a picture of it there are rags, axes, hammers, pails, etc all over. The porch is a regular workbench. Why don't you try taking some pictures inside the house and send them to me. I'd like to have a picture of my room upstairs. And other rooms in the house. So I won't feel lonesome.

Please take a picture of the kitchen and you cooking dinner. That would be great. And I can dream I'm coming home for one of your delicious home cooked dinners. Sometimes I day dream we are at a bar in the upper peninsula and I'm sharing my war stories with you all over a cold beer. I can dream can't I?

Well so far today this is what happened. We are now having formations at 6:20 a.m. each morning. They want to make sure we get up. Then after chow at 7:30 a.m. we have our daily rifle inspection. Then I go to work at 8:30 a.m. five hours have passed since then and I'm still sitting here—working.

There are a bunch of Rotation men leaving here today. How I wish I were one of them. All of them are grinning from ear to ear. Well I guess I'll cease fire until later today.

It's later, now. Worked so hard, I'm sweating like a pig. It's pretty dark now so I'm going to bed. Will write tomorrow. Your loving son, Willie.

—ꟿ—

May 8, 1952

Dear Mom, Dad and Carol,

So Father landed a few trout. Good deal. That's a lot of fish for the first day, usually the river is pretty high and you do good to get a couple. He went to the AuSable didn't he? Probably would have come home with a few more if I had been along. I would have spent less time in the beer halls.

I got my fingers crossed hoping Dad will win the power mower. Who are you going to pay to get rid of the old lawn mower? I'm sure no one would buy it and I doubt you can give it away.

So Daddy snores quite a bit. Is that new? You'll have my talking in my sleep to contend with when I get home. Let alone his snoring. The guys here say that not a night passes that I don't hold a conversation with myself.

> *(Years later, Bill often talked in his sleep, reliving his life in Korea. This was in addition to the nightmares he had which woke him up.)*

What the heck could be wrong with our car that it needs rings already? You know darn well it wasn't me any way. My being a hot rod I mean. That sure was a bad deal on the car. Maybe a Chevy is better.

About Carol driving—if you want my opinion I wouldn't let her drive my car. Pontiac is a hot-rod city and it's pretty dangerous unless you can do some quick thinking. Especially on Friday night, Saturday night and Sunday all day. I couldn't see it then but now I see there was many a fool behind the wheel of those cars. I may have been one of them but I know better now. Surprised to hear that I've finally learned?

That's it for today. Write more tomorrow, Love Bill.

—w—

May 9, 1952

Dear Mom, Dad and Carol,

So Father won the power mower, Hip, Hip Hooray for him. At least we can stand up while mowing the lawn instead of crawling on our knees and trying to manipulate a short handled thing. Send me a picture with proud papa with his new grass cutter. I'd like to examine it with my magnifying glass.

Would I ever like to have one of those Buckskin jackets. I'd want one with the fringe on it too. I think those are the number one. I'm gonna get one when I get home for sure. What do they cost? About 30 or 40 dollars? I don't care-I'll have "tak-a-san" money when I get home. I'll charge it like Carol does and worry later about paying for it. The R & R I'm going on means Rest and Recuperation-not rotation. That's the big "R".

Did I tell you I wrote my Arkansas gal a mean letter? She wrote back and was worried I was giving here the cold shoulder. Even I have quarrels. It isn't only Carol and Bob. I don't give a care. How many pebbles are in the beach for me to worry about her?

I'm a jeep driver again. I was chosen by the Major to drive for him. I get a brand new jeep too. Really sharp. I'm putting mud flaps and fog lights on it. Ha. Ha. I still work in F.D.C. though. Two jobs. Love, Bill

—w—

May 12, 1952

Dear Mom, Dad and Carol,

Two days ago the Major asked me to drive for him and I accepted. During my spare time I was also to work at FDC. Well, driving has ceased as of today. I haven't had a chance to sleep any and I've been on the constant go. I admit I've seen lots of country but it just doesn't quit. I actually HATE driving the jeep around here. Army driving and civilian driving are entirely different. And bouncing around in the jeep all day. Wow! Have I ever got a sore bottom. I know I could do a lot better at FDC. I already know how to drive so what will I gain?

The weather has been fine and dandy-real hot. Tonight the weather took an unusual turn. It's real cool and the wind is blowing like mad. My face and arms are sunburned like a beet. It'll probably be gone in a few days. I'm sitting here writing this letter by candlelight and I can't see so well so I'll quit for now and write more later, tomorrow. I'm tired.

Received the box with the cookies and Tums today. I'll hit the sack. Your loving son, Bill

—w—

May 12, 1952, Journal Entry:

Driving for the Major. That's a full time job, plus my work at FDC. I worked round the clock and caught myself sleeping standing up. And driving to the front lines is no picnic. The roads are horrible, what we call non-roads. They don't have pot holes, they have valleys you can sink a jeep in. We were headed for a radio shack one day and when we got there it was all blown to hell. It was hit by an air bomb. The four boys manning the shack were dead, all horribly burned, one of the boys, a sergeant, had burned out blackened holes where his eyes had been. Not much we could do but radio the medics and give them our location. Then we headed for the front.

—~—

May 14, 1952

Dear Mom, Dad and Carol,

Working in FDC and driving for the Major really kept me on the run and I didn't get any sleep. It was round-the-clock. So I quit driving for the Major. Now at least I have a little time to shower, sleep and maybe write a letter or two. I didn't mind driving for the Major, but that's a full time job by itself.

Yesterday morning we went out and found some logs to make our clothes line. It mainly serves the purpose so we can hang our sleeping bags out to air them. Had to dig holes 3 feet deep to bury the timbers so they wouldn't fall over. The Army can think of more silly things for the men to do then ever I did see. A bunch of us guys really played it cool yesterday afternoon though. We took off for the shower and happened to go the long way around and finally ended up in the Inchon River. Is that ever a beautiful place to swim. The shower was forgotten and we swam all afternoon. It was Number One. There was white sand on both sides of the river, just like Port Huron. The water was a little on the chilly side but all in all it was O.K. That's the first time I've been swimming since the first of July before I came in the Army. I'll have to do it again, soon.

Had a game again last night with the 11th Marines and 'natch' we beat 'em again, 3-2. After the game the PX comes twice a month so consequently we only get two chances out of every 30 days to spend our dough. They ain't got hardly anything to buy. After the PX, a movie was showing—"Flaming Feathers". It was one of those cowboy and Indian pictures. I went to bed before the first reel was finished. I knew how it would end anyway. The bad guy wore a black hat and good store bought clothes concealed his hardware, while the hero rode a white horse. The other reason I know who the hero was because the gal in the movie fell in love with him in the first act. They're all the same aren't they? Of course he gets shot once an everybody thought he was dead. I know better. You don't kill the hero.

We haven't had a bad day here for nigh on to two or three weeks. Beautiful weather. I expect any day now it will make a drastic change.

I'm getting some more film when I go on R & R. I'm gonna be a picture taking fool when I get to Japan. I'll have my album all filled up. I haven't got the album yet, but I'll get one in Japan. Post all the pictures I take over here in the album will you so they wont get lost. I'd like to look at them when I get home.

We have a Sergeant that came here a few days ago that at one time studied for the priest hood. Anyway he has started up a good idea here. At 7:30 p.m. every night we (all us Catholics) get together and say the rosary. It won't hurt me a bit so I'm going every night I can. Can never tell, it may do me some good. When's the last time Carol went to confession? Is she going to church all the time or not? I'll sign off for now. Write again tomorrow. Lots of love, Willy.

> May 15, 1952, Journal Entry:
>
> *(Funny, I should think about attending church when I was a kid. Every Sunday, sometimes with Fred, and we'd go to confession before we went to our jobs at the bowling alley. So, it's sorta comforting to attend Mass here in Korea. The chaplain is a good guy and he talks straight. Feels good. Say, I need all the help I can get. God, are you listening?*

May 15, 1952

Dear Mom, Dad and Carol

Had a hectic day today. Me and another fellow climbed a mountain near here to set up a couple of radios and stayed up most of the day. You should see me now, I'm so red, I really got a sun burn. That's what I wanted, and that's what I got. But what really hurt was the long climb up there. It took a good hour to climb that mountain. It's really a high one. I'll be a jack-of-all trades when I leave here. Mountain climber and the whole works. I also checked out a set of field glasses and did a bit of looking around while I was up there. You could see for 50 miles! If those glasses were powerful enough I might have seen Joe Chink parading around in his territory. I wished I could have stayed up there for a while. A person is alone up there and there's no one to bother him.

Got back down about 2:30 just in time to catch the shower truck and incidentally we done went and lost the way again. Had a wonderful time in the Inchon River swimming all afternoon. I should volunteer for a few more years. What am I saying? Sure is beautiful weather here. Are you getting any of it back there? There isn't even any mud here yet. When the rain starts probably we'll get a lot of mud. Write again, soon, Love Bill.

—∾—

May 16, 1952
"Letter to sister Carol"

Bon Jour Queenie,

I'll sort of change my stride here and write you a letter for once. I think maybe it would be a good idea to write you once anyway before I come home on rotation. I got myself a pretty fine deal now. It finally worked out so that me and another guy are going on the hill to take care of the radio which was recently set up. Up there away from everyone and live a life more or less on my own. I hate people telling me what to do every move I make.

I'm also going to get myself a pretty good sun tan. You should see me from the waist up, now. Really got a dilly of a sun burn. From my neck up and wrists down I've got a real tan. We are not allowed to run around the camp with our shirts off.

What a deal we had the last couple of afternoons. Our shower trucks get lost all the time but we eventually end up at the swimming hole. It's really fine out there. I'd flip if they put a stop to that, too. But first of all they have to find out we're doing it. It's unknown to them so far.

You sure seem to be having a time with the senior prom. I've got my fingers crossed for you. Hope you're not left out. Be a bad deal if you were, wouldn't it?

What's Patsy's motto anyhow? Cheaper by the Dozen? She's having a baby every time you turn around. Everybody will be gone when I get home. They will be on their way over here while I'm on the other ship going home. Sounds good but it's still a long way off. I feel like a citizen here already. Won't believe it when I can come home.

Au Revoir, Bill.

—ʍ—

May 17, 1952

Dear Mom, Dad and Carol,

What the heck kind of deal is that when you sell my car and don't even know what you got for it. I'll find out tomorrow most likely.

The weather has changed just a little today. it's been overcast but still it's warm. Pretty soon now the rain will start. I've got that feeling and I don't like it. I believe I'm going on the hill next week some time for a spell. The guys up there now say they have some deer up there. I'd like to get permission to do some shooting up there. Be pretty nice to drag a deer back here to have a few pictures taken. It sure is nice that father has a movie camera now. Has he got a projector for it? It'll be a thrill to take movies. I hope he gets some good ones of Canada. That will be a good show.

About the letters I'm getting. I'm still corresponding with some gals. The one from Arkansas writes on a regular basis, all the time. Pretty good girl. She's getting real serious. I hear wedding bells every time she writes. She's a sweet gal and I like her, even love her, but Curly and I have plans to do a bit of running around before we settle down. He told me that he is now getting three points too. We'll be going home about the same time. Sounds good to me.

They cut this R & R out for a while now. Silly people here. I don't know now when I'll go. Pretty soon I hope. About it for now. Till tomorrow, Love Bill

—ʍ—

May 18, 1952, Journal Entry:

That letter from my sister got me to thinking about Anita. And about what am I going to do? Sure, I love her, but there are a lot of buts. I sometimes forget what she looks like unless I pull her

photo out of my wallet. Sure, I love her, but will she like Michigan? Will she like my parents? Does it matter? Too many questions, eh? I'm all mixed up. I've got to concentrate on getting out of this hell hole alive and not in a body bag. The Army seems to be playing games with us. Well, that's what I think sometimes. Cutting out R & R, raising the points.

—ııı—

May 18, 1952

Dear Mom, Dad and Carol,

You sure had me all mixed up on that deal about selling my car. It finally ended up that you didn't even know yourself. I sure hope I got $650 for myself out of that deal.

So Carol finally got her driving license eh? So she's playing the same tricks I used to. Turning back the mileage on the car, I mean. That brings back memories of you telling me how the boys were following them around. I did the same thing myself. Wish I was back doing it again.

About that foreign dictionary you're sending. I said I wanted a Finnish-English dictionary not a German one. You got that Finlander? The reason I wanted the extra 50 bucks is because I want some extra money for R & R. I wanna buy lots of souvenirs I don't have to pay my own expense there. I'm in the Army now and I don't pay for going any place. This is the life! No worries, a carefree life. Ha! Did I tell you I heard talk they are cutting out the R & R.

I have 16 points as of the end of June. They have the points computed that far ahead. I wish it were a 3 instead of a 1 in front of the six.

I hope that new diet you are putting Ollie (my bird) on will improve his personality and activity a bit. I hate to see $5 go to waste. Gotta fight a little to save him. What will we do with the boid cage if Ollie dies? That's a tough question. Maybe I shouldn't ask it.

Are there any new songs out now? We'll never catch up to the hit songs over here. "The Blue Tango" is just starting to be played on the radio. It will be popular over here in about two months. We're living in an ancient world over here. The weather has changed back again to beautiful days. Will write more later, love from your son, Bill

—∿—

May 18, 1952, Mon.

Dear Mom, Dad and Carol,

The days are so full that it's pitiful. The letters I get are the only things that keeps me going. I did something different today. I went down to the creek near here and bathed. The creek ain't over your knees but cold. Wowie, is it ever. I just about froze myself to death. But it felt nice cause it was a pretty warm day anyway. I saw a fish in the creek too. It was only three inches long, but never the less a fish.

I'm not going up on the hill anymore to operate the radio. It was a voluntary job and I turned it down. I'd just as soon do my regular job down here. I'm just lost for words tonight. Best I cut this short and wait till tomorrow. Love and kisses, Willie.

—∿—

> May 19, 1952, Journal Entry:
>
> *When I went down to the creek, I thought about the times Anita and I would swim in the river in Arkansas. That gal is something! A sweet thing and beautiful. I sure enough miss her. Don't know what to tell my folks about her. Best, I keep my yap shut about our plans. I'll just go along with what they want me to do, to keep them happy. I don't know what they've got a bee up their ass about Anita. Cause she's not from Michigan? That's weird. I was taking a chance going into that creek. One of the boys here got a fever from swimming in one of these creeks and wound up in the hospital. Well, I took a chance, so what?*

—∿—

May 21, 1952

Dear Mom, Dad and Carol,

I now found out that my car is sold. Don't tell anyone how much money I have in my bank now cause if any woman finds out I'll probably have them hanging all over me when I get home. A good-looking man with money has such a heck of a time.

Don't tell me that Carol is back with Bob again? This is starting to look like a never ending circle ain't it? I'll probably be home and married to Anita before Carol even finds out she's going steady. Yes, I think I'm serious about that Arkansas gal, in spite of what you and Daddy think. She's the one for me. Don't forget I'm a man now and should know. I can't think of anything to write about.

I did hear a rumor that we may go to Japan. The whole outfit I mean. I won't like that because it means I'll have to stay here until spring. But then again I would anyway. Do I make sense? I'll go where they send me. Why am I worrying? I have no choice in the matter in this Army. Till tomorrow, love Bill.

—~—

May 22, 1952

Dear Mom, Dad and Carol, I got the pictures. I notice you still haven't cleaned that porch. You got rags laying all over it. You did get rid of the pail and wrenches though. That sure does look to me like a keen new lawn mower.

I worked the night before so I went to bed around 7:30 a.m. and never got up till 5:30 p.m. I missed dinner. I was really tired. I had guard that night too, but I didn't sleep any this morning. They had me and some other guys out there digging bunkers. I filled sandbags all morning long. If I have to fill another sandbag again I'm going to bury myself in the bunker. I hate sandbags.

I went to the shower instead when I found out I wasn't needed. Talked to a few Marines while I was down there. They told me about the harsh winters in Korea. That's not what I wanted to hear. Those Marines are talkers and once they found out I was from Michigan, they told me about a Marine from Michigan, a Sgt. Bill Gobert, who was in Korea in 1950. His company was rear guard coming out of the Chosin reservoir. Well, as they told the story, it was the winter of 1950 and these Marines were freezing and hungry. Their c-rations were frozen and they were out of ammo.

And to top it off, their rifles were frozen, too. So you know how they thawed them? Now, I'm going to get a bit raw here, but it's the truth. They "urinated" on their rifles to thaw them out. No kidding.

But, I'm getting away from the real story. So they were out of ammo, and they relayed the message for more ammo using the code words "Tootsie Roll" for ammo to the Air Force. So what did they get—dropped from the sky? Yep! Lots of Tootsie Rolls. Really, honest! Well, the Marines were starving and the Tootsie Rolls were welcome cause they had lots of sugar in them for energy. Finally, the Marines got their ammo on the next run. Quite a story. From then on the 1st Marine Division was known as the "Tootsie Roll" gang. That's the way Sgt. Gobert told it to the guys back in '50. Some story, eh?

They had some more stories about frost bite, but I'll save them for another time. Those Marines sure know how to tell a story. Almost forgot, when those Marines started peeing on their guns to thaw them, unknown to them Maggie Higgins, a war correspondent, saw them, and there was hell to pay. Cause she got mad, real mad! Whatcha-gonna do?

It started to rain now. I was lucky to have guard last night instead of tonight cause those poor guys are getting soaked tonight. I found out I'm going on R & R on the 8th or 9th of June. Happy Days are coming when I get out of this place for a while.

Till tomorrow, Love Bill.

—~—

(May 25, 1952: Raid on Agok. Nine tanks of the 245th Tank bn. 45th ID, retaliate for three raids on the division's sector.)

—~—

May 25, 1952—Monday

Dear Mom, Dad and Carol,

I'll go back to yesterday and say a little first. At 9 a.m. they asked me to make a run for them to go to a leadership school which is located a few miles from our old area. Naturally I accepted. Anyway I hopped into a jeep at 9:30 a.m. and took off. I was 45 miles there and about the same back. It took me until 3:30 p.m. before I got back. It was a nice ride, I saw a lot of scenery. All kinds of mountains. I had to take some training aids to them. When I got back it was almost chow time.

At night they showed a movie, "Aladdin and His Magic Lamp" That wasn't so good, But we had a good one the night before, "Ma and Pa Kettle at the Fair."

In a few minutes I'm going to church, bye for now. Write soon, Love, Bill

—≈—

May 25, 1952, 6 p.m.

Dear Mom, Dad and Carol,

. . . . Received a letter from my Arkansas gal. Yep, she still loves me, lots, she says.

Still wants to marry me, can't resist my charm, even though I'm a million miles away. She's looking at wedding gowns. So———we shall see. . . .

What a day I spent today. It's that kind of day I like to spend. I got up this morning at 7:30 a.m. ate, then went to church. I got back a little before ten and from then till now, I've read and written letters. No body came and bothered me either.

We had a game yesterday with another battery and we lost by a score of 8-1. We didn't play worth a hoot. In other words we played like the Detroit Tigers. Better quit before I start telling you already what I said. Till tomorrow, Lots of love, Bill. . . .

—≈—

May 26, 1952

Dear Mom, Dad and Carol,

I worked all night last night at FDC so it gave me a chance to sleep through the morning. Had a chance to catch up on my reading in the afternoon. I'm reading a good book about Alaska and the dogs they use to pull the sleds. That's the first book I've found in a long time that held my interest to the end. I'll be anxious to get to Japan just to weigh myself. I think I weigh about 170 lbs. I should anyway because I've been eating. Enough.

The P.X. got here today and I bought myself writing paper and envelopes. I got the last ones they had. I was just lucky. I also loaded up on tomato juice, orange juice, and I figure that's better than potato chips, pretzels and Ritz crackers.

Last night I was talking with one of the guys most of the night. He got on the subject of how he almost lost his girl friend but finally won her back and married her. What a tearjerker that was. He almost cried while telling me and I was getting a lump in my throat. I was thinking about Anita. I don't want to lose her. I think I know what I'm doing. Or did I say that a couple of times before? Till tomorrow, your loving son, Bill

—w—

May 27, 1952

Dear Mom, Dad and Carol,

. . . . Didn't get detail today, but that was unusual because they sure pick on us guys from FDC. I know that the other guys resent FDC men, because they think our job is cushy. I have to keep remembering what the Major keeps telling us. "We are the guys who tell the men on the front lines where to shoot the howitzers. We have a very important job and we have to keep our wits about us and our mind on our work."

I work till 8 p.m. We work 12 hours on and 12 hours off. When our shifts work the night shift, if there's no action, it's not bad. I worked two nights this week and next time when I'm suppose to work nights, I'll be on R & R. . . . Love, Bill

—w—

(May 28, 1952: A patrol of the 179th Infantry Regt. 45th ID, is hit by two Chinese companies.)

—w—

May 28, 1952

Dear Mom, Dad and Carol (Queenie),

What a hectic day I endured today. I volunteered and was chosen to acquire some logs. A truck brought us within walking distance of the mountains side. I was all pooped when we reached our destination. (we had to climb up the mountain). After a brief rest, I commenced chopping trees. I first had to figure out which end of the ax to use (both ends are sharp). I reckon I found the right end cause within 30 minutes I succeeded in felling my first tree. I chopped three of them before they finally ran up to me and told me to stop. I would have cleared the land if they had let me go. Then after a moment of rest we proceeded down the mountain with our burden. It surprised me just how difficult it was to drag logs down hill. Maybe if I would have dragged two at a time I could have made it with out much trouble, but I went and dragged all twelve of them at once. (Bulldozer Ahnen).

We used the logs to put around the sides of our tent. It's a skeleton wall if you know what I mean. It works pretty good. It'll make the tent a lot more sturdy for the oncoming rains and winds. It had that "rainish" look now for a few days, but then again, it might clear up pretty good later in the day.

We're having a cinema tonight. It's all about horse racing and stuff like that there. I'm waiting for them to show, "The Wild North" here. That's more up my line.

Oh yes, one of the guys on our logging expedition shot a pheasant. I'm not about to shoot my carbine out there. I don't know if it's right or wrong. So I'm not taking any chances. The shot tore the bird all to heck when it hit him. So we had to just leave him lay.

Received the box at long last today. Writing paper and the whole darn works. Also a newspaper. Everything in the box is what I've been craving for, and that's the kind of stuff I like to see. It really goes over swell. That all Folks! Till tomorrow, Love, Bill.

—ɯ—

May 30, 1952

Dear Mom, Dad and Carol,

I didn't get a chance to write to you yesterday cause I had guard. On top of it all it rained like heck. I never saw it rain so hard in all my born days. I ducked inside a tent nearest to my post and waited for a while.

We were going to have a movie too but it was rained out. The name of it was "Flight to Mars" one of those fantastic rocket ship shows. They are going to show it tonight, that is if it doesn't rain again. That rain sure did cool it off considerably. I had to wear my field jacket all day. And windy. Wow! It almost blew our tent down.

I'm going to try to get out of FDC. Everybody is griping, right and left. And as for the Captain and the Major, I'm often tempted to—well you get the picture. This is chicken shit all the way. Maybe I'm just sick and tired of all this crap. There comes a time when a man says, "What the hell!" I know this is getting to me and also getting to some of the other guys. Maybe it's too much stress. Sure, we joke and laugh, and kid around, but then there are times when—Oh, I don't know—I'm just fed up.

I'm going to see about driving again and not for the Major, that's for sure. There's a guy here that drives a $^{3}/_{4}$ ton and he's going to leave soon. I'm striking for that job. No lie, a person lives a life of misery in this place. I think their main objective is to make life miserable for you while you're here. I swear I'll be a different person when I get home.

So you hope I get a nice girl and get married. Well, Mom, I think I have one.

She lives in Arkansas, and her name is Anita. Her letters keep coming and make me happy. Sometimes she sounds like she is sad, maybe for me. But sometimes it's more than sad—I can't put my finger on it. She is a sweet kid and I do love her, honest.

I got a laugh out of Daddy when he called to make that connection in the Sportsmen's Club Magazine. And he got in it, too. Publicity hound hey! Well, I guess he's right though. Speak for yourself John, or you'll never get what you want. Till tomorrow, Love, Bill

—ııı—

(May 31, 1952; Enemy fired 102,000 rounds on 8th Army positions. The assault struck the 8th Army near the Imjim River. At that time, the Engineers of the 8th Army were working on the X-Ray Bridge, on the Imjim River, 38th parallel. Corporal Gust Anton, of Coloma, Michigan, of the 8th Army , assistant battalion photographer, took photos of the bridge, which was saved from attack, while grenades exploded. Seconds later a burst of small-arm fire killed three Chinese, crouched in underbrush just yards away.)

—ııı—

May 31, 1952

Dear Mom, Dad and Carol,

I'm still disgusted with this FDC stuff. I guess I'll get into something more in my line, like mechanics. I think maybe I'll be a lot happier.

Well only a few more days to go before the coming event—R & R. That's going to be a big thrill to remove myself from this place for a while. I got paid today the enormous sum of $51. I think I'm getting gypped on my longevity pay. I'm going to see about it sooner than immediately. I should be getting more than just $101 a month.

Yes, yes, yes, I'm getting the newspapers. Thank you! I know this is a sko-sha letter but it's dark now so I'll hit the sack. Write more tomorrow, Love Bill

—w—

(June, 1952: Cpl. Joe Butkus, of Fairfield, Conn. was one of the first 20-year olds drafted from Fairfield. In Korea, he was a member of the 84th Engineers. He helped construct the building for the truce talks in Pamunjon, July, 1953. Butkus also was responsible for assigning construction supplies and equipment for the building of bridges and structures. He was discharged on Mothers' Day, May 8, 1954. "My Mom said I was her best gift, that Mothers' Day," said Butkus.)

—w—

June 1, 1952

Dear Mom, Dad and Carol,

Carol sure is doing a lot of traveling lately. She's really gone all the time. I hope she gets to go to the prom. She and Bob are really having a time of it, aren't they? Why don't you worry about your daughter, instead of me and my Arkansas gal. Besides, Carol's only eighteen years old, just a baby. So please get off my back. I've got enough to worry about being here in this hell hole. They don't even call it a war. I'm pissed off and have been for a while.

I was sorta in a bad mood yesterday and I wrote my girl, Anita, a sarcastic letter. Now I got three letters from her today and I wish I hadn't written it. She'll probably be a little peeved but it won't last long. She loves me too much. Things have been going too smooth anyway. I would have to say something to start an argument. Wouldn't I be surprised if she quit writing.

There's a storm brewing out there now. Looks like a pretty wicked one too. The wind is blowing like mad. Hope it doesn't rain when I'm on R & R on the 7th and 14th. Yes, I finally found that I was going. I hope they don't change their minds again. I'm all set. This Army does things a silly way, I tell you.

I tell you what you can send me, some of those 25 cent pocket books. See if you can find "Blood Brother" or something good and exciting. Enclose the books in a box when you send the next box.

Starting today we buy all our rations. They consider us not to be in a combat zone. (10 cent for cigarettes, etc.). They sure are getting fastidious around here. Before long I'll have to pay for my return trip home. That's about all around here. I'm going to get a different pen in Japan.

Till tomorrow, Love, Willie.

—ɱ—

June 2, 1952

Dear Mom, Dad and Carol,

Another hectic day. We had a big inspection this morning. Some big brass looked the place over. I guess we were rated pretty good cause we haven't been chewed out by the Battery Commander for being unsatisfactory. Those inspection officers looked everywhere and at everything. They never missed a thing. I'm glad that's all over with now. Another highlight of the day was that I found out I'm really going on R & R. That was big news to me after all this suspense. My buddy and I were lucky enough to get to go together. Tokyo is the spot. We leave the morning of the 7th and come back either the 12th or 14th. I'll send you all some souvenirs. I've got a little over 100 dollars to take with me.

The one thing I'm going to do is eat, eat and eat.

There's a guy here that was looking over my photograph collection and noticed Carol's picture. He said he'd like to start writing to her but he wants her to write the first letter. I told him, that would never happen cause I know Carol better than that. He may get up enough nerve to try to write a letter. Well, I guess that's about it. I'll hang up this time. Write soon, Lots of love, Bill

—ɱ—

June 3, 1952

Dear Mom, Dad and Carol,

Believe me, we really have had the rain. It started at eleven and quit at two and during those three hours we had it. A few of the tents here still haven't got floors in them and the Inchon River was flowing through the middle of them. We're lucky enough to have a floor in our tent so we didn't experience that.

Right now it looks as though this place is set up in the middle of Oakland Lake. I'm gonna get me a fly rod and do a bit of fishing out here.

Been nice in Fire Direction lately. The Major had the carpenters build us some new tables. They are big ones too, about three to four feet high and 7 × 3. we have our charts and maps set up on them. Looks nice in here now but I don't understand how we will get all this stuff moved when we have to move again. (Yes, that's right, we are moving again) I guess we'll have to rent a moving van of some sort. (joke). Or else put the FDC tent on wheels (another joke).

Only four more days to go till I'm on R & R. The guy I'm going with to Tokyo used to be in show business back in New York. That is he and his wife. He's only 21 years old and a heck of a nice guy. Next letter I'll tell you about the guys we have here. Till tomorrow, Love, Bill.

—~—

June 4, 1952, 10:30 p.m.

Dear Mom, Dad and Carol,

That one letter Dad wrote sure did strike home. I mean talking of all that fishing and stuff. Sure be glad when the time comes when I'll be one of the fellows on those fishing trips. I didn't get a chance to look at the fish over here so I don't know what kind of fish they have here.

Hey what a surprise to hear that Rod is home. How does he look and all that stuff like that. Bet he's pretty busy catching up on lost time. I know I would be especially after four years over seas. I can hardly stand nine or ten months more of this.

This week is our turn to work the night shift. But I won't get the full advantage of the night shift cause I'm going on R & R. What a shame! Oh well I'll have to make some sacrifices.

Went to church again today. I don't know if I told you or not but we are having a mass every Wednesday in the area and still the Sunday mass in the Marine area. I attend both of them. Good Boy Willie, that's me.

As I told you before we have some Koreans do our laundry at a very reasonable sum but lately things have been getting messed up, like lost clothes. So I have decided to let one of those house boys in camp do my laundry. It costs a little more but at least I'm sure of getting my clothes back.

I said I was going to write about the guys here but I'm too tired tonight so I'll wait till next time. When I feel more in the mood. Don't know yet whether I'll be getting a letter off every night when I'm on R & R but I will resume when I return. Till tomorrow, Lots of love, William

—ω—

June 5, 1952

Dear Mom, Dad and Carol,

Received a letter from Anita today. I must be in a bad mood or something today cause you should have read the letter I just wrote to Anita. I think she might get sorta peeved at me. I don't give a hoot though. I guess true love doesn't ever run smooth does it? I'll probably be sorry for it. She's a sweet kid, and I don't know why I get in these nasty moods and write her those letters. It's this damn situation I'm in, can't think straight some times and write a decent letter to my girl.

Well I worked all last night and so I slept most of the day away. It's a beautiful day today, too. These are the kind of days I'd like to have. To get away from all this area for a while I went and took a shower this afternoon. One of these days I'm going to try and find Fred. I think that his Marine division is nearby. Be nice to see someone from home.

Don't worry about your writing. You are doing O.K. Anything from home is welcome. A lot of days I don't know what to write about, either. Like now, I'm lost for words. Love, your son, Willie

—ω—

> June 6, 1952, Journal Entry:
>
> *Why am I writing those mean letters to Anita? What's the matter with me? This war is getting to me. I don't tell my folks half of what is going on here. Those gooks are closing in on us. Some Captain came in from the front line and told us that the Chinese are sweeping through our lines, and sometimes it's hand-to-hand battles with Americans and Chinese fighting it out with rifle butts*

and bayonets. Grenades exploding everywhere! They are so close, our guys can hear the commies swearing, in English, "Son of bitches, we kill you! Son of bitches, you die, now!" So why am I taking it out on Anita, that sweet little southern gal? I don't know. Sometimes, when I read her letters, I can feel something is happening there in Paris, Arkansas. Something she is not telling me.

—m—

(June 6–14, 1952: Operation Counter. 45th ID launches a two-phased series of attacks to establish 11 patrol bases in the Old Baldy area. 2nd and 3rd Bns. 180th Inf. Regt., fight fiercely for Outpost Eerie on Hill 191, which is counterattacked by two Chinese battalions.)

(June 10: Raid over Kwaksan. Three U.S. bombers shot down.)

—m—

(This letter was written by the camp Chaplain to Bill's father, Nick.)

June 12, 1952

My dear friend,

On Sunday, June 8th, I offered to write to the father (or any other person named) of the men who attended Mass that day. Your son, Bill, gave me your name, so even if my greeting is a little late; "Happy Fathers Day".

There is no use in my telling you not to worry about your man, because I know you will, no matter what I say. But perhaps an explanation of our life here will lessen your worries somewhat.

We are on the western side of Korea, north of Seoul and close to Panmunjom, where the peace talks are being held. You will not believe how well we live, any more than I did before I arrived in Korea. But we all agree that our food is superior to the food in states (with the exception, of course, of Mom's cooking). I do not know of any outfit in our sector, no matter how small, which does not have a ball-field and a volley-ball court. A rather regular supply of reading material (magazines, paper-covered books, etc) is available, and our mail usually arrives a week after mailing. All in all, things could be a lot worse for us.

But do no get the idea that all we do is eat and read and play ball. The boys work hard every day, keeping the guns in shape, building bunkers, maintaining roads, and doing the hundreds of other things that keep our fighting potential at top level. Matter of fact, there are men here who are sure we are fighting the war with shovels rather than with weapons.

But with the hard work, good meals and life in the open, then men are in fine physical shape, tanned from the sun, and are doing a job that you folks can be proud of. Naturally we would all like to be home with our families, and God willing, it will not be long.

As I said in the beginning of this letter, the names were taken at Mass, so that, by the fact that you receive this, you know that your man in Korea is keeping up the religious practice he learned at home.

Keep on writing lots of letters, and keep on praying for your serviceman and for all of us.

Your son, Bill, is doing a fine job here, you should be proud of him.

WILLIAM P. LANE
Chaplain, 11th Marines
Hdqtrs., 11th Marines
1st Marine Division, FMF,
c/o FPO, San Francisco,
California

—m—

June 13, 1952

Dear Mom, Dad and Carol, Well today is my first day back at camp after my brief absence of 5 days, and all five days of living the life of a human being. Sure would like to spend the rest of my time in Japan. As you know I went to Tokyo and Yokohama. They are the best places to spend R & R! We left camp at 5:30 a.m. June 7th and arrived in Seoul and waited around until 1:30 p.m. to catch a plane to Tokyo. We rode in one of those big four motor jobs. I might as well tell you I got airsick again. That was nothing though just so I got to Japan is all that worried me. Arrived in Japan at 7 p.m. and proceeded through to Camp Drake which consists of obtaining khakis and all the other necessary clothing.

On the way to the R & R center the bus broke down and we were detained until the early hours of the morning. Finally pulled out at 6:30 a.m. and slept until noon. After we caught up to ourselves and got everything straightened out we commenced to look the place over. This guy I was with hadn't been to Japan so I showed him around. During all that time we visited the Emperor's Palace. What a beautiful Oriental Place that is! And I couldn't find any 616 film anywhere. So that did away with my picture taking. I'm going to get some of my buddy's negatives though and send them home to get developed.

Also bought some stuff and sent it home. You should be getting it in a month or less. I sent it parcel post. I got that box you sent, too. I sent some pajamas, a bamboo tray set but most of all a fishing set. I think that's really a No. One set. That one rod consists of a fly rod, casting rod and some other types. It's a 3 oz. rod and one of the best you can buy in Japan, I guess. There are a few cards in the box to tell you more about it. I also sent a photo album.

You won't believe this but I danced with a W.A.C.S. Lieutenant! It was a regular stateside ball room or whatever you call them. I danced with a lot of other girls too. We had a good time. I took in all the sights and high spots. Took in a few shows. I covered all of Tokyo and Yokohama. They are pretty cities.

I've been thinking of buying a new camera. The one I have is out of date. I might get an Argus C-3. A lot of the guys have them and they're good. That camera costs about $50. is that too much for a camera?

Now that I'm back, I'm more disgusted with this place. I though maybe I'd have a different outlook, but I haven't. I've got lots of letters to answer. So I'll close now and write more tomorrow. Love Bill

—w—

June 14, 1952

Dear Mom, Dad and Carol,

Today has been a dull day being my first day back at the old grind. Haven't fired a mission all day long. As I mentioned earlier, we don't get any more free rations. Have to buy everything. Cigarettes are a buck a carton! What a robbery! It's getting more like state side here by the day. They are talking about getting us footlockers too. Just like basic training.

When you get that fly rod I sent you tell me what the name of it is. I'd like to send a letter to Outdoor Life and get some dope about it. It's supposed to be one of the best. Should be good for Canada fishing about next year, eh?

I wish I had a few more hundred bucks to spend over in Japan. There was a lot of stuff I wanted to buy and send home. I weighed myself in Japan and I weighed 175 lbs. With my uniform on. I look the same though. More muscle!

Our Major is sitting in here bull shitting about the early days of his career in the Army. Talked all about their horses and everything. He's one of those hillbilly officers.

I just got back from R & R and I swear I can't think of a thing to write about. Lots of love, Willie

—~—

(June 16–28: Chinese launch a series of attacks against Outpost 9 (Snook). Outpost 10 (Pork Chop) and Outpost 11 (Old Baldy), all defended by the 179th Inf. Regt. 45th ID.)

—~—

June 16, 1952

Dear Mom, Dad and Carol,

We were pretty busy firing missions from 6 to 10 p.m. a full four hours of nothing but mission after mission. Every once in a while it gets like that. As some of the old FDC guys say, "When the shit hits the fan in FDC you don't hide, you just throw it back at Joe Chink." There was no let up. It was something big, can't tell you much about it, but believe me, we were scrambling in FDC.

It's getting hot. It darn near hit 90 degrees yesterday and today too. Sweat weather we call it.

Went to church yesterday. Haven't missed a Sunday. It feels good going to church and listening to the chaplain say Mass. And yes, I pray that this war will end and soon, and I pray that I get home in one piece.

Enclosed you'll find some negatives of some of the pictures we took on R & R. These are from my buddy's camera. Some are of the area here and some of in Seoul at the airport. When he gets his other pictures back I'll send some of Japan too. Those that I already have at home now plus these I want put in the album. In fact I want all the pictures I sent home put in the album. Thanks.

Did I say anything about that big construction going on out here? Across the road they're building a landing strip for these light observation planes to land on. We will have a little excitement now watching the planes take off and land. We're also building a shower about 500 yards from here, by the little creek. We won't have to go to the Marine shower anymore once ours is built. It's only 10 a.m. now so I'll close for now and write more tonight. Lots of love, your son, Bill.

—∾—

June 18, '52

Dear Mom, Dad and Carol,

It has been a very dismal day. There are low hanging clouds all over. If we straighten up they say we'll have our heads in the clouds, that's how low they are. It's been misty here, too.

There's talk we might be going on one of those practice moves again. Of all the nights they pick, it has to be one when it's raining. Isn't that the berries, though. What-cha-gonna do? Haven't fired a shot all day today. Nobody can see twenty five yards in front of you, that's probably why. I've been catching up on quite a bit of reading during this lull.

It seems to me as though Carol is getting good use out of the car. She's getting it more than I ever did. So everybody is disgusted with their jobs? What's the problem in Father's job? I know why Carol doesn't like her job, and you know how I feel about this job.

There are 39 guys leaving in the morning for Rotation and they're out here now in formation and the Battalion Commander is awarding them their campaign ribbons. Big deal. I too will be coming home with one of them. I hope this G.I. Bill gets passed because I might take advantage of it and attend some school.

Well I guess I'll write my Arkansas gal (Anita) and tell her about the weather too and some other stuff, of course. She is a faithful gal and a good letter writer.

Write soon. Love from your son, Bill

—~—

June 19, '52

Dear Mom, Dad and Carol,

No letters today for anybody in FDC. I guess the boat never came in.

Our shift is working nights this week and it's my turn tonight. I would have worked last night but guard duty got in the way. I'm not complaining though cause I had a chance to sleep all morning long. After dinner we sit around and talk to pass the time away till 2 p.m. so then we went and took a shower. They're building a shower in our area now. It's such an ancient type that I don't believe I'll go to it. The one they're building is just a high stand with 3 50-gallon drums on top of it. They take water from the creek and put it in the barrels and you're supposed to run under it until the water runs out. I'd just as soon wash in the river instead of doing all that. I'll hitch hike down to the Marines' shower.

Anyway after the shower I just cooled my heels until chow time. Saw a real good movie last night, "My Six Convicts." Don't miss it if you have a chance to see it. It's really Number One. It's not exactly what you'd think it would be, it's better.

Well I guess that brings you up to date. It's 11 p.m. now and all is well so nothing to say about that. Until tomorrow, Lots of love, your son, Bill

—~—

(In 1952, Sgt. Arthur G. Wigdahl, a member of the 84th Engineers, was a welder doing iron work on the bridges in Korea. He worked on a bridge across the Taedong River. The 84th Engineers worked on one side and the 62nd Engineers on the other, building the bridge to meet in the middle. "We never finished the bridge because the Chinese entered the war and we ran out of time. So we blew up the bridge we were working on," said Sgt. Wigdahl, who now lives in Mexico.)

—~—

June 20, 1952, 4 p.m.

Dear Mom, Dad and Carol,

Received your letter today along with the enclosed pictures. Very good pictures too. I got a kick out of the one with Daddy and Pat M. in it. I like those poses of Pat. So we got cats' eyeing our fish pond already huh? Let's hope those fish are a little smarter than the other ones were and not get eaten up by a cat. I paid 360 yen for this pen in Japan and it ain't worth 1 yen. The thing scratches and just about tears the paper each time I go to write.

I worked last night so again today I slept all morning. I was laying down in my bunk most of the afternoon until the mail came. But I'll have to get up for chow, can't miss chow. Oops, the point on this pen broke. Good pen, eh? Now I'm using another pen, the one you sent me. It ain't much either. It'll do though.

So my dear sister finally got her diploma. Wish I could have been there to see her get it.

I don't know too much about that guy I went on R & R with but he and his wife are a dance team. They have a studio of their own and they teach dancing. Maybe they don't own the studio, but they teach dancing there. He was in the entertainment field when he entered the service but somewhere along the line he got fouled up and he's here. He's a nice guy.

Being here in Korea, I seem to be left out of all this marriage business. I ain't ready yet anyway. Or on second thought—but I'd better leave well enough alone.

I'm not being mean to the girl in Arkansas (Anita). I'm just giving her the low down. I'm getting her to think my way. If she says things I don't like I say so. I don't let it just slip by. She's a good girl though and I shouldn't be too rough with her. She got wedding plans for us, but whatcha gonna do?

While on R & R I bought myself a wallet. It's got a lot of picture windows in it and it looks pretty nice. Flashy.

All those pictures you are sending me I'm keeping in a little tin box and now and then I get my little tin box out and look 'em over to think about home.

Look around there and see how much those Argus C-3 cameras cost. Or send me a few rolls of film so I can take some pictures around here. Have no film around here for my camera, but could buy a lot of 35 mm film. Bye for now, till tomorrow, Love, Bill.

—∾—

June 21, 1952

Dear Mom, Dad and Carol,

Letters from you today? Nope. I just got one from Anita. As usual, she writes a good letter, lets me know what's happening. I keep thinking about that gal. Or have I told you that lately?

What a scorcher we had today. It was hot! Our shift works nights this week so it wasn't hard at all for me to sleep through the morning. Went to take a shower in the afternoon and before I got back I needed another shower. How exasperating!

We played a friendly game of ball this afternoon. Anybody and everybody got to play if they wanted. And you'd be surprised at the number of guys who can't even hit a ball let alone catch one. I'm going to go to the cinema now so will finish this later. The name of the movie is "One More Chance" with Janet Leigh and Peter Lawford. Boy that was a really good movie. I thought it was funny too. Janet Leigh is really Number One.

It's about 11:00 o'clock right now and did the weather sure change. During the night we have to sleep with blankets and sleeping bags, or freeze to death. (I pity those guys on the front line.) It's really crazy weather over here, almost as bad as Michigan weather. One of the guys here got a radio a while back and the other day the battery went out. So we took it to the radio section. They fooled around with it and now it won't even work. They burnt out the tubes, condenser and even bent the hands on the dial. How they did all that damage is beyond me. That goes to show you the type of skilled technicians we have here. I doubt if they even knew how to turn the thing on. Well some more later. Till tomorrow, Love, Bill

—∾—

(June 23, 1952: HYDROELECTRIC PLANTS STRIKE. FEAF and 290 carrier planes bomb 9 hydroelectric power plants in North Korea.)

—~—

June 23, 1952

Dear Mom, Dad and Carol,

I was sorta burned up at Korea in general yesterday. When I'm peeved at the whole set up I can't write a half way decent letter so it's all the best I didn't mail the letter I wrote yesterday.

The weather around here? Whee! I've never seen it so hot since I left Camp Chaffee. It's impossible to keep a T-shirt dry for two hours during the day. Wish it would cool off.

One of the cooks here is from Park Rapids, Minn. It's about 180 miles from Duluth. He owns a big resort up there. I looked at some of his pictures and it sure looks like a beautiful place. He wants me to come up there when I get out of the Army. Me and my bride, he says. He's anxious to meet my Anita. We can honeymoon there, he said. How about that?

They've got me working on the radio for the FDC. They got a radio truck across the road and I work with three other guys there. We work two at a time. It's not too bad but I still don't like the idea of them putting you wherever they want to and whenever they want. I'd better be quiet or else I'll get mad again.

My buddy got some more negatives back and I'll enclose them with this letter. I want you to have two pictures made of my buddy and me and also of him alone standing by that little stone structure. Just those two pictures and send them back to me, okay? Don't forget. That girl in the picture works in the P.X. on the compound. He took her picture too so I'll send them along. Pretty cute for a Japanese girl. Well, that's all for now. Lots of love, son, Willie

—~—

June 23, 1952, Journal Entry:

I was pissed off, really pissed off. I know what to do at FDC backwards and forwards. Even the Captain asks me things when he's caught in a bind. Then this chicken shit Major comes in—well he—I'm so mad I can spit or ram my fists through something. But I don't dare. This isn't a war, this is madness in hell! Sometimes we're so dead tired, so exhausted, but we get the job done. We're the best

FDC battery in Korea. Sometimes the tension here is unbearable especially when we've got mission after mission. We've got to think straight, man! And those boys in the front line think we have cushy jobs back here. Don't they know that we are the brains of this damn war? Anyway that's what the Major keeps telling us.

—~—

June 26, 1952

Dear Mom, Dad and Carol,

I missed writing last night cuz I had guard duty. I try to write every day but once in a while I slip up a little. The main topic around here is the weather, the hot weather. Everybody is griping about how hot it is here. Can't do much about it; just have to sweat it out. I wring out my clothes every night. No kidding. The sweat is like glue, sticking to my body. But sweat is better than no sweat. When that happens, you're bound for the medics cause you've got sun stroke.

I saw two pretty good shows in the last two nights. "Girls in Every Port" with Groucho Marx and Marie Wilson, and tonight, "Fort Osage" with Rod Cameron. It was one of those hero-cowboy westerns but good. When I skip a day of writing I can't seem to think of anything to write about.

They finally got some brains here. They now have those radios set up in the FDC instead of across the road in a truck. Makes things a little easier. We don't have to relay all these fire missions down by phone anymore. Of course it was nice in a way. We who worked in the truck got away from it all.

When you send the next box I wish you'd enclose a songbook of all the latest hillbilly songs and a popular songbook. We're a bunch of singing guys here but we don't know all the words. Also put in a box of foot powder. My feet sweat in this heat. Throw in a little chop-chop (food) on the side. I'm starving. I guess that's about all for now. Write more tomorrow. Lots of love, son, Willie.

—~—

June 27, 1952, Journal Entry:

Can't get this out of my mind. I'll have to talk it out in my journal. When I was driving for the Major we went to the front a couple of times. Didn't tell my folks about it. But it has been bugging me. So I'll jot down a few things. Saw many wounded. We got there after a blast and before the medics. One soldier's lower body and legs were burned and bleeding, the flesh burned black. Another had third-degrees burns on his face and neck. His face was scorched like he had been hit by a blow torch. All purple heart boys, if they live to have the medals pinned on them. The worst I saw was a dead soldier, had been dead for a few days. Medics didn't have time to remove the body. Starting to decompose, and recognition of his face was impossible. The medic said they'd use finger prints to identify him. He had lost his dog tags.

—m—

June 28, 1952

Dear Mom, Dad and Carol,

Sure would be nice to head for that old swimming hole on nice sunny days like this but the best we can do is dive in a steel helmet full of cool water. If you have a good imagination you could call that swimming. I got a letter from Curly yesterday. He sent me a few good pictures, one of which I've enclosed for you.

It seems like every time they have the Baccalaureate Services it's always hot. When I graduated, I sweated it out too. I guess Carol's excitement is about all over with now. She sure seemed to have an exciting time though graduating from high school.

I hear that Fred was coming home and he's getting married. I wonder what she'll do if he has to go overseas? His girl has been down there with him ain't she? She probably will go overseas with him, too. Inseparable!

I just traded jobs. I'm now a radio-telephone operator. Things are going a bit easier. I don't get my head screwed off every time I turn around now. I'd like to get transferred to where Curly is but if we put in for a transfer we can't get any preference so I'll just forget about it. I'll just struggle through these last six months. Just don't anybody mention Army to me when I get out of here.

Guess that's about it for now. Write soon, Lots of love, your son, Bill

—~—

June 27, 1952

Dear Mom, Dad and Carol,

Thanks for the box of cookies and that stone for sharpening knives. I've got the stone now, but the problem is I ain't got a knife to sharpen. I done lost it. I'll have to buy another one before I lose the sharpening stone. If it's not one thing, it's another. Oh well, what-cha-gonna-do.

We've got a switchboard all set up here in the FDC now. We got 11 phones in the place. Another guy and I take turns operating it. While the other guys operate the radios. Oh what fun we have!

I'll tell you about another incident we had today while firing a mission. This goes to show you how uncanny we are. We fired a mission at some enemy artillery and missed it and lo and behold the observer sent back to us this message—"Missed target but hit small village, observe six casualties." That was a bad scene. We don't do that often, thank God. I mean miss the target. Usually we are right on.

I'm not going to write Fred anymore. I wrote him three letters and he hasn't answered a one. Let him get married without my congratulations. See if I care. So there! When I get married. I'm not even gonna tell him.

We've got a movie again tonight but I hear it's the same one they showed last night because the Col. didn't get to see it last night. I'm sure they wouldn't show it over for me. Today I celebrate 4 months, 2 days in Korea: 6 months, 12th day overseas. In about 15 minutes I'm going to sleep. I'm tired. I'll have to rest my weary bones. Love, Bill

—~—

June 28, 1952

Dear Mom, Dad and Carol,

I'm still waiting for a letter from Father telling me of his time in Canada. Haven't heard from him in quite a while. Come to think of it Carol hasn't written either.

We finally got a change in the weather today. It's not much cooler but it is raining out a little now. That's a sign that it might cool off. I hope so anyway.

Cool weather would be a nice welcome. I despise the rain for only one reason. That's when I go to chow. When going from and to the mess hall you get all wet. I'm all wet now anyway from the sweat so what's the difference?

A bunch of PX items came in yesterday and I didn't have any money, won't have for a few days. I don't know what I want to buy but there sure is a lot of stuff there to choose from. They have everything except film for my camera. They've got every size except 616. My R & R buddy just got back and brought back my pictures too. I gave him my negatives to have them developed in Japan. Another buddy wanted some of my pictures too so I had some extras made at his expense. That's why I didn't send the negatives home like I said I'd do.

Went down and took a shower in our new shower unit here. As you know we pump water out of the creek into barrels overhead. Well, the creek water today was a bit colder than usual. A cold shower wasn't too bad. Like showering in cold water? I do that all the time. Showers not only gets the grime and sweat off me, the showers also releases the stress we all have at FDC. One false line on the map and whamo! We have to be accurate and calm all the time. No time for jitters when we are working on a mission. It's life and death.

I'm starting to grow a beard. About time, eh? I'm almost 22 years old now. Just a month and a few more days. Write soon, your son, Bill

—~—

June 29, 1952

Dear Mom, Pop and Carol,

They've got a guy here right now that takes wire recordings of service men and then broadcasts them over the air. It's going to be broadcast over W.C.A.R. You be sure to listen in and hear what I said. I talked about my job at FDC and what Korea is like and the Battalion and I said hello to you all. I understand it takes anywhere from two weeks to three months for it to get on air. Also the radio station will notify you in advance when my recording is on. You also may be able to get a record of it from the station. It's a nice set up. I hope it works out. He said sometimes the records get dented coming out but I pray mine doesn't.

The weather has changed quite a bit. It's raining pitchforks outside now. It's also cooled considerably. Those cool breezes really are welcome. Well it won't be long before you will be going on your vacation, eh? Where do you plan to go if you take a jaunt into Canada?

Boy, I didn't know what to say on the recording. That's the highlight of the day so I'll sign off now and go to a movie and it's "Flesh and Fury". It sounds like it will be pretty good. Write soon, love, Bill

—~—

June 30, 1952

Dear Mom, Dad and Carol,

Received Father's long awaited letter today. Sure was nice hearing from him and about his trip. About that fishing rod that I sent home, well it cost a little more than $7.50. It cost $13.00. It's a more expensive and better one. It's supposed to be the best in Japan. I can see myself now fishing with my fly rod in hand and pulling in all the big ones. Well, find out about that rod for me and send me the dope whenever you get it. I'm anxious to know whether it's really any good. It'd better be.

We've got another movie tonight, "One More Time." We got paid today and I got $93 and $60, which I will send home. I hope that bankroll is pretty big when I get home. With my next allotment in there and this 60 bucks I should have about eleven or twelve hundred. I'd like to have a few thousand in it when I arrive home.

They had us outside on the roof of this place fixing the leaks in it while it was raining the hardest this morning. I was a drenched lad when we came back in. It gave me a little chance to get washed up anyway, ha! Write soon, Love, Bill

—~—

July 1, 1952

Dear Mom, Dad and Carol,

My Arkansas gal wrote me. Nice to hear from her. She writes a good letter, or have I told you that before? She's getting mighty serious. She also sounds kind of sad or worried or something. Don't know what it is, but I can sense the tone of her letters are a wee bit sad. Something must be happening in Arkansas that she's not telling me.

By this time I guess Fred is all hitched up. I guess he knows what he's doing. It's starting to get monotonous about Carol and Bob. Everything is apple pie for a while then "Boom!" I know what I'd do if I were her, but I'll keep my opinion to myself. What's the big problem with them? Can't they get along ? If not, why do they go out with each other ? Whatcha-gonna-do?

I never saw Jack Selberg, but I do know where Fred Blough is located. He's off the line now and about 5 to 7 miles from here. I tried to call him by phone but there are too many switchboards to go through and by the time I get there the connection is too weak to hear anything. I haven't had a chance to get over that way either. He's written once and I answered him. That's it for Fred.

Did I forget to enclose a picture of Curly? Will try to remember and enclose it in this letter. I'm going to hold off sending you the money order until you get back from vacation. Unless I can send it to you before you leave. I hate to have that money around here.

The show we saw last night was "The First Time" with Robert Cummings and Barbara Hale. It was a good picture. If you haven't seen it, be sure to see it, it's funny. "Flesh and Fury" is playing tonight.

Had another warm day today. I'll be sweating my 175 pounds down to a mere 150 if I don't watch it. Had steak for dinner tonight and it was like shoe leather, but that's just the way I like it. Ha ha. Well must leave now, Love, Bill

—m—

July 1, 1952, Journal Entry:

Something's going on in Anita's life. Does she have another guy in Arkansas? Nope, don't think so, she's the loyal type and she says she loves me. It's something else. I can feel it, I can read it in her letters, between the lines. They are not the same kind of letters she used to write. Maybe it's because I wrote her a mean letter or two. But I'm going through hell here. Keep in control, the Captain says. "Watch those lines. Aim for the right target. No mistakes, soldier! No mistakes!" Can't tell my folks the true story, can't let on it's a hell hole here. Make nice with the letters. Shit!

—m—

July 2, 1952

Dear Mom, Dad and Carol,

I'll tell you what I want now, some points that go in this fountain pen. I took the point from the pen you sent me to stick in this pen that I bought in Japan and it worked real good until I dropped the pen on the floor on its point and now it's writing wrong.

Well tonight our shifts start working night shift. From 8 p.m. till 8 a.m. I work tonight and then I'm off two nights and then work again. It's not a bad deal this night work. You get quite a bit of sleep during the day. Today we sat around all morning in FDC. without firing a single mission. Then just as if it were timed at noon they start calling down missions, and we fired steady from noon until 5:30 p.m. It was mission after mission. We must have gotten a lot of those Chinks. Didn't even have a chance to look out the window to see what was going on outside.

Forgot to mention, I got up early and went outside. There were a bunch of Korean kids. They usually hang around the camp. Well, they've invented a game and it's quite interesting. They have a paper ball (rolled up paper) and a stick. The object is to juggle it in the air with the stick. Those little kids, some are maybe six or seven are fantastic with that paper ball and stick. They keep the ball in the air for a long time. Those poor kids. We give them fruit, candy and food, and most of them wear our cast off fatigues. They look funny but sad. Kids will be kids, no matter where they are, I guess.

Before I went to work at 8 p.m., I read in Stars and Stripes about the heat you're getting in the states. Bad, eh? I've been thinking seriously about attending school on the G.I. Bill but I don't know what I'll take. I've got some time to think about it. Well I guess I'll quit so I can go out and wash up before it gets dark. Till tomorrow, lots of love, Bill.

(July 3, 1952: 7th Marines, elements of the 45th ID and units of the 7th ID engage CCF units along various sectors of the front.)

July 3, 1952

Dear Mom, Dad and Carol, There is going to be big doings today. "Operation Fire Cracker" we call it. We are going to fire 1,000 rounds at Joe Chink to remind him of the 4th of July. We really are going to give them hell tonight! That ain't swearing is it?

There was only one letter for the whole FDC section today and I didn't get it. Speaking of letter writing, we got a fellow here that writes fan letters to the movie stars once in a while. He's a lot of fun. One of those guys that doesn't stop talking unless he's sleeping. The life of the party. A few days ago he wrote a letter to Marilyn Monroe. She's the number one movie personality in FDC now. She's really a Wow! That's what our discussions are usually based on. That and baseball. I haven't got much to say about baseball cause look where our Detroit Tigers are now (last place).

All the guys here think Marilyn Monroe is hot, but personally I go for Janet Leigh. I believe I'll write her a fan letter. Probably never get an answer, though. I wouldn't want to include my picture cause she'd probably fall for me, ha! Then I'm going to write Liz Taylor. Speaking of movie stars, I'd appreciate it if you'd send me Photoplay, or some such magazine. How much would it cost to send it airmail? That's one magazine we don't get here. If it cost too much, just sent it regular mail.

Since I worked last night, I slept all morning long and took a shower in the afternoon. Then I have work all night again.

Evening shadows are upon us now, and cool breezes are flowing after this humid day, I've endured. Sorta poetic, eh? Well till the 'morrow, Lot of love, Miss you all, Bill

—ʌʌʌ—

July 4, 1952

Dear Mom, Dad and Carol,

Bang! Bang! Yep, here it is fourth of July. Did they have some pretty fire works back home? I suppose there will be fire crackers going off until the sixth.

Wow what a blast that was to hear that Carol is going to remove my Hawk from the wall! I'm pleading with her. Leave my Hawk where it is. I can't stand the thought of it being stuck in some dark corner.

I was wondering about that Marine that Daddy said he got a letter from, and then I remembered, that was the chaplain. I thought it was pretty nice of the chaplain to write a letter to Daddy. He's a real nice guy. He's a major but you can talk to him as if he were just one of the guys.

I sure envy you people back in the states enjoying all that nice warm weather. It has only been 90 degrees here the past week. Sweat! Sweat! And I hear it's gonna get a lot hotter.

We work nights again this week, so we have free time during the day. I just can't understand why Carol doesn't want my prize possession (the Hawk) hanging up where it has always been. The Hawk is nice.

Till next time, Love Bill.

—~—

July 5, 1952

Dear Mom, Dad and Carol,

Got the newspaper from home. That's it. I guess Curly is stationed around Seoul somewhere because he says he gets passes to go in to Seoul quite often. I'd like to get down there and see him but it's too hard to get any time off around here. But I'm going to try and call him on the phone soon as I can find out how to get him. There are umpteen switchboards you have to go through.

I heard that they've been computing the points and juggling them and may even cut them a bit. The whole idea is so they can get as many guys home for Christmas that didn't get home last year. That's just a rumor though.

The stuff I sent home should be there about now. I hope it arrived safely. I have to work tonight. They've got a good movie on, "Steel Town" I'm going to try to get off to see it. Just have to talk fast to someone and get them to take my place. Lot of love, Bill

—~—

July 6, 1952

Dear Mom, Dad and Carol,

We were busier than all get out this morning and I lost track of the time and when I ran for the truck that takes us to church, I missed it. Right after that I went to see the Captain about getting a pass to go to Seoul and he obliged me with one but I ended up with negative results in respect of hitching a ride. I may have been able to make it hitch hiking but I wasn't sure about the ride back. I was just taking a chance on Curly being there anyway.

Just witnessed another bunch of rotation guys this morning. Wish I were among them. That fellow with the recording machine never did come back. I sure wish that first one he recorded with my message home was good.

How about sending me post cards along the way when you go on vacation? Scenic views, you know. That's about it. Till tomorrow, Love, Bill

—᠁—

July 7, 1952

Dear Mom, Pop and Carol,

I guess that wedding reception was really something. All were inebriated and all were having a fun time. Sure must have been a brawl. I don't believe I'll have it when I get hitched. I wanna remember it. So Jack Selberg is in Pusan with 36 points uh? Beats me why he has to stay there. Maybe he hit the Captain.

Slept all morning long this morning, and have the same plan for tomorrow. I got guard tonight so I'll have a reasonable excuse. Just now got back from taking a shower this evening. Like to take 'em at dusk cause if you take them during the day you're all sweaty again by night, anyway. Got a good movie again tonight, which I will probably see. It's call "Hoodlums' Empire," or some such name. I have relief guard.

Anita wrote me a letter today too. She said she heard a nice song by the four somebody's called "I'm Yours." Now what I want to know is who are the four somebody's? She has a very vague way of putting things. I think I'm writing her some mean letters because she's crawling on her knees trying to get me on her good side. I don't know what gets into me. Her letters sound different. I think there is something bothering her. I keep saying she is eating out of my hand. But best I cool it a little, or she will find somebody else's hand to eat out of. How uncanny!

The "Love Sick Blues" is playing now. That guy sure is blaring out with the corny voice of his. My favorite now is "The Black Smith Blues" I know what you can send me for my birthday, a pen, a good pen, and some shorts (BVD's). I got three pair of shorts and I can't get any here. I've tried, I get socks and stuff but no shorts. I bought a roll of 35mm film today and used my friend's Argus C-3 camera and took a few shots.

Another thing I'm pretty low on is envelopes, lots of paper, though. When I buy envelopes here paper comes with it, all for 75 cents. It's too much, since I don't need the paper. Bet you'll be glad to see me come marching home so you won't be sending all that stuff over here. I'm keeping ya-all broke 10,000 miles from home. If that Argus camera costs that much, don't buy it. I'll buy a different kind when I get home. You know, the heck with it. It ain't compulsory. As a matter of fact, DON'T buy it. It's too much money for me anyway. I can draw them cheaper than that.

I made out a $60 money order today. Will send it tomorrow as soon as I get it. That's $60 more toward my $2,000. You think I'll make two "G.s" before I draw it out? What's the present total? What a miser, hey? When I get home I'll sit in the parlor and count it. Well, I guess that's about it for now. I gotta see the movie now and then go guard the premises. Write. Love, Bill Ahnen,

Money order enclosed.

—∾—

July 8, 1952

Dear Mom, Dad and Carol,

I had third relief guard last night so I slept all morning long. Could have been a tornado going through here this morning and I wouldn't have heard it. That's the soundest I've slept for a long time.

This afternoon after chow I went and took another shower and stayed down there till 3:00 and did I ever get a sunburn, look like an Indian now. In the area we are not allowed to strip any further than our T-shirts.

While at the showers, I got to gabbing with the Marines and they told me of an incident that happened yesterday at one of the nearby checkpoints. It seems one of those old beat-up farm trucks was tooling toward the checkpoint with a load of straw or hay in the back. Of course those South Korean guards were suspicious of the driver. (All those Koreans look alike, south and north.) So they hauled him out of the cab and started searching him and the cab. Nothing there. Then they went to the bed of the truck all full of straw and started stabbing it with their bayonets. Yep, they killed two North Koreans who were hiding in the straw back there and pulled another one out.

Tonight is our last night to work nights. It's been quiet on the fighting front for the past few days. Must be something going on at those secret sessions of the Peace Talks. I hope they come through with something this time. It might mean I'll have a better chance of getting home for Christmas this year. I'm praying I get home for the holidays. I think I'll make reservations on the new ship they just built—"The United States". What a ship that is, eh?

The boys here know I'm Finnish and when that gal from Finland won the Miss Universe contest, did I tell them all the beautiful women come from Finland, and of course the handsome men, too. This Greek guy here was peeved because his babe from Greece came in third. We talk endlessly about such silly things. Have to do something. Well enough for now. Your loving son, Bill.

—~—

July 8, 1952

Dear Mom, Dad and Carol,

Today I received a package from Anita. I guess it was somewhat of a birthday present cuz it had a birthday card in it. A logical conclusion, eh? But my birthday isn't for a month. The box contained cookies, gum and other assorted stuff. Had a real nice birthday card with it though. Just between you and me, the cookies she baked weren't as good as yours, Mom. But I don't tell her that. My mother's cooking is still the best. Guess I'll have to live at my house when I get married, and eat at your house, Mom. Kidding, of course. Anita is a good cook, good southern food.

The monsoon season must be here now cuz it's been raining for a few days steady. Just enough to antagonize us. Just a drizzle that keeps it damp and muddy. I'll have to be getting a set of snowshoes so I won't sink in the mud.

Witnessed another bunch of guys on rotation leaving today. The more that leave means the shorter my time is getting. After this I'd better go into detail about the day's happenings instead of skimming over them, thus it will make my letter longer. I'll try it tomorrow. Till then, Love, Bill

—~—

July 8, 1952, Journal Entry:

Why do I mouth off about Anita and her cooking, trying to put her down to my folks? I'm an ass hole, that's what I am. I don't know why I do those silly things. I love that southern gal and I'm going

to marry her. Sure, I am trying to play both sides against the middle and I'm stuck in the middle.

—∞—

July 9, 1952

Dear Mom, Dad and Carol

Yesterday some of us FDC guys that were off were put on detail digging a bunker. We didn't dig it all though. Only got about two feet before quitting time. During the evening we saw a movie "Peking Express." We're getting movies quite often now. We get one every other day weather permitting. Today is my first day back at the FDC on days. And believe you, me it's hard staying awake. I was used to that morning sleep when I was on nights.

Guess I'll hit the sack early tonight, listen to the radio a bit first. I just love the "Black Smith Blues" sung by that girl (name?) Write again tomorrow, Bill.

—∞—

(July 11, 1952: Pyongyang Raid, 91 U.N. aircraft hit 40 targets)

—∞—

July 11, '52

Dear Mom, Dad and Carol,

There wasn't but two letters for the whole FDC section today and I was one of the unfortunate ones. Not one single mission was fired at FDC today. Not one! I spent the time reading a book, checking the charts and other FDC work. The book is called "Never Love a Stranger." It was quite a tear jerker toward the end.

Whew! Has it ever been hot today. I'm going to sweat all my 175 pounds away. I'd much rather see it rain than be hot. I'm going down to the showers at 8 p.m. after I'm through with work. Maybe I hear some more war stories.

I'm using this lined paper it's getting kind of dark now and I can hardly see the lines, so I'd better stop. Hope to be home by Christmas. Love, Bill

—∞—

July 12, 1952

Dear Mom, Dad and Carol,

I had a fairly interesting day today. Didn't work at all in FDC. Everybody here is supposed to have a government driver's license so a few of us went today to take a driver's test. The class lasted all day and was composed of everything mechanical, why and how the engine runs—to how to drive it. Then we took a driver's test. Drove a $^{3}/_{4}$ ton truck. We will get our license in a few days. Getting the driver's license doesn't mean that we are going to drive, though. Actually, I don't want to drive any vehicle until I get out of the Army. I tried a couple time already and there are too many Army rules and regulations. I can't cope with them. So, I'll wait till I get home to do my driving, in my own car.

Today has been the hottest day so far, that I have experienced here. A 100 degrees if not higher. Really a scorcher! I was out in the sun most of the time too which made it all the worse. Our classes ended at 4:30 and I went down to the showers and showered for an hour before it was time to go to chow. After sitting in the sun all day, my clothes were soaking wet.

Top tunes here now are "Kiss of Fire," "Tell Me Why," "Blacksmith Blues," "Blue Tango," "Wheel of Fortune." That's it. The bugs and 'skeeters here sure are getting to me. We spray the tent every night. I keep a net tucked in over my cot during the night. No bugs will get to me and bite me. Summers are worse than the winters on account of the bugs. It's getting near midnight, so I best close for now. Love, Bill.

—w—

July 13, 1952

Dear Mom, Dad and Carol,

Received Carol's letter today. It was very nice hearing from her again. She writes a very nice letter. Being today is Sunday, we didn't have any formations so I took advantage of it and slept in until 8:00 a.m. Went to church this morning at the 9 a.m. mass. That's the only one they have. Went to communion, too. Feels good to listen to the chaplain, he's an all right guy.

We have a big inspection tomorrow or the next day so we had to clean up the place. We spaded around the outside of our tent and raked. She looks pretty sharp, now. Everything has to be uniform, the tent too. Everything has to be in a certain place. I tell you it's worse than Basic.

When I finished with cleaning and all that, I went down and took another shower. Boy, does it feel good to stand under that nice cool (cold) shower. But a half-hour later, you're all sweaty again. I went out for my final driver's test this morning when I returned from Mass. I thought I was finished last night. They brought it on me by surprise. Well, anyway out of fifty questions on the test, I only missed one. Pretty good, eh? When you're in low gear and coming to a stop, do you depress your brake or clutch first? I said your brake. I was wrong. Woe is me.

I'm studying a book on aviation mathematics. All the way from adding, algebra, geometry, trig and stuff like that there. I'm trying to beat it in my thick skull. I love challenges. That's all for now, Lots of love, Bill

—w—

July 14, 1952

Dear Mom, Dad and Carol,

Boy, I am tired boy today. Had guard last night and then had to go to work today. I'll get caught up with my sleeping within the next week though.

We're not busy at all in here today. I've been sitting on the breeze porch all morning with a pair of high-powered field glasses and looking over the area. It looks the same as it does with the naked eye. Watched a few planes and jets go over loaded to the gills with bombs and come back empty. They've been flying into Chink's country day and night and literally bombing the hell out of it. One of the officers here went up in an observation plane over the country and he said, it's really torn up.

> *(About this time preparations began for the Battle for OLD BALDY (Hill 266) 23rd Inf. Regt (2nd ID) sustains 39 KIA, 234 WIA and 84 MIA from July 17 to July 21.)*

We got our big corps. inspection in a few days. This area around here sure looks sharp, all cleaned and shaped up. We should pass with high honors. We even G.I.'ed the floor in our tent. How'd you like that for a basic training reminder? Mail just came in. Got a letter from you. So you finally go some chilly weather hey? Bet it really feels good. Wouldn't I love to get some of that. Wheeee! Well, till tomorrow, Love, Bill

—ɯ—

July 15, 1952

Dear Mom, Dad and Carol,

I did receive a paper today and it was fairly new too. Dated June 4th. Today was a bit cooler than it has been lately. Sure is a relief to get a few cool breezes once in a while. I sure was sweating off the pounds. Super hot!

I got guard duty again tonight. It comes around my way about once a week. So I'm writing these letters a little early, about 5 p.m. Do you know what we've go for supper. Hot dogs! I go to the PX to buy cookies and stuff so I can survive from one meal to the next. (That's a slight exaggeration.)

We got electric lights on in our tent now. No more lamps. Just like downtown. The lights are on until 10:30, and then, boink! It makes it nice having real light. One bad thing about it is that the light bulbs are good bug collectors. (But I best not complain when I think about those poor bastards on the front lines. What they would give for a tent and a light bulb, even if the bugs collect around it. Oh well, we all have to do our jobs, get this damn war over with, and go home.)

I just found out today that the rainy season is all over. It was supposed to rain like hell all during June but it didn't. Now we just have a few hot months to contend with until winter. I was just interrupted by an airplane. We have a landing strip out here and they buzz the FDC before they land.

I wrote my Arkansas gal that enemy planes were bombing nearby and they caught Chinks a mile from here. You should have seen the answer I got to that letter. Was she ever scared! Love, son, Bill

—ɯ—

> July 15, 1952, Journal Entry:
>
> *One GI here has clearly gone out of his head. He's a quiet one, doesn't get any letters from home and I know darn well he's homesick and scared. A skinny kid. I tried to talk to him a couple of times and he he told me to shove off and leave him alone. Well*

yesterday, he woke up and started waving his hands, screaming and swearing. No, he wasn't talking in his sleep, I know that for sure. He was just going crazy. "Son of a bitch, bastards," he shouted. Then he tore up his cot, threw the blanket at one of the boys. He lifted his cot and bang, it hit the floor of the tent with a crash. When he reached for his rifle, we ganged up on him. He was a handful, wild! Someone called a medic.

—w—

July 16, 1952

Dear Mom, Dad and Carol,

Got a letter from Anita. I think she's a little worried about me. I'll enclose the letter for you to read. Boy oh boy has it been hot today. Sweats been rolling off me all day and I've been trying to take it easy. One of our air observers landed and started gabbing with us. I sure would like to be one of those air observers and fly around in those planes, all day long.

They finally got smart around here and brought in several Koreans from outside to do a little work for us. They will work all day for a meal. They had them cutting down weeds and sprucing up the area. That's what we used to do.

Thank God I start working nights tomorrow. Now I can go and cool my heels down to the showers once in a while when I don't have detail. Oh yes, in one of your letters, please enclose a comb. Now and then I can't get them over here, and my last one is broken. I'm combing my hair with a seven-tooth comb. I hope you received the rest of my packages. How do you like the photo albums from Japan? Pretty detailed and neat, almost like a painting. Write soon, Love, son, Willie.

(Bill enclosed this letter from Anita to his parents on July 16, 1952)

July 8, 1952
Paris, Arkansas *(letter written in red ink)*

Dear Bill,

It has been so long since your last letter was written that I am beginning to worry about you again. In fact, I have been for a long time now. It has been about two weeks since you wrote last. Honey, what's wrong? Has something happened? What is it? You aren't still mad at me are you? I'm beginning to think now that I really am getting the cold shoulder and it is kinda hard to take. I can't understand why I don't hear from you. I care for you very much.

Both my mother and sister-in-law aren't helping either. My mother says, "Maybe he doesn't want to write to you anymore." And the other one says, "He has to have time to write to his other girls." Are they both right?

I went to my brother's house this morning and made two new skirts for myself, one red and the other green checked. Bet you didn't know I could sew, did you? Well, I can.

We had a nice little shower of rain this morning. It really cooled things off too. It sure feels good. Mom and Dad are going to the show tonight. It is my night off, but I don't want to stay home by myself so I'm going with them. Gerald just came after Nadine. They are going to the show, too.

Well I guess I had better close and wash the dishes and then get dressed to go to the post office and the show. Answer soon. I'm lonesome for you. Stay safe. Bye for now.

Love always, Anita.

> *(This was probably about the time Anita discovered that she had bone cancer. But she did not mention this in her letters to Bill.)*
>
> *(Note written by Bill on Anita's letter: Get the red ink? I told her to change colors of ink because my eyes were getting blood shot. I like her very much, maybe love her. I'm not mad at her. Don't know what gave her that idea. Guess she thinks I'm leaving her.)*

—ꟺ—

July 18, 1952

Dear Mom, Dad and Carol,

Well my shift is working nights this week so here I am at 3:00 in the morning fighting to stay awake and writing this letter. One nice thing about it though, I get to sleep tomorrow. It's been hotter than blazes. You just can't find a cool place anywhere.

I suppose about now Daddy is out fishing somewhere or at the conservation headquarters in Wakefield, in the upper peninsula. I sure would like to be up there now. Just the thought of it makes me homesick.

We had the big Corps. inspection yesterday and everything went off fine. Our captain said the general passed us with flying colors. The only thing he found wrong was in the tents. He looked under our air mattresses and lo and behold he found everything from comic books to C-rations. I had a set of my fatigues under mine. I was trying to press the wrinkles out of them. That's the way we iron our clothes here. Pretty shrewd eh? That inspection lasted all morning and during the afternoon I sat and listened to the radio. Listened to everything from concerts to hillbilly music. Even a few Japanese numbers. They sure have a variety of them on the air. Never had heard the soap opera "Helen Trent" though. Maybe her life is finished at 40 now.

I wrote Curly about a week ago and told him that I would see him in Seoul this coming Sunday. Sure hope I can make it down there and further still I hope he can too. I didn't think those pictures were too good so I didn't send one to my Arkansas gal. Didn't want to disillusion her. Too bad I couldn't record my voice. That would have been nice to send to her. She said she'd like to hear my voice. She's lonesome for me, I guess. Love, Bill

—ʍ—

July 18, 1952

Dear Mom, Dad, Carol, (2nd letter)

One of our Marine observation planes crashed today in Chink territory. There was a lieutenant and master sergeant in it. Other planes went on a search mission and found where he had crashed, but they couldn't find anything but two parachutes. The Chinks have two more prisoners.

This happened another time and I wrote Anita about it. You should have seen the letter I got from her. She was so scared for me and worried sick that the Chinks were in our tents. She loves me. Wants to marry me. But maybe you all are right, I shouldn't get serious. I'm still young. Well, anyway that's what Daddy keeps telling me. Right now I feel like an old man.

I worked all last night. I really had a heck of a time trying to sleep after my shift, it's so darn hot. I'm melting away, sure I am. When I first got here I was griping about the cold. Never satisfied. We got another movie tonight, a training film. It's all about how to shoot guns and that there stuff. Last night they were showing "Angels in the Outfield" but they shut it off in the middle of the second reel because some guys said something that the Colonel didn't like so he got mean and took it out on us by turning off the movie. So tonight we have a training film. Silly, don't you think?

It's 10 at night now and I'm sweating like a marathon runner. Boy it's hot. Starting today we have to start dunking our clothes in some sort of solution, a disinfectant, I guess. It's supposed to help prevent hemoalga (spelling?) fever, too. Something to do with the blood.

Guess I'll go hit the sack, now. Your loving son, Bill

—ɯ—

July 19, 1952

Dear Mom, Dad and Carol,

Worked all night again. Got myself another sunburn. It rained like the dickens this morning and all last night and this afternoon it was hotter than hell. I stayed at the showers for a while and every so often I got under the shower to cool off. Some of the guys came down with sun stroke and went to the medics. I can't believe how hot it's been. Over 100 degrees some days. Reminded me of what happened when I was in Basic, and all those guys had sun stroke, bad. When you stop sweating, that's it!

This evening from 6 to 7:30 we had a U.S.O. show here. They were all Special Service Men and they put on a very good show. Had a big band and played quite a few good numbers. Also had a comedian. He acted like Jerry Lewis. He was very good, and had everybody laughing. Then after the U.S.O. show we saw a movie, "Bugles in the Afternoon." Good too, I like that kind. Now it's 10:30 and I'm ready to hit the sack. I can afford to stay awake late this week cause I can sleep all day. Tomorrow night there is supposed to be a U.S.O show at the First Marine Division, starring Patricia Neal and Troupe. I don't believe I'll be able to see it cuz I'll probably have guard duty or something. It always seems to happen that way. I go sleepy-bye, now, Love, Bill

—ɯ—

July 20, 1952

Dear Mom, Dad and Carol,

I've never seen a day like this before, rain, cold and hot. To start off, this morning I went to church and all during mass I was sweating. When I came back they had us digging bunkers, but they finally let us quit cause one guy passed out, sun stroke. It was too hot for that.

Then this afternoon we went to the Patricia Neal show and it rained all during the performance. They weren't going to put the show on today because of the rain. Finally they said as long as we didn't mind sitting out in the rain, they'd go on with the show. And that they did. I had to laugh one time when Pat Neal ran out on the stage. The stage was wet and whoops, there she was sprawled all over the stage. She didn't hurt herself though. There were others there, too. One was Tony Windsor or something like that. And there was a Jenny Jackson or Jackie Jenson. The last one was a singer. It was a pretty good show. But I practically froze to death before I changed my soaking wet clothes. Then the rain stopped and it got hot again.

Now it's evening and it's raining again. Cats and dogs. You've never seen it rain until you see it rain in Korea. It literally pours in buckets. But it doesn't cool it off for long. Water is leaking all over and everything is soaked.

There's a rumor going around that there is going to be a hillbilly show here in a few days. There is lots of entertainment here. Got one letter today from Anita (my Arkansas hillbilly). Sure enough she still loves me. How about that? More on the morrow, Love, Bill

—ʌʌʌ—

July 21, 1952

Dear Mom, Dad & Carol,

Seems funny to be getting letters from you from home and all the while you're vacationing in God's country, up north in Michigan. I have the same gripe again that I had in previous letters. It's too damn hot! It's ten o'clock at night now, and I'm actually sweating. I've been sweating as though I'd been in a sauna.

During the morning we had to work on our bunker. We (FDC guys) have to dig a bunker 8×8×8. It's not too easy, either. There are a lot of rocks and gravel and what not to endure. We've been digging for two mornings now and got about two feet deep. Besides I don't believe in working too hard in hot weather. It could knock a man out. (It has knocked out two of our guys). This afternoon I went to the showers again. A couple more days and once again I'll be cooped up in FDC for a week and won't be able to take advantage of this nice sun outdoors. It rained a while today but that didn't stop the sun from beating down on us. It'll shine come hell or high water. What a place!

Here's what we did today. First, we have a five gallon water can in our tent which needs to be taken over to the water truck and filled up. We do that twice a day. It's getting so nobody wants to go anymore so four of us sit down and play a game of cards (hearts). The loser goes and gets the water. We started that today and guess who went and got the water? Yep, me. I'll have to learn to play that game.

I quit eating out of that tray they gave us. I went back to the good ole mess kit. I'll probably be eating out of the mess kit when I get home, I guess. It's too awkward to carry the tray. I've dropped it three times in the hot water where we wash them. Then on the trays you have no handles to slide your silverware and cup. It's hard to hold on to all that stuff and wash it at the same time. I lost my spoon in the bottom of the wash can too and had to wait till they dumped the dirty water out so I could get it. I always did like to eat out of a mess kit anyway. I sure hope those packages I sent while I was on R & R got there all right. I sent them parcel post so they should have gotten there at the same time. I had that fishing rod insured for $25 in case it gets lost. I didn't insure the other stuff though. Maybe I should have.

So Carol is going with Bob again? Two little love birds for a while probably. Now isn't she too young to be going steady, Daddy? What is she, eighteen? My little sister can go steady, but if I mention anything about my Arkansas gal, I'm too young! What's the deal? I'm old enough to be in this hell hole fighting for my country, right?

Have to cut this short. What delicious meals you have at home. Did you say hot dogs? Yum! Love, Bill

—m—

Journal Entry, July 21, 1952:

Same old crap with Carol and Bob. I'm getting sick of it. She's just 18 and Mom and Dad don't see anything wrong with her constant back and forth with Bob. But man, if I mention Anita and our plans, whamo! They say wait, they say no, they say I have plenty of time. Time. Who knows how much time I have? Only God, knows. What the hell is wrong? I know I've said it often, so why do I give a damn what they think. I love this gal, and I'm going to marry her. This long distance romance is getting under my skin. Somehow, I can feel that something is happening in Arkansas. Something that Anita is not telling me. Or am I dreaming? Too much, too much. I'm getting to sound like that GI they carried off to the medics a while back. Last I heard, they were shipping him out to the states. They had him in a straight jacket.

—~—

July 22, 1952

Dear Mom, Dad and Carol,

. . . . What a Skosh mail call we had today. Only five letters for the whole darn place. Probably get Takson mail tomorrow though. I have a tough time sleeping in all this heat, but I manage to make it all right. I'm getting so I can sleep anywhere, anytime.

Only a few more days now till payday rolls around again. I can see the ole bank book climbing. I was sitting here tonight looking over my fishing lure book again. Every now and then I get it out and look it over. It rained again today while the sun was shining. If that ain't the craziest weather I seen in all my born days. I'm at a loss for words again tonight. Write more tomorrow. Love, your son, Willie, Lump, Lump. . . .

—~—

July 24, 1952

Dear Mom, Dad and Carol,

I neglected writing yesterday cause we were kinda busy up until evening and after that we had a movie that I didn't want to miss, "Bend of the River." It was a darn good movie.

Tomorrow night, "The Marrying Kind" is playing. I hear that Judy Holiday doesn't play a dumb blonde in this one.

I started working days today. . . . I just heard the four top tunes a little while ago when I was eating chow. "Blacksmith Blues" (4), "Anytime" (3), "Blue Tango" (2) and "The Wheel of Fortune" (1). Are we much behind?

What a blow that was to find out you weren't going on that trip to South America or Alaska. I thought for sure you would be going. That letter you wrote in the post office sure surprised me. Did you run out of ink or a pen?

Fred G. I guess has got a pretty good deal in Georgia. Heard he's a supply clerk and lives off the post with his wife.

Tonight is another one of those nights I can't think of anything to write about. Two more weeks and I will be twenty-two years old. An old man!

Write again tomorrow, Love, Bill.

—ʊʊ—

> July 25, 1952, Journal Entry:
>
> *I'm in another world here in Korea. Might as well be on Mars. My folks are going on vacations and I'm fighting a war. Not by my lonesome, that's for sure. Okay, sometimes it's cool here. In the dayroom, when it's quiet some of the boys play craps and poker, others are at the ping pong table or dart board. And then there is the softball games outdoors, which of course, FDC always wins. Well, almost always. It's not always like that.*
>
> *We have some near battles when the Chinks fly too low and scare the hell out of us. But somehow those Gooks don't know we're here. Lucky us. Or are they just teasing us, and waiting for the big blast off! Who knows? Whatcha gonna do? That's why us Catholics line up outside the priest's tent for confession. "Father," we'd say. And then confess to everything including drinking, screwing (on R & R) and gambling.*

—ʊʊ—

July 25, 1952

Dear Mom, Dad and Carol,

I wish you'd cut out the notices of guys entering the service, etc, and send them to me. That paper you sent me today had four guys in there that I know. One of them is now in Seoul.

You heard about the 45 extra dollars we are going to get over here (combat pay)? If that goes through and I think it will, that bankbook of mine will really climb. What a miser I've become. The combat pay is effective from the day we arrive in Korea. So I should be getting quite a chunk of back pay.

Business was slow today so I requested permission to leave for the tent for a little while. I was gone precisely two hours. I lay down and fell plum asleep. It did me good, because this morning I was so tired I could hardly move. You remember how I was in the morning at home? Tired and sleepy, then toward evening I was 'up and at 'em.' I haven't changed in that respect. The show, "The Marrying Kind" is going to start in about a half hour. I hope it's as good as the other one she played in. Judy Holiday, I mean.

We have been busy firing lots of missions. Will cut it short.
Love to all, Son, Bill

> *(The missions Bill mentions, was a continuation of the Battle for Old Baldy (Hill 266) which began on July 17 and went through Aug. 4: 23rd Inf. Regt. (2nd Id) sustains 39 KIA, 234 WIA and 84 MIA by July 21.)*

July 26, 1952

Dear Mom, Dad & Carol,

I've often heard about that new Ferry that goes across the straits in Michigan but never did see it. It sure is a beautiful one (from the postcards you sent). I suppose it's really modern compared with the older ones, eh? Those cards sure brought some memories flooding back.

About that fly rod now. Daddy says it's too heavy. It's only a 3½ ounce rod. I didn't think it was heavy. I figured it to be just about right. You'll notice that there's about four rods in one there. You don't have to leave it in the box. I'll give you permission to take it out of the box and experiment with it. You know, break it in for me. It's got nice tip action to it, too. I think.

There's been a slight change in weather today and tonight. So far it's been raining with a capital "R". It's been like this all day and hasn't let up a bit. There is mud up to my ankles here. To top it off I have guard duty. I just got off my first two hours and I'm a little wet you might say. Being a rainy day as it is, it was considerably cooler, and we didn't have a single mission to fire. It really was a dull day just sitting around in there and looking at the four walls all day. It's much better when we fire something. Time passes faster.

Well, I guess I'd better hit the sack now and get a little sleep before I go on guard again. Only 23 more times to pull guard. Lots of love, Bill.

Journal Entry, July 26, 1952

I have to let this all out. My Dad, yes my father sometimes is a pain in the ass. Now about that terrific fly rod that I bought in Japan and sent to him. First he says it's too heavy, and it's only 3½ ounces, then it doesn't handle right, then something about the tip action. Hell, why doesn't he say right out that he doesn't like it, and leave it in the box for me, when and if I get home. I just don't get it. Enough griping for now.

July 27, 1952, 7 p.m.

Dear Mom, Dad and Carol,

Received the box of cookies, song sheets and magazines today. They sure will come in handy. I'll be singing and telling jokes and what not all night. The movie magazines really go over big here. The cookies got here in sorta poor shape, this time. They were kind of busted up, but they really tasted good. A funny thing about those envelopes you sent me. Five of them were sealed, and the rest were stuck together, but I managed to get most of them apart. The kind I have been using are the best for hot weather, I guess. Thanks for everything.

We had a full day of rain today up until 4:30 anyway. Then it cleared up just all of a sudden and now it's starting to get a little cloudy again. Hope it doesn't rain again tonight because we have a movie, "The Red Ball Express." It's another one of them war movies, I guess.

Boy you should have seen me after I came off of guard duty last night. I was soaked through. Really drenched. I'd like to know who would be dumb enough to be sneaking around in all that rain, anyway. The Chinks were probably snug and warm in their own tents.

Since it's Sunday today, I slept in until 7:45 in the morning and at 8:30 I went to church. After church I turned in a set of my fatigues for new ones. It will take about a week or two before I get the new ones. The pair I had were a mite too large, 32 waist for the pants and a 40 jacket. I still can squeeze into a 28 inch pants and a 34 or 36 jacket fits really good. You can imagine how those others looked on me. Like the drape shape or something.

Well I'm nearing the end of the page so I'll sign off for this time, once again. Another visit, tomorrow. Your loving son, Bill

—∿—

July 29, 1952

Dear Mom, Dad and Carol,

Received a letter from Ma and one from Pa. Also one from Fred which knocked me off my feet. That's the third time I've heard from him since I've been in the Army. Also got a letter from Anita and she's telling me how nice it will be to become a Yankee soon. The girl seems to be jumping to conclusions. Oh well that's what I get for being so darn handsome.

It's still raining and it hasn't showed any signs of letting up either. It may rain for a month for all I know and as a matter of fact for all I care. I just can't figure out how I'm going to get my clothes clean. They don't seem to dry very well hanging out in the rain.

Nothing doing in FDC yet. I've been reading, writing, checking charts, going over graphs and what not to keep myself busy. The meals seem to be few and far between when there's nothing to do. Time goes too slow. It's true what that say about the Army. "Hurry up and wait." I get hungry at 10 a.m. instead of 11:30 like I'm supposed to do. Too bad it had to be raining while you were on your vacation, or R & R as Father calls it.

I haven't heard anything else about me coming home for Christmas. As I said before it was only a rumor. Sometimes we are lucky enough to learn a few things ahead of time but most of the time, that's what they are—rumors. You never know what will happen, until it happens. That's the Army. Those pictures you sent were the right ones. Did you have trouble with the car? Well I got a little more written this time. Will quit for now. Your loving son, Bill.

—∿—

July 29, 1952, Journal Entry:

Anita! She wants to know what it will feel like to be a Yankee! Yipes! Sure will be nice for her to become a Yankee. That girl is something else. And I sure enough miss her sweet face and body. I'm not telling Ma and Pa the whole story about Anita. Sometimes I think I'll let well enough alone. I don't want to get any more lectures in the mail about not getting serious until I get home. Don't want to make waves. Besides what am I ? A child? What have they got against my Arkansas gal? Beats me!

—w—

July 30, 1952

Dear Mom, Dad and Carol,

It finally decided to clear up and we had a bit of sunshine for half a minute. Then the sun went behind the clouds to hide the rest of the day. The temporary ceasing of the rain gave me a chance to take a shower after 3 or 4 days without one. Instead of the little trickling creek we had a big gushing stream before us. I showered first and then laid in the creek and cooled my heels. It was almost deep enough to go swimming. The Inchon River, so I have heard is up about 25 feet. It has washed away three vital bridges and is really doing a lot of damage. One of our firing batteries is completely isolated because the bridge is gone. Most all telephone lines are out. The only way we have of getting supplies to them is by helicopters. The supplies consist of food, ammo, etc.

This flooding is bringing more disaster than anything else. I suppose you're reading about the rain in your newspaper. We still are carrying on the normal duties of the day though. I sure do feel sorry for those poor guys in the infantry. They are knee deep in mud.

Starting today I work the night shift. I got tonight off but I work tomorrow night. It'll give me a little chance now to catch up on my sleep again. This life ruins a man. No sleep one week and then work the next. You just can't go over and go to sleep any old time.

Had pretty good chow again tonight. Turkey this time. Seems to be getting better but it probably will slack off again, like it always does. Well I guess I might as well hit the hay for tonight. Your son, Bill.

—m—

July 31, 1952

Dear Mom, Dad and Carol,

Makes it a lot easier to answer a letter when I get one. Had a little break in the weather today. For a change the sun was shining in the afternoon. You'd think with all this rain we've been having it would cool off around here. It didn't. Soon as the sun comes out it gets hotter than the devil again. The sun looked pretty good, never the less.

I spent the morning until noon sleeping and the afternoon trying to find something constructive to do. Don't forget I worked last night. But nothing to be found so I cooled my heels until 5 p.m. when we had mail call. Oh yes, I also received another newspaper.

The papers are coming pretty good, no complaints. No complaints about the mail either, or for that matter chow, it's better, too.

The Colonel had a birthday party last night and he had an extra tent pitched to celebrate the occasion. All the officers were invited. They had a big birthday cake, wine and the whole thing. The officers had a high old time. If that ain't silly. A big party in the combat zone. He's the berries, I tell you. Till tomorrow, Son, Bill

—m—

Aug. 1, 1952

Dear Mom, Dad and Carol,

According to the letter and post card I got today you are on your way home. It sure didn't seem like you stayed up North long. Sounds like you had an exciting trip coming back. Besides taking pictures of the bear did you get any deer at all? When you went to the drug store in Wakefield what did you have to say about that girl there? I haven't written to her in three months. She probably doesn't even know me any more. Oh my poor breaking heart.

Things around here have been just as hard as always. Had to go to sleep again this morning after working all night and the Sergeant came around and woke me up just to clean some old rusty shovels. Of all the stupid tricks. These shovels were used by FDC guys to dig bunkers and must have left them in that sad shape. We were the only ones available and got stuck with the job. I wouldn't have minded doing it if I had been awake.

The highlight today is that it's payday. I got 73 bucks and about 50 of it I'm sending home again. Money, money, money. When we start getting that 45 extra bucks combat pay that should put up the account a might more.

I gotta work tonight and can hardly wait until tomorrow when I can get some sleep. I'm tired. I gotta write Anita a letter yet tonight. Been four days since I wrote her. Love from, Bill.

—w—

Journal Entry, Aug. 1, 1952

Well, I finally wrote to Anita after four days. Why am I doing this to her? Why am I doing this to me? Her letters sound sad sometimes. She IS missing me. I know that for sure. But this is a different kind of sadness. I can't quite put my finger on it. What am I going to do with my Arkansas gal? Lord knows. When and if I come home. I don't know. Those gooks are getting mighty close. Don't want to scare the hell out of my folks or Anita. Sometimes I can actually hear those Chinese breathing. Only kidding, it's all in my mind. I'm playing mind games.

—w—

Aug. 3, 1952

Dear Mom, Dad and Carol,

I'm working all night tonight and I just woke up a few minutes ago to finish off the rest of the night. I slept the first part of the night and my partner on duty sleeps the second half. It sure is hard to get up at 3 a.m. and just sit here and listen to the stillness of the night, unless we have a mission. When I get off this morning, I'll get a chance to sleep until noon. I'm so tired now, I could sleep all day.

Two guys from FDC are going on R & R this morning. I have to go over and wake them up in a little while (3:30 a.m.). Wish I were going again to get away from this place for a little while. My turn should be coming up in a while to go down to Seoul for a three-day rest. During my R & R then I might get to see some guys that I know because they are stationed near Seoul.

Another five days from today and I'll be 22 years old. Remember how I celebrated my last birthday at Camp Chaffee? I was on the firing range target practicing with my carbine. This year I'll be directing fire for 155 Howitzers.

Had a fairly cool day today again. It rained a little off and on and mostly cloudy all day. Got until the end of September before we can even think about cool weather coming here to stay. They have funny seasons here in Korea, compared to Michigan.

You know those songs I mentioned—"Wheel of Fortune" and the others. Well they are at the height of popularity over here now. Everybody is playing these tunes and that's all you hear on the radio. Probably by now those songs are fading out in the states and new ones are taking their place. The movie was "The Golden—". I saw it once before and I saw it again anyway. It was pretty good. Better than seeing Tom Mix or Gene Autry.

I've been writing this little by little in between work. It's almost 6 a.m. now. I gotta turn in a morning report and a few other things. Write again tonight, Love, Bill.

—w—

Aug. 3. 1952, Journal Entry:

Another birthday in a few days. God, I'll be 22! And what the hell am I doing with my life? Got to get this Army and war stuff behind me. Keep thinking that way, that's the only way to get through this mess. Too much going on, not enough going on. Am I making sense? Shit! So the big guys tell us we are the "brains" and without us, all is screwed up! Those other guys think we have a cushion job. Sure, all that tension, all those decisions, all that moving around so the gooks can't find us. It sure is a "soft" job, a job that will drive you crazy, if you don't watch out. Enough dribble for now, I'm getting the high sign to get back on the charts and maps.

—w—

Aug. 3, 1952

2nd letter Dear Mom, Dad and Carol,

Sure do like hearing from Carol, cuz she really writes a good letter. Was tough to hear that you had to do that to my $5 boid, Ollie. Gone but not forgotten.

You're going to get another bird aren't you? This time find out how you're supposed to feed the bird and other important details so that you won't have to give him the axe, like Ollie. Carol you didn't mention if you took down my Hawk. Let me know.

We heard some bad news today. The Major mentioned that we have to finish our bunker. That means, without a doubt, that I'll be digging a bunker tomorrow. I hate the very thought of it.

Today turned out to be a very nice day for a change. No rain at all. A nice clear blue sky and a hot sun. I wanted to go down to the showers and get a little more than but I done went and fell asleep and when I woke up it was too late.

You're reading about all those flying saucers over there? Have you seen any yet? There's an article in Stars and Stripes every day and the July 1st one has a big article. Strange what people can imagine. Well guess I'll quit now.

(An ocean full of fish that kiss every wave—1925 saying) I don't think that's right, or is it? Love, Bill

—~—

Aug. 4, 1952

Dear Mom, Dad and Carol,

Got rid of 3 bucks right quick and fast this morning. Paid for my laundry. Three bucks a month is pretty reasonable to have all your clothes washed as many times as necessary. Didn't have a chance to get my morning sleep today. Had to pull a detail. Some of us guys had to put new cloth and paper on the firing range. This afternoon we finished it up then went to the showers.

This evening we played a little ball and that's it. Now I have to work all night again. I'm going to see about bringing our radio in and listen to it. There are some good popular songs playing every night from 11:30 p.m. to 6 a.m. Love, Your son, Bill

—~—

Aug. 5, 1952

Dear Mom, Dad and Carol,

So you and Father were feuding a bit on the way home eh? That sounds familiar. It happens just about every time.

Remember that time when we were going West and you all were feudin' and you saw that mountain goat in the hills and you wouldn't say anything about it? Thanks for sending a comb too. The one I have is toothless. Like combing your hair with a stick. Got the pictures too. So Father is repainting the windows again, eh?

You mentioned something in your letter about TV. Tell me what exactly is TV? Ha. Headquarters Battery played a game against Able Battery. They beat us 4-3. The game started at 2 p.m. the hottest part of the day. I wouldn't play in all this heat for anything.

I got guard again tonight. I get it every fifth day around here. Well I only have five or six more months to pull this crap. Write more tomorrow, got guard now. Love, Bill

—m—

Aug. 6, 1952

Dear Mom, Dad and Carol,

I just finished watching a movie and it's after 10 p.m. now. It was a really good one with "Betty Grable" in "Meet Me After the Show." I guess it's old, but I haven't seen it.

Tomorrow we start days and that means working from 8 a.m. to 8 p.m. with no sleep. This morning was wholly composed of detail. First we posted bulls' eyes on our targets and later all I could see was bulls' eyes. After we finished two of us headed for our unfinished bunker and started bailing water out of it so we could get to finishing it one of these days. I dread the thought of it.

Oh yes, I also received the OCSC magazine and the box that you sent July the 4th. Everything airmailed is in excellent condition. Those were Number One books and everything else. Thanks. I sweltered through another hot one today. Hot and humid. The nights are cool though.

I thought that I had mentioned that I received those "dog tags" you sent a while back. They got here safe and sound. As long as the pen you sent me is guaranteed, I'll send it back if it gives me any trouble. It's getting kinda late so I'll sign off. Love, Billy.

—m—

Aug. 7, 1952

Dear Mom, Dad and Carol,

Well today is my birthday and today I received the newspaper and box that you sent. It's the one containing the shorts, candy, envelopes and comic books. If you had sent the fountain pen along in that box, I didn't get it. It was nowhere to be seen. Maybe you forget to put it in the box, or someone could have copped it along the way.

We fired the longest mission today that we ever had. Started at 4 p.m. and continued firing until it was too dark for the observers to observe anymore. We fired a hundred and forty eight (148) rounds at one target before we finally got it. It was out about 2½ miles and there was quite a bit of dispersion by the time they got there. Many times we can fire six rounds and knock out a target.

After I got out of work at 8:00 p.m. I went down and took a shower in the dark. There was a nice big moon out so I really shouldn't say it was dark. Just jumped in that cold water and there was no sun to warm me up. All I can say is Brrrr! I feel a lot better with that sweat off me. I think I'll quite writing and go to bed. Good night, Love, Bill.

—~—

Aug. 7, 1952, Journal Entry:

It's my 22nd birthday and we fired 148 missions, non-stop. We were a sorry lot when we finished. We rocked the hell out of those Gooks! Even the priest joined us in FDC. He said, "Bless us oh Lord, And help us give them commies hell!" He's a priest, but also an all right guy, one of us. The priest has guts!

All day the FDC tent stank of sweaty men. We had been at it for 15 hours and it was even hotter and stickier then it was outside with the sun burning down on you. I tried to look on the bright side, I figured that the misery of the hot tent would keep me awake during the missions. It sure as hell kept everyone else awake. For once, gabby Pete had nothing to say. He was too busy reading charts and maps, just like the rest of us. And the Captain became one of the "boys." The only "bad guys" were the North Ko-

reans and the Joe Chinks. Well, Happy Birthday to me! Oh yes, my pal Pete wished me a Happy Birthday in Greek! Something like "Kala yenethyah" or whatever. Hey, where is my ice cream and beer? I'm got to celebrate, right? Wrong!

—~—

Aug. 8, 1952

Dear Mom, Dad and Carol,

We were supposed to have a few TV films rolled off for us tonight in place of a regular movie. We were supposed to see Sid Caesar and Imogene Coca and some other programs but the movie projector broke and we didn't see anything. So I cam back to the tent and I'm writing letters now. All day long we have been sucking on candy and eating pistachio nuts. My fingers are all red from the nuts. They're good!

You know how hard it is to get me up in the morning? Well this morning the guys said they kept yelling at me but I swear I never did hear them. Everyone is supposed to make a formation at 6:30 a.m. and I've made it every morning except this morning. I was a might late for it and consequently I had to put in two hours digging a bunker tonight from 6 to 8 p.m. There were three other guys in the same situation. I guess that might make me get up a little earlier. I keep telling them to roll me out of bed. They all obliged. It seems that's the easy way to do it.

Now you mention Flying Saucers. That's the last straw. That's all I've been hearing in the news and reading in the newspapers. Some brain has seen them I suppose. Sure! There are probably some one-eyed green men with six arms coming from Mars or some far off planet. I think it's all in the mind. One person thinks he sees something and then everybody else agrees. Have you seen any yet?

Well, I've got about five more minutes before lights out so I will sign off. Love, Willie

—~—

Aug. 9, 1952

Dear Mom, Dad and Carol,

The insured box with the pen in it arrived in good shape. I don't know what to say except "Thanks a lot". I really appreciate it. There's one request I'd like to make. In that box you had one piece of Finlander Toast. I would like you to send me a 2-pound box of that toast. It's really delicious. Next time you do that, eh?

The weather is still hot here. Shows no sign of relief what so ever. Have to change clothes everyday. Lucky thing it only costs three bucks a month for laundry or I'd be broke. Talking about broke reminds me of money. Are you still getting my allotment checks? Still coming O.K. huh? I better get off the money subject or I'll be inquiring again the amount of my bank account.

Even with the new pen, my penmanship is still bad as it always has been. I thought I could write better with a new pen. Boy this Parker '51 really works fine.

Getting late again and have to write to Anita, my Arkansas gal. Till tomorrow, Love, Bill

Aug. 10, 1952

Dear Mom, Dad and Carol,

I got guard again tonight so I'm writing this before I have to go out. It's a beautiful night out tonight. Big full moon almost. It's starting to change now. It's about an eighth now. In another week there will just be a banana in the sky. It's nice and bright during this clear warm evening. Notice I said warm and not hot. That's quite a difference around here.

Saw a real good show tonight. "Mr. Belvadere Rings the Bell." That show even made me feel younger. You probably know what it's about so I won't go into the plot. It was very funny. I'm writing this letter by candlelight now. They just turned off the lights for another night. I've got another hour to sit here before I go on guard. I'm listening to nice soft music too. Without a radio or going down to the shower to cool my heels, I could not survive (kidding). Just three more days before I go on night shift at FDC for a week.

I can hardly wait for those weeks to get here so I can catch up on my sleep. But to tell you the truth, I'm waiting for the big Rotation, when it's time for me to come home. But it sounds so unbelievable. No kidding. It's hard to explain it but it seems funny.

Will write tomorrow, Love, Willie

Aug. 10, 1952, Journal Entry:

I dream about going home all the time. Will I ever get home, and in one piece? Damn it! What the hell is this war all about? Police action? Shit! This is war, man. And I want to get out of it. God? Are you listening?

Aug. 11, 1952

Dear Mom, Dad and Carol, There was a drop of approximately fourteen men that left here a week ago and now they're all back. They got down as far as Saesabo, Japan, and they sent them back cuz they couldn't handle them. Sure hope they clear that place out before I get there. That's a sad feeling to be turned back when you are on your way home.

They've got that old Army plane flying low around here again this evening spraying the area. Bet the plane ain't but 100 or 200 feet off the ground. It's the main event at present. Everybody is out gawking at it including me. There are more planes flying over here to bomb Joe Chink. Air strikes have been called into FDC all day. We have to plot them on the charts so we don't fire in the area during the strike. Only had four hours sleep last night so I'll cut this short and hit the sack.

Roger and out, Love, Bill

(Aug. 12–16, 1952: Battle of Bunker Hill (Hill 122) First major Marine ground action in western Korea is fought by the 1st Marines: 48 KIA, 313 WIA)

Aug. 13, 1952

Dear Mom, Dad and Carol,

We were super busy up till 8:00 p.m. Plenty missions to plot. Can't tell you much about it, but I think we got many, many Joe Chinks! Go, Go, Go! That's what it was like in FDC. Sometimes it's amazing how we work as a team, all business, like clockwork. It seems as if we can read each other's mind. The charts and maps and everything is there and we manage to get it right and it falls in place. That's what it's all about. After work, I was too tired to do anything but sleep. So I did.

Here's something humorous. Yesterday morning another guy and I were picked to mix some white wash to use to paint the white lines on the airstrip. Well, we got a pail of water and put some lime in it. We stirred it up and lo and behold it was too thin and we were out of lime. So someone got the idea of putting salt and corn starch in the mixture to thicken it up. So after stirring it for a few minutes you should have seen the chemical reaction taking place! It started popping, boiling and foaming all over. It looked precisely like lava flowing all over the place. We never laughed so hard in all our lives. We were actually scared to go near it. The stuff and the pail was hotter than hell.

It's near a hundred and the humidity is about the same. I just went out and checked the thermometer and it says 106 in the sun. Whew! I am slowly melting, melting. But the old timers, said I should enjoy it, cause it gets mighty cold here in the winter time.

I'm enclosing another letter from Anita. She sure is the berries. She must like me but then again I don't see why she wouldn't. Also got a letter from Curly yesterday too. He's gotta stay there until his discharge. So he won't be leaving here until 40 days from his discharge date. If I'm back in the states three months from my discharge, I'll get discharged 21 months. That sounds good.

A while ago there was an officer here looking for men who want to re-up for another three years. I almost laughed in his face. Some guys do it though. Crazy in the head. I've been thinking quite a lot about what I should take up in school when I return. Should I go into night school or full time? Been meditating on some sort of mechanics such as diesel or hydraulics. Or even civil service. Maybe I could wiggle my way into a school of forestry or conservation. All of them sound good. I know I'm old enough to make up my mind but the thought of continuing school has penetrated into my thick skull.

Best I find out what is available for me to take and then make the decision. I'd like to hear Father's and your opinions. I know you'd like me to go to school. I know it's all up to me, but I'd like your say on it, too. It might throw a different light on the subject.

I'm going to start sending home some pictures with my letters. All of them were taken during my R & R in Tokyo and Yokohama, Japan. Got about 50 of them. Just got them back from being developed. Write soon, Lots of love, your son, Bill.

Anita's letter—written in green ink on August 3, 1952, Paris, Arkansas

Dearest Bill,

I will answer your letter that I received yesterday afternoon. I planned to write last night but we got home a little late and I was so sleepy so I went to bed. I started to work again today. You know something, I think I like the idea of a vacation better than working.

I'm glad you like the idea of me saving the red ink to write to my other boyfriends. Honey, didn't you know that you are the only boy I write to? The only reason I said that was because you have been talking about writing to all your girlfriends. And I really believe that you are writing to someone else. Like Beverly, for instance. I still believe you write to her. You won't tell me for sure, you just keep me wondering and worrying.

Ruby stayed with me last night. We had a nice time, but I missed you. Ruby and Hogan are getting along just fine. They say to tell you Hello. I still don't have any pictures. I can't even remember to get any film. I'll have to have my picture taken in a studio. How about that?

I didn't finish this letter last night so I will finish it this morning. We are working and I sure am working hard! I think that it's going to rain today. It's cloudy and I hope it does rain to cool things off a little. Well honey I have to close now and go to town to the post office. Answer soon.
All my love, always, Anita.

—~—

Aug. 14, 1952

Dear Mom, Dad and Carol,

I don't' see how people can stand weather like this year after year. It'll drive a man insane! But this month is going pretty fast. I expect that September will be cooler. This morning I caught up on my sleep. We're on nights again. I usually get to snooze a little during the morning hours, but in the afternoon, when they find us they give us trouble. Well, this afternoon they found us so we had to bury some hooks in the ground on the airfield to moor the planes during high winds.

I would not doubt it in the least that very shortly we'll be constructing a hanger out there. I wouldn't put it past them. After we finished with the hooks I took my sweaty self down to the showers and stayed there for a while. That's the only way to combat the heat.

About my pay for the month—I'm getting about $123 and some odd change. That's with longevity and overseas pay added. I sent $50 money orders and that leaves me $23. Are you still trying to keep track of my money for me? Remember when you used to bail me out when I didn't have any money left come Wednesday or Thursday. "What on earth do you do with it? You just blow it all on foolishness. You just can't stand to save a little." You said this every week just as regular as your morning argument with Carol. Do you two still argue about what she should wear or she didn't iron the night before? "Or where did you put that and I had it here last night. Honestly, Carol, it just didn't get up and walk away." Sounds familiar. Those were the days.

So you are going to buy another Buick? Remember what I said. Once you get a big car you won't want to change anymore.

You think my Arkansas gal will sue me for breach of promise if I don't marry her? Well, maybe I won't disappoint her, but I'm not home yet. She wrote me today and told me she hadn't gotten a letter from me in five days but still she's faithful enough to write anyway. I guess I got the right kind of girl this time. I believe you'd like her. I don't think it'll be like that merry-go-round that Patsy put me on.

Did I ever tell you about Anita, my Arkansas gal? Well to start off. She's 20 years old, five foot 3 or 4, 112 pounds and cute too. She dresses nice, nice personality and all that. Crazy as it seems, I believe she loves me. She's faithful and I guess she wants to get married. She graduated from high school and she says she's a good cook and all around housewife. Has dark hair, dark complexion and a few freckles. She seems intelligent although you can't judge by her letters. She's considerate and everything. You'll probably be meeting her in less than a year. That's about it for now. Any questions? Love Bill

—m—

Aug. 14, 1952, Journal Entry:

Why are my folks so against me marrying my Arkansas gal? That's the same old question that has been buzzing around in my mind all these months. They are driving me crazy with their "wait till you get home" and "she might sue you for breach of promise" and all that other crap they are dishing out in their letters. I have said it a hundred times, but I'll say it again. What about Carol and Bob? And their silly romance, always fighting and then making up. What about them? I can make up my own mind. I can! And I will!

Aug. 15, 1952

Dear Mom, Dad and Carol,

I'll answer a few questions that you asked. That 20 dollar increase in my pay must have been some back pay. That box that I received a while back had the foot powder in it. So far I have gotten everything that you have sent me with the exception of a few newspapers and letters, which are probably on their way.

We had what you'd call a "different" day. It was so hot until 3:00 p.m. a person could hardly bear it. "Heat stroke weather" we call it here. I worked all night last night.

This afternoon we all went to fire and familiarized ourselves with the 50 cal. machine gun. I fired a belt of ammo. Can't hit nothing though cause the gun jumps around so much. After shooting it I looked like a drug addict for a few minutes. I couldn't stop myself from shaking.

You should have seen the place they put that 50. Right square on top of a mountain. I was almost too pooped to shoot the thing when I got up there. We fired across a valley into another mountain. I tell you it's no trouble finding a mountain over here.

Right after we got back I went down to take a shower and I'll be darned it wasn't five minutes after it started raining. It came on all of a sudden. All day long the sun had been shining. It only rained for two hours and the sun came back out again making it just as hot as ever. It better start cooling off soon or I'm going to see the Captain about coming home.

You hear Eddy Fisher sing very much over there? He's really made a hit hasn't he, especially with the song "Anytime." He sounds like Don Cornell who also is a good singer. Till tomorrow, Lots of love, Bill

—w—

Aug. 16, 1952

Dear Mom, Dad and Carol,

Good to hear you're getting my money orders all right. There's one important letter going home each month and that's the one with the money order. Did you get the allotment okay?

We had sorta a cool day today. It only went up to 92 degrees. I worked last night from 8 p.m. to 8 a.m. I'm going to be lazy when I get home, sleeping all morning and taking afternoon naps. Ha. Can you see me doing that?

Got a good show tonight—"The San Francisco Story." Our shift goes to work at 8 p.m. tonight but I hope I'll be able to get off to see the show. Right now I'm listening to Eddy Fisher's program. He plays over the Armed Forces network. I don't know if he has a program in the states or not. Has he? I think he's a really good singer.

This afternoon everybody had to get another shot in the arm. This time it was a typhoid shot. Lots of love, Bill

—w—

Sunday, Aug. 17, 1952

Dear Mom, Dad and Carol,

Today being Sunday I went to church this morning to start off the day. Another thing I can say for myself, I didn't go to sleep at all at any time today. That's unusual for me especially when I'm working nights. I generally sleep in the morning. I gotta work tonight so I guess I'll make up on my sleep tomorrow.

I got myself another sunburn today. Like a fool I went out and played ball this evening and got all sweated up and hot and didn't feel good. Never again will I do that. I'll wait till cooler weather before I start running around. Remember the typhoid shot we got the other day? Well, today more than half of the Battery got sick from them. I feel a little woozey too. I wonder what caused it?

Our Battery Commander got relieved of his duties as of this evening. He still retains his rank but another Captain is taking over. The Colonel did it. The Captain wanted to put up another squad tent cause one of the tents here was getting pretty crowded. And the Colonel didn't like the idea and so the Captain and him had a few rounds of words and presto—"You are relieved of command." It was all very interesting to watch. I guess he will start his duties in FDC as a liaison officer. That will work out just dandy because the Major at FDC and the Captain don't like each other. It's getting a bit exciting around here now.

Well, I've got to get to work, so I'll cut it short. Lots of love to all, Bill

Aug. 18, 1952, 7:00 p.m.

Dear Mom, Dad and Carol,

I suppose you're reading in the papers about this hurricane that is sweeping through the Far East? We are expecting it here tonight. I don't know whether it's going to hit us full force or just the tail end of it. We've been getting an awful lot of rain all through the day but the wind hasn't been blowing hard. All day long we've been tying down the tents and putting sandbags on everything. I hope it ain't as bad as they expect it to be.

It's the same old story as the last time when it rained. You're always wet and waddling in the mud knee deep. It's cool though. That's one good thing about it.

Only got one letter today and that was from Anita. She sure is a faithful kid. It's been nine months since I've seen her and she writes four or five times a week. I guess she really loves me, and all that stuff. But she sounded a bit different in this letter, kind of sad. Something is bothering her, I know that from the tone of her letters.

A little while ago I was sewing a patch on my pants and I happened to think about the time way back when I was about nine or ten years old I guess and Father and I were home alone. The insurance man was there and he and Father were talking. Presently I came in with a needle and thread and started to sew a tear I had in my over-alls. Now I'm sitting here laughing at the incident. Daddy probably remembers it too.

Nothing else to write about today. Love to all, Bill.

—✥—

Aug. 19, 1952

Dear Mom, Dad and Carol,

Remember the storm I was telling you about in the previous letter? Well there wasn't a storm. It was just a nice cool night. That was the only thing different about it. It's usually hot! The cool night made it nice sleeping anyway. They really must have expected the worst because they made us sleep with our clothes on.

It was cloudy up till noon today then it cleared up with only a few clouds in the sky. A nice cool breeze blew all day too. In other words, it was a Number One day. The Battery had a little get-together today for about half an hour and they explained the procedure of submitting your vote. I believe I'll send in to get a ballot and give my two cents worth toward the Presidential nomination. My vote may be the deciding one.

I'm working nights again tonight. I don't know which I like best—nights or days. When I work days I can sleep during the night, but when I work nights, I can sleep during the days—sometimes. Both are the same I guess. Lots of love and stuff, Bill

—✥—

Aug. 20, 1952

Dear Mom, Dad and Carol,

Had another beautiful day today. It was slightly cloudy with a nice breeze blowing. It actually got cold last night too. I had to cover myself up with blankets. It's getting so you can sleep pretty comfortably now. I feel guilty telling you I sleep comfortably and eat well and those poor infantry guys are sleeping—God knows where and are eating God knows what. But as the Captain says we are doing an important job here at FDC, and if it weren't for us, they wouldn't know where the hell to shoot their Howitzers, and lo and behold, the Chinks would be at us, one and all.

They started issuing our winter clothing today. As of now I have three tops of long underwear and a pair of gloves. It's a good start anyway.

Please don't write any more letters with those long sentences. I start turning colors before I get to the end of the sentence and take a breath. I found out one of my worries are over anyway. You received my 50 smackers and added it to my bankroll.

So Carol is through with Bob again? That boy is too stupid to stay away. And you are worried about me and Anita, my Arkansas gal? I think you have some big worries, and I mean Carol and Bob. Too much fighting going on for it to be true love. And besides, Carol is too young. Till tomorrow, love, Willie.

—⁂—

Aug. 21, 1952

Dear Mom, Dad and Carol,

There were twenty-four very welcome men that came into the Battery today. They are replacements, and the more that come in the more going home and that puts my name a little higher on the list. I also heard some bad news. We aren't getting combat pay. I don't believe it's definite yet. But it still will probably work out that way. That's quite a blow as I was figuring on that little extra money.

Had a busy day in FDC. I was out on our breeze porch for a few minutes with a pair of field glasses watching the air strikes over here. It's interesting the way they dive, let loose of their load and "Boom." Like an air show, but for real.

> *(What Bill was working on when he said he had a busy day in FDC was probably the continuation of the Battle of Bunker Hill, which began Aug.12. He also probably saw the planes' assaults.)*

I've been thinking about that girl in Arkansas. I don't know if I should lead her on, because I don't know what I'm going to do. I don't want to be mean to her. Sometimes I think it's kind of stupid thinking about marrying her. And then sometimes I think it's a darn good idea. She's nice and she loves me. But I haven't't known her that long. Maybe, I should pick me a slick chick from Pumpkin Creek around home. There's no sense of me rambling on about my love life. I'll have to figure it out, I guess. Can't think of anything else. Love, Bill.

—m—

Aug. 21, 1952, Journal Entry:

Same ole, same ole, battles, planes bombing the hell out of those gooks, and here I am, confused, damn it, about me, about Anita. Am I screwed up? You bet I am. What the hell am I going to do? Sure, I love that sweet gal from Arkansas. Sure, my folks want me to forget about her. Sure, Bob and Carol are going round and round, fighting and making up. The same old shit. Say, man, there's a war going on. Haven't you heard?

—m—

Aug. 22, 1952

Dear Mom, Dad and Carol,

So, Carol's been swearing again? I'll see what I can do about that when I come home. I can imagine you two sitting in the bedroom having a good time and laughing at all hours of the night.

To speak of myself a moment here. I have been doing quite a bit of talking throughout the night in my sleep. I get up in the morning and the guys have a pretty good time relating all I've said in my sleep. Last night I was talking about music. I said, "Bring on the band boys, what am I doing dancing without any music." They said I was talking just as if I were holding a conversation with someone. Sometimes when I talk in my sleep they answer me and darn if I don't answer them back, in my sleep! Oh, we have a lot of fun here. They're starting to call me "Chief Gab in Sleep."

Again today I had a difficult day. I came into FDC in the morning and within an hour I found myself and two other guys in a truck looking for empty ammo boxes at the neighboring firing Battery. I was the driver because I was the only one who knew how to drive a truck. We drove around all morning—but came back empty handed—no ammo boxes.

I spent a hard afternoon, also. After just a half hour at FDC I was called out to do a little cleaning up around our tent to make ready for another big inspection coming up shortly. I worked like crazy for and hour and a half. Then I walked to the Marine camp and took a shower. By that time it was 5 p.m. and I went to mail call. Got a letter from Anita. I believe she is peeved at me. She didn't receive a letter from me in a week. She wrote me and tried to chew me out. Silly girl.

Saw a good movie tonight, "African Queen." It was a Jim Dandy!

I sure hope Carol gets a job at GMC (General Motors) in the office. Maybe she can work in a section to juggle some books. Seriously though, I think that working in the office would be a good deal for her. Now she can start paying room and board! Ha, ha.

You know about those blue gills Father caught and left in the basement in a pail? Why don't you put them in the fishpond? At least you wouldn't be wasting them. Lots of love, Willie.

—m—

Aug. 23, 1952

Dear Mom, Dad and Carol,

My friend got back from R & R yesterday and he brought back a bunch of pictures. I gave him some of my films to have developed. There are quite a few pictures of Japan again and also a lot of pictures of the area and the guys around here. They all turned out good. I wish I could find a box or something to send them all to you at once instead of dwindling them out a few at a time in my letters. But I guess that's what I have to continue to do. Instead of writing on the reverse side of the photos, I'll explain them to you when I get home.

Had a slow day at FDC. Today it's been rainy and cloudy all day so we haven't any missions. Our radio went on the blink about 3 or 4 days ago and I took it over to the radio shop and had it fixed. Now we'll get to hear music again for a little while. One day probably before long it will go on the blink again. The radio must be jinxed.

I have a chance to buy a good 35 mm camera here for 30 bucks. I believe I may take it. It's a darn good deal. Oh well, lots of love, Bill

—m—

Aug. 24, 1952

Dear Mom, Dad and Carol,

I pulled one of my old tricks again last night. I took the radio and set it along side of my cot and was listening to some good programs and presto I fell asleep. I woke up again at 2:30 a.m. and it was playing some nice cool music. Just like I did at home, fall asleep with the radio on. I guess I won't lose any of my habits. I'll be the same old chap when I return. Sleeping with the radio playing and talking in my sleep!

What a miserable day it has been. All day, too. It's been drizzling all the while but every now and then it would come down in gushes. It's a crazy world over here.

This morning during the best part of the day we had another Corps inspection. When it's time to pull an inspection, they inspect come hell or high water. Never seen the likes of them.

I must say that Pontiac sure is gonna look like a changed city when I go home. All new roads and new factories going up. It makes it sorta business like around there, especially with the new factory almost in the backyard.

I see that Carol's picking up some of my habits. Takes the car out and brings it back with the tank M.T. Well, at least I put a dollar's worth in it. "But you took two dollars out of it," Father would say. The show is about to start—"Lone Shark" is playing. Love, Bill

—๛—

Aug. 25, 1952

Dear Mom, Dad and Carol,

I neglected to finish this letter last night, so I'll try tonight. I sure am neglecting my letter writing lately. Well, next week I work nights and I'll have time to catch up. Oh, I forgot to say this is Aug. 26th today and it's still raining and it's getting cold. I put on one of those long john tops that we got a while back. What am I gonna do when it gets really cold? I got guard tonight too and I have to wander around outside for two hours. Oh well, I'll get away from all of this.

Saw a pretty good movie last night for a change, "Just Across the Street" with Ann Sheridan and John Lund. It was goofy for a while but turned out O.K. Well, that's the news for the day. Til tomorrow, Love, Willie

—~—

Aug. 26, 1952

Dear Mom, Dad and Carol,

They thought of something new for us to do again. We now have to dig more bunkers and these will be along side each of our tents and they are to be as long as the squad tents and five feet deep. All we got is a mess of bunkers around this place. Well starting tomorrow I work nights so that'll mean I will be among those digging the silly thing in the day. No sleep!

So Dawn and Chuck are back from their two-day honeymoon. I wonder why they stayed so long? Ah sweet mystery of life! Maybe I shouldn't say that but I showed the letter about the short honeymoon to my buddy and we had a good laugh over it. That's mean though, I guess.

Walt Heck is getting married? Even Pat is getting married? Geez, I'll be the only single man around the place. I guess I'll marry one of these Korean gals. Ha. I'm gonna hit the sack early tonight. Had guard and didn't get much sleep last night. Lots of love, Bill

—~—

Aug 27, 1952

Dear Mom, Dad and Carol,

What a day we had today. I sure was glad to see the sun set to finish it out. We had to dig in our new bunkers all day long. My poor back is just about broken. It ain't done yet, either. We have to keep right on digging tomorrow. Then about 4 p.m. we had to go out and get some logs to put on the thing. It seems mighty strange but the only place we can find any trees are half way up a mountainside. I was too tired to pull them down when I got up there. Boy, I sure am getting a workout over here if nothing else.

Also this afternoon, we had a championship softball tournament. No, we weren't playing in it. Although our Charlie Battery did play a game against another Battery. They played two extra innings and Charlie Battery lost a tough game to the score of 1-0. It was a battle of pitchers and really a game to watch.

Our firing batteries are from six to nine miles from here, and the front is three miles beyond that so that puts us quite a ways back and makes it reasonably safe.

That's in answer to one of your questions. Now, don't worry, it's safe here. (What did he say?).

Well just another three days until pay day. You know these months seem to be going by pretty fast for me so far. Been in Korea six months, not counting the two in Japan. Those were a waste of time. Lost six points in Japan and haven't as yet applied what I learned there. Love Bill.

—𝔪—

Aug. 28, 1952, Journal Entry:

How safe is it here? Well, I ain't telling. That is I'm not revealing any information to my folks. Can't tell them the hell that is going on here. Can't tell them about the reports we get from the front, the bloody reports and the men wounded and dead. Can't tell them. Can't tell them about the nightmares when I wake up in a cold sweat, and imagine the gooks in our tent.

—𝔪—

(Aug. 29, 1952: War's Largest Air Raid—FEAF and carrier planes bomb Pyongyang in a 1,403-plane assault—the largest single day raid of the war.)

—𝔪—

Aug. 29, 1952

Dear Mom, Dad and Carol,

We had a good lecture tonight on the subject of security information. The whole thing in a nutshell rounded out to be just this—"Keep your yap shut!" He related some surprising incidents. They have been continually picking up on the average of 50 North Korean and Chinese espionage agents that have infiltrated through the line. Surprising, but true. One of the interrogation officers came up to give us the talk.

If you haven't read it in the newspapers or seen it on TV, we had a lot of fireworks going on and it wasn't even the Fourth. I mean we had a super duper air strike, lots of planes, lots of bombings. It was the largest air strike ever! There was a lot of hooting and shooting! So, it continues, war is hell!

To change the subject, I've been figuring out my funds until I get discharged and I'll have over two grand. Quite a tidy sum huh? I don't know what I'll do with all of that money although I grant you this; there are many things and many ways I can get rid of it. What with a car, clothes, going to school, and buying this and that. I sound like you with an extra 20 bucks. You're going to remodel the whole house with the 20 bucks, right?

I endured the hardship of staying awake last night in FDC cuz I worked. While I slept this morning the other guys displaced dirt (dug a bunker). In the afternoon I did some digging too. You think they would let me get away without digging? Nope! That's it for today. Lots of love, Bill

(Aug. 30, 1952: Ocean tug Sarsi is sunk by a mine off Hungnam. KIA, 4 WIA Last U.S. naval vessel lost in the war.)

Aug. 30, 1952

Dear Mom, Dad and Carol,

It's been drizzling off and on all day. I'd just as soon it rain instead of playing around like this all day.

If you want an example of chicken shit—here, just bend an ear to this. It's just an example of one officer. We got 6 men working on one shift and every one of us had to stay in here from 8 to 10 o'clock at night. Every other officer lets four men go and two stay on. By go, I mean go see the movie. But this one doesn't like movies so he won't let any one else see them. We are all burned up about it. But no use griping about it.

My day was taken up by digging bunkers again. A very interesting and worthwhile occupation I'd say. Something happened today as far as the food was concerned. This evening for chow we had Turkey! It was good too. I don't see how they happened to find a turkey here.

We got rid of one of the officers here at FDC. Since the Colonel left, everyone moved up a step and that took the major out of here. He is now Battalion executive. I was glad to see him go. He wouldn't even let me have a birthday party. (Kidding, of course)

Have you heard the latest Shaggy Dog story? "And after dinner Gentlemen, a shaggy dog will pass among you." Funny, huh? Lots of love, Bill

---

Aug. 31, 1952

Dear Mom, Dad and Carol,

The rain has ceased once again but I have no ideas just how long the lull will last. All the stars are out and a big full moon but that doesn't mean it will be nice tomorrow. It's fooled me before. It best not rain cuz I have to get some clothes washed. I have to put a clean set of clothes on every other day here. I don't know how I get them so dirty so fast. Lucky it only costs 3 bucks a month to get them washed.

"Teresa" was the name of it. Pier Angela played in it. I must say it was a number one picture.

Don't start posting those pictures in the album yet because I've got a lot more to send home. There's quite a few of Japan yet and also lots of everyone around here and various scenic shots of the place. Best maybe wait till we get them all together. I may be sending another album home if I get the chance to pick one up. They are pretty albums aren't they?

Right now at the end of August, I have 21 points and I get 3 points a month so that figures that I'll have 36 at the end of January. I'll be gong home for sure in January. But seeing how I wasn't home last Christmas and I'm so close to Rotation in December they might get kind hearted and send me home then. Never can tell.

I got paid again today. Got another 74 bucks, 60 of it will be on the way home soon. If I could send home 60 every month will the allotment that makes $110 every month. Better than I was doing at home huh? A fool and his money are soon parted. Gad! I hate to think of that. I'm not really that bad, I just love to hear myself talk.

Carol really is in the dough now with a $113 burning a hole in her pocket. I'd like to be there to watch her blow it away. I bet it will go easier than mine did then. It's getting a little cool here and it gets chilly at night. Don't wish the cold weather on us. Well I'll sign off. Love, Bill

—w—

(Sept. 1, 1952: Largest All-Navy Raid. 144 planes from three carriers destroy the oil refinery at Aoji, North Korea.)

—w—

Sept. 2, 1952

Dear Mom, Dad and Carol,

I was intending to write last night but we got so busy from 5 till 8 p.m., had many, many missions. All those missions and we were working our tails off. Team work, that's what it's all about. Another giant strike at the enemy.

(An all-time single day high of 45,000 rounds fall on the 8th Army front during September.)

It gets quite chilly in the morning. It's getting so I hate to get out of a warm bed and put my warm feet on a cold floor and dance around trying to keep warm and put your clothes on. I don't envy those guys in the infantry. (There I go thinking about those poor bastards on the front line. I should be grateful to God that I'm here, and not there.)

I'm glad I don't have the full winter to spend in Korea. Before long we will have to start going down to the Marine showers again. Our makeshift shower up here is getting pretty cold. That creek water doesn't seem to get warm.

Better sign this and get this out while the getting is good. Lots of love, Bill

—w—

Sept. 3, 1952

Dear Mom, Dad and Carol,

Had a fairly quiet day at FDC. . . .

Among the other letters I got one from Anita. Struck it rich again. She says she loves me. I'm at a loss again for words tonight. I can't think of a blame thing to write about. Maybe I'll be more in the mood tomorrow. Well anyway, love to all, Bill. . . .

—~—

Sept. 3. 1952, Journal Entry:

Yipes!! She loves me! And I love her! So all is right with the world. Now, maybe I can get some sleep tonight. Not that I was worried about her. Damn it to hell. Hurry up, hurry up. I want those points. I want to get home to my girl. Yes, I do!

—~—

Sept 3, 1952

Dear Mom, Dad and Carol,

. . . . There's a good movie playing tonight-Tony Curtis and Piper Laurie in "No Room for the Groom." They didn't show a movie last night. I guess those three in a row were sort of an added attraction because the "big man" left. Everyone was happy because he left.

(Later-much later) It is about 9.p.m. now. About those "men in service" clippings you have been sending me, well I found Nelson Fizzard's address in them and wrote to him. Carol should know him. I know quite a few of the guys listed in the clippings. If I get a chance to go on R & R again I'm going to try to go to Osaka, Japan. That's where Nelson is stationed.

That picture of that girl setting the pins in the bowling alley sure does belittle me. I worked so hard at it and I made a saw buck a night. Now they've got beautiful gals in shorts doing the work. It will be a pleasure to bowl now.

I've been sitting here for an hour trying to figure out why everyone is going on vacation for the weekend. You see the funny part of it was I didn't know it was Labor Day weekend. Dense me! Well I thought it was funny, anyway. It didn't seem like Labor Day to me. I took a shower but that was on the Fourth of July. Ha!

I heard about that program that Patti Page has on TV. I bet she's really good. Speaking of songs have you heard "Bermuda" by the Bell Sisters? I think it's perfectly dreamy (like they say). I do though. I think it's a beautiful song. No one else can sing it better than the Bell Sisters.

Getting back to TV now. When you were talking about having such good luck with it well I also knocked on wood for you. It'll probably blow apart when I get home. I miss switching the channels and adjusting the silly thing. I suppose they got just about all-new programs now. Any good hillbilly programs on it? I go crazy over here when I hear hillbilly music. Not really crazy, I just like to listen to that kind of music.

You sound as if you believe in those flying saucers. How many have you seen so far? Did you read about the one that swept down from the sky and almost hit a car somewhere in the states? The driver drove to the police station shaking because it almost hit him. It sounds more dangerous being home then in Korea.

I sure hope you can buy some of that Finnish toast and send it to me. I'll take it to the mess hall with me in the morning and dunk it in my coffee. I'll just take two pieces at a time cause I don't want anyone else getting their hooks in it.

There are two guys leaving FDC this month. Then next month two more, and then the next month, two more, and then the next month, which is December, I will be counting the days. Time seems to go by fairly fast. If we could be kept busy at something all the time it would fly by. Well they're trying to keep us busy. Lots of love and kisses, Willie

—~—

Sept 4, 1952

Dear Mom, Pop and Sis,

Whee! What a busy day we've had today. It feels good to relax for once. We've been running around like chickens with their heads cut off. Didn't know where to turn next and it got so confusing in here it actually was comical and we all started laughing and having a good time. Sounds crazy but we laugh at anything.

The reason we were running around, securing everything is because we had another storm warning last night but like the last one it never did reach our area. Thank God. We had everything roped, tied and sand bagged down. All we got was a little rain and mild breeze and by morning the sun was out again shinning for a long time.

Here's a funny incident that happened to me today at lunchtime, which I will relate to you. There are a lot of these yellow jacket bumblebees flying around here now for some unknown reason and it so happened that one was making a survey of me so I made a bat at him and lo and behold he got stuck in my paw. I let out a yep and went off to the medics. My finger swelled up as big as my thumb. It's hurting now. That will teach me to keep out of their way. I guess my letter was too long yesterday cause I seem to be out of words. Love and kisses, Willie

—w—

(Sept. 6-8: Outpost Bruce (Hill 148) During a 51-hour siege, U. S. Marines sustain 19 KIA and 38 WIA.)

—w—

Sept 6, 1952

Dear Mom, Dad and Carol,

I'm working all night again. Sure hope it isn't busy like it was last night.

I didn't work then but those who did said they were firing missions all night long. They shot over 500 rounds last night. It must have been a bloody mess on the front.

(For security reasons Bill could not mention the destination of the missions he fired. They were often briefed about security and told not to reveal any information pertaining to the firings.)

I went over to the mess hall about an hour ago and got myself a pot of coffee and sandwich, and a few rolls to help me get through the night. That's the first time I've done that, having a midnight snack I mean. Of course, when I get a box from home I take it with me to FDC and munch on the goodies from home.

Remember when I told you about digging bunkers? Well, the first bunkers were dug and then we had to fill them all in because they decide they wanted the bunkers next to the squad tents. So we did that and started digging them along side the tents and got three or four feet down and struck water so we had no other alternative but to fill them up again and now they are thinking of another place to dig those bunkers. I hope they make up their minds. I have been contemplating just digging half a hole until I find out if they want them in another place, again!

A joke: There were two men talking to each other and one said, "Look here, we've been talking for ten minutes now and you haven't even asked me how I'm doing in my new business."

So naturally the other man said, "Well, how are you doing in your new business?"

The first man replies, "Don't ask"

He! He! And so I'll end this letter. Now a shaggy dog will pass among you. Love Bill.

—~—

Sept. 6, 1952

Dear Mom, Dad and Carol,

I received the box containing some Finlander toast. I haven't opened it but I presume that's what in it cuz I also received a letter from you stating that the toast was in the next box. The boxes usually get here a day after the letters.

I received another letter from Anita and I'm enclosing it with this letter. She's worried for fear I'm going to leave her—me, the dashing debonair man. I was meant to be a lover not a soldier. I also received a post card from Grayling. It looks familiar. I like to get post cards of places where I've been. See if you can get a post card of the metropolis of Pontiac, my hometown.

I worked all last night and this morning I slept. During the morning they had a pretty rough inspection. Very thorough from what I hear. I'm lucky I slept through it.

We got a new Battalion executive in today so that put the major back here in F.D.C. The new fellow is only 35 years old and he's a Colonel. Pretty young hey? He's been a Colonel for seven years. He served with McArthur and Ridgeway. I guess he was their right hand man.

I'll end this now. Love, Willie

Anita's letter written in purple ink. It was enclosed in Bill's letter (Sept. 6, 1952 to his parents. His comments are included in parenthesis.)

Paris, Arkansas
August 28, 1952

My Dear Little Boy, *(Get that?)*

I received your letter just a few minutes ago. You say you just received my letter where I was attempting to give you hell. Well I guess you think I should apologize *(she apologized anyway.)* for writing such a letter. Well I'm not as stubborn as you are. If I was wrong, I'm sorry but honestly Bill, I didn't get a letter from you for one whole week. *(my! my!)* I don't know why I didn't get any, you say you write so I believe you. I'm really sorry that I wrote that letter and I won't do it again. Don't you wait two weeks or even one week without writing to me. *(I threatened her that I wasn't going to write for two weeks)* I guess I would really be worried. I know I would. Now I have apologized. Are you still mad at me, Daddy? *(I guess her Daddy gets mad too.)*

Hilda, that girl that works at the theater with me, is spending the night with me. I stayed with her last night and all day today. We walked two miles to the store to get some stuff for a picnic lunch and then we went swimming. And talk about sun burn, boy we did! We looked really cute, you know red all over, especially my face and arms.

I am so tired I can hardly move or even hold this pen, but I have a good excuse this time, it's because I walked so much today and stayed in the water too long. We are going swimming again tomorrow. Hilda is sitting in the middle of the bed reading. Every few minutes she stops reading long enough to gripe at me. That's what I like about Hilda, we can just tell each other what we think of each other and we don't get mad about it. She's my pal.

We are listening to the "Hillbilly Hit Parade" and Hank Thompson is singing "I didn't Know God Made Honky Tonk Angels." I like that song. I hope we have passed the rough spots in our road, and every thing is all right now, okay?

I'm getting so sleepy now that I'm going to close and fall into bed. (Plop!) I will write again tomorrow night. Until then good night and be good.

Love always, Anita

(Although Anita knew she had cancer, she did not tell Bill)

—w—

Sept. 7, 1952
Sunday

Dear Mom, Dad and Carol,

I started off the day by attending mass. It's a good way to start off I guess. Keep praying for this war to end, but I guess God has other things to take care of first. When I came back I plunked myself down in FDC and ain't moved yet. Got a good movie tonight, "Marco" or something like that.. It's the one with Jane Russell and Robert Mitchum. Why do we get to see so many movies, while those poor bastards on the front line are stuck in a hole? According to the Captain, we watch movies to relieve the tension of our job. We have a very important job, the Captain says. Yes, we pour over maps and chart in our tent plotting out where the enemies is, and we do this for hours. We have to have clear, cool heads, and know what we are doing all the time. Does that make sense? Don't forget this is a war!

I opened up that box yesterday and just as I hoped it had the Finnish toast in it. I went to the mess hall and got myself a cup of coffee and sat there at 9 p.m. eating toast and drinking coffee. I still got some left so I'm gonna to have some more Finlander toast and coffee tonight.

I remember you said that you wrote to Curly once. Did you ever get an answer from him? I swear I can't think of a thing to say. My letters keep getting shorter all the time. Love, Bill.

Sept. 8, 1952

Dear Mom, Dad and Carol,

It's hot today, about 80 degrees. I wonder when the cold weather starts here in Korea?

And then I don't want the cold weather to start. From what I hear, it's colder than northern Michigan in the dead of winter. Spine chilling cold, fingers falling off from frost bite, COLD!

I was waiting today for the letter from you telling me about your trip up north. I suppose Father caught a mess of fish. Did he happen to hear anymore about making a profit on those fly rods like the one I sent home? Maybe pick up a few extra ones if and when I go on R & R again. . . . Write more tonight. Love, Bill.

—~—

Sept. 9, 1952

Dear Mom, Dad and Carol,

I enjoyed reading your letters. I got a good laugh of what Father said when he saw the picture of me with a cigarette in my "puss". I sent that one on purpose cuz I don't think he ever saw me smoking and I was right. Yes Mother is right. After all, I am 22 years old. Can I smoke, Pa?

That Finnish toast you sent got here in good condition. It was crisp and not soggy. Very good. About taking pictures over here with the movie camera. No one here has a movie camera. I'd like very much to do that but it's pretty hard without a camera. Don't you think? I turned my name in for R & R again for the 20th of this month. It's possible I might get a chance to go. It will be darn nice to get away from this place for a week. It may put a new slant on things around here and it most likely will make it all the worse.

Had a movie in FDC today. It was based on procedures and operations of the Fire Direction Center. It was a very interesting movie. Also tonight we have another movie, and it's one of those TV movies—"Man Against Crime" or some such thing.

Well I will close now. Love, Bill

—~—

Sept. 10, 1952

Dear Mom, Dad and Carol,

Got up as usual at 6 a.m. Ready to meet fate of the day. One important thing happened today. I must write about it. No doubt it will interest you. I imagine you have heard of the education program that the Armed Forces is sponsoring.

Well, today I enrolled in the program and am taking a course in Forestry. The way it works is they send you an application (that I filled out and returned to Japan). There in Japan they have the Education program headquarters. The enrollment fee was $2.10. Then they sent me a text to study on my own for a certain length of time. When I finished or think I know all about the subject, I will submit a request for a questionnaire. When I get the questionnaire, I fill it out and send it back and they grade me accordingly.

They give you credit and you can use this when you enroll in college or a trade school. They have various courses including auto mechanics, business courses, drafting, vocational courses and more. I'm going to give it a try and if I get good grades, well I'm on my way. What do you think of the idea?

I went down to the showers, got rid of the grime and sweat, not that I sweat a lot. Kidding, of course. It's just another way to clear your head, the showers I mean. Anyway, that's what they tell us. Have a clear, cool head, soldier, take a shower! But that just means us guys in FDC. No, it means everyone, but especially us FDC men.

I tried calling Curly again tonight and I got all the way to his company and spoke to a fellow who knew him but Curly wasn't there. He said he left for a few weeks and when he returns I will call him again.

Well I guess that's it for now. Lots of love, Your son, Bill

—✲—

Sept. 11, 1952

Dear Mom, Dad and Carol,

So Carol has herself a job now. You didn't keep me in suspense a day though. I just went on to the next letter and found out she got the job.

Yes, Mother I will watch my Ps and Qs. Did I say anything wrong? I had a good laugh out of it anyway. Before we know it we will be slipping a dollar bill in the token box of the Pontiac bus. Inflation is getting here.

Sure was bad news to hear that Fred Blough was wounded. He was probably up on "Old Baldy." When did the Bloughs get divorced? Everybody is getting married or divorced around there. What a fad! About all you have to do now is sit on the court house steps and write me a letter. You've tried every other place.

There's a U.S.O. show at the 1st Marines tonight and tomorrow night. I'm going tomorrow so I'll tell you tomorrow what it was all about. That's it. Will try to write a longer one tomorrow. Love, Bill

—~—

Sept. 12, 1952

Dear Mom, Dad & Sis,

We did it again ! We dug more holes today. This time we dug individual holes for ourselves. I suspect we will be filling them up pretty soon. After we got all of them dug, we had a mock air raid warning and every one ran and jumped into these fox holes. We are having fun playing war here all by ourselves.

Had another cool day today. I guess ole man winter is just about here. I don't know whether I told you this or not but I changed my allotment from $50 to $75 the other day. That's $25 more I can't get my hands on. I believe the increase will come in October's check. I will save next month's pay that I get here in my pocket because I may go on R & R and I'll need some money. I don't know when or if I'll go on another one.

I heard about the big heat wave you're having there in the states. Came on quite unexpected like didn't it? Also read an article in the Stars and Stripes concerning Flying Saucers which amused me quite a bit. It said that in West Virginia a Saucer landed and five people went to investigate and low and behold they found a man from Mars. He was about 12 feet tall, green skin, big buggy funny eyes and had a spade-like tail. Have you ever seen one of them yet? It sounds safer here in Korea, than at home. No one here has seen a Green man from Mars or a Flying Saucer, yet! Will write more tomorrow. Lots of love, Bill

—~—

Sept. 13, 1952

Dear Mom, Dad and Carol,

I had a full Friday night last night. First I went to the U.S.O. show and when I got back here the movie had just started so I stayed for that, too. Doris Day and a guy (I can't think of his name) in the movie called, "Moon Light Bay."

Good show at the U.S.O. too. They were Darlah Murray, Gloria Foster, Linn Maybury, Jack Jecker, Barbara Banks and the Rio Bros. They put on a very good show. After that hectic day, I turned in, I enjoyed it.

Today we changed our squad tent for a new one. What a job that turned out to be. Taking the old one down and putting the new one up. We had frames built around the sides and had to walk the new one into the frame. The frames and the tent are sure heavy!

This darn paper I'm writing on ain't worth a hoot. The paper seems more like a blotter, the ink in my pen seems to go through it. It's not the pen, it's the paper.

I guess winter will soon be here. We were issued our winter sleeping bags, long johns, sweaters and the whole works. I wish I didn't have to use all that stuff. Just as soon would be heading for home. That's all, love and kisses, Bill.

—~—

Sept. 14, 1952

Dear Mom, Dad and Carol,

Being Sunday today, I attended church once again. Still praying, and I think it's working, cause I'm still here. Thank God! When I got back from church, washed, shaved, and combed my hair and brushed my teeth. Didn't get too much to eat for dinner, but it was food. This afternoon the majority of my precious time was taken up in work. I also slept from 2 to 5 p.m. The reason I did this is because I have to work all night, tonight. By working I'm missing a very good movie, "High Noon." I heard it was good so I guess it must be.

I must say we had an educational evening. They blew the familiar whistle at 6 sharp and "Fall Out". We had to pull grass. Imagine that! Acting like kids out there on our hands and knees making hay, or pulling grass. The Army hasn't heard about the scythe. Our captain must have rocks in his head. He strolled out there while we were working pulling grass and one of the guys shouted, "MINGLE", implying we were a bunch of prisoners plotting a break. Everyone had a good laugh except the Captain. He still doesn't know who said it. Our new captain is an illusive person. Then again we could say he is uncouth.

If I stay in Korea much longer, this place will be my legacy. Well, farewell for another day, Lots of love, Bill

—~—

Sept. 15, 1952

Dear Mom, Dad and Carol,

Has Daddy been practicing much with his bow or has it been just sitting in the corner gathering dust.

I got a pretty long night again tonight. Got guard duty again. Only got about 20 more times to pull guard. I just finished my first relief from eight to ten o'clock then I have to go on again at 2 a.m. until 4 a.m. Don't have to go to work tomorrow at FDC so I will get some sleep in the morning anyway.

Had an hour of manual labor again tonight. From 6 to 7 p.m. we pulled grass (of all the intelligent jobs). Other than that I spent a fairly decent day. Slept all morning cause I worked last night, and rested in the afternoon cause I have guard duty tonight.

Don't tell me you are going on a diet again. That makes the 12th time during the past year. Speaking of the dentist, as you were, I also have an appointment with the man. I go in Wednesday and have him start drilling. I believe I have decay in one of my teeth. I dread going to the dentist.

Carol still can't get to work on time, eh? Get her a job where she has to be there at 11:30 and she won't make it till 11:45. Ha.

Well I guess I'll go and hit the sack now. Have to rise at 2 a.m. What a dreadful thought. Love, Bill.

—~—

Sept. 16, 1952

Dear Mom, Dad and Carol,

I agree with you. It is hard to find something to write about. Especially around here. It seems like I go through the same ordeal and routine day after day. Today I endured practically the same thing as I did yesterday. Work all night, sleep in the morning and part of the afternoon.

They got another good movie tonight, but I'm not going to get to see this one either. I have to work again this evening! "Carson City" is the movie. Received a letter from Anita. I've been slacking off on writing to her quite a bit lately and it seems the less I write the more letters I get from her. She's getting worried about her one and only.

We didn't pull any grass this evening. Guess something went wrong and we had a night off. This evening we all sat around the tent gabbing and got into the subject of what are we going to do Christmas Eve. Guys that are going home said they would send us fruit cake and Christmas tree lights and stuff like that there. I've been trying to make myself believe that I'm going home too and that I'll be sending them stuff back in Korea.

Now I have to holler at Pop and Carol for not writing. Why don't you write? Why don't you, huh? Well, that's it. Love, Bill

—෴—

(Sept. 17–24 , 1952, Korea; Outpost Kelly, 65th Inf. Reg.3rd D. is besieged by Chinese Communist Forces. The regiment sustains 350 casualities.)

—෴—

Sept. 17, 1952

Dear Mom, Dad and Sis,

I visited the dentist this morning again and lo and behold, nary a cavity. I was really surprised. It's been almost three years with no trouble with my teeth.

I'm working all night again tonight. It seems to be getting habit forming. In the afternoon we hauled some more lumber. . . . A hectic day. Love, Bill

—෴—

Sept 18–21, 1952, Korea; Battle for Hill 266 continues with the 38th Inf. Regt. (2nd ID)

—෴—

Sept. 19, 1952

Dear Mom, Dad and Carol,

What a surprise I got today. I received the box that you sent Parcel Post about a month ago. Usually you write and tell me you're sending me a box but you surprised me. I sure did need that paper and envelopes. Good magazines and everything, etc. Gee thanks loads. I really appreciate it.

Today I dunked all my winter clothing in some liquid that they say is somewhat of a bug insecticide or something. I'm playing it safe and taking all the precautions. Other activities consisted of digging a little more in my fox hole and a brief rest after that. I'm beginning to arrive at the conclusion that I spend more time waiting—but that's the Army for you, hurry up and wait.

Here's a joke I'm going to pull on some girl when I get home. I will ask the gal, "Has anyone ever told you how beautiful you are?" She will say, "Why no, Darling, they haven't." Then I come in with the punch line. "Who the hell ever gave you that idea." And then I'll snicker. Not funny, you say?

I had two blankets over my sleeping bag last night. I learned from the night before, when I just had the sleeping bag and got very cold. We haven't got our winter sleeping bags issued to us yet. Just have to wait it out.

We are going to try to get some lumber to build the sides up around our tent and try to winterize it a bit. It would help a lot to keep the heat in and the cold winds out. I don't suppose they will let us though cuz it might be too comfortable for us.

In closing I will say good night. Write more tomorrow, Lots of love, Bill

Sept. 20, 1952

Dear Mom, Dad and Carol,

Father seems to have given me a little lecture on my future in his letter. All about my Arkansas gal and my plans for marriage. Well, I'm thinking about it. Don't forget I'm 22 years old. Has he given Carol and Bob a lecture? I wonder.

Well, we finished up our bunkers today. Have to carry a flashlight with you at night now or else there is a chance of falling in one of these holes and breaking a leg or something. Now I hear talk of digging a FDC. bunker. I wonder when they are going to stop around this place. Our battery will be sitting at sea level soon.

One improvement which they started today is building a little movie theater, P-X combined. It's mighty thoughtful and considerate of them I must say. It's a Quonset hut style. Very modern.

Did I tell you that the Major said that we who work nights (8 p.m. to 8 a.m.) won't be able to see the movies. We used to go and watch them and leave just a couple of men in FDC. Now the whole shift stays in till 10 p.m. and two men stay in until morning, unless it's extra busy. The reason I brought this up is because I'm going to miss a real good movie tonight, "Singing in the Rain" and my girl Debbie is in it too.

They finally got some PX items in today. They'll start selling 'em tomorrow. And how I needed them. I'm running short on soap, toothpaste, hair oil and about every other thing. I hate to ask you to send me stuff if I can buy it here. Stationery is about the only tough thing to acquire. But cookies and such like you've been sending are greatly appreciated.

The sergeant that left on rotation this morning gave me a couple more pairs of fatigues. I asked him for them. Now I'm pretty well set.

Have you heard the song, "I Love you Twice as Much as You Love Me"? Rosemary Clooney sings it. It's a pretty song. Love, Billy

—∿∿—

Sept. 20, 1952, Journal Entry:

Father and his lectures. I know that my Mom puts him up to it. What's wrong with my Arkansas gal? They don't even know her. I'm getting pissed off about this whole two-sided thing. I mean Carol and Bob, why that's fine and dandy, even if they fight like cats and dogs most of the time. It's okay with Mom and Dad. But, they don't even know Anita, and they have their minds set against her. What gives?

—∿∿—

Sept. 21, 1952

Dear Ma, Pa, and Sis,

I just got off of guard half hour ago and I'm darn near frozen. I didn't have my jacket on and when the sun went down behind the mountains, the warmth went from the air. You can believe I'm gonna wear a sweater and jacket when I go out again at 12 to 2.

We dug a little more today on our foxholes. At the rate we are going I do believe we'll be digging two days from now. I believe I'll get to work and finish mine up tomorrow. Have to also get our stoves set up tomorrow. They finally got 'em in yesterday. It might be a little warmer in the mornings now when we pull our toes out of the warm sack and place them on the cold floor.

Went to another U.S.O. show this afternoon. Saw Frances Langford, her husband, Jon Hall, and a few other people who sang and danced. They weren't important because I forgot their names already. The comedian's name was Wally Vernon. You've probably heard of him ain't you?

It was a pretty good show. After the show, they stayed on the stage and talked a bit. I managed to get close and got a good look at them. What bags they are, they look like they are 50 years old. I was disappointed when I saw their wrinkled faces.

After the dusty ride back I went down and took a fast and brief, cool shower.

There have been a few guys here who are still using their mess kits when we have trays at our disposal. The battery commander didn't like that so he gave an order that everyone must eat from the trays. How silly, eh? There are a lot of silly things we have to do around here.

I guess I'd better go hit the sack again. Have to get up in two hours for more guard duty in the middle of the night. Lots of love, Bill.

—~—

(Sept. 22, 1952, Korea: 245th Tank Bn. 45th ID. Launches an attack on the Chinese.)

—~—

Sept. 22, 1952

Dear Mom, Dad and Carol,

Received a picture post card from you today. It's a very nice picture. Seems good to look at the old clubhouse again. It looks different to me but I guess its just because I haven't seen it in so long.

Pop's getting all set for deer hunting, eh? What did he say about his new gun. I bet that's really a rifle. I've read quite a bit about it and I believe he'll be satisfied with it all right. Daddy's been taking quite a number of movies ain't he? I'll have to sit home two nights in a row in order to see them all. He's still got all his hunting movies too. Hope father takes some good snapshots of the deer he shot, and the cabin and stuff like that so I can see what he did.

How is my sweet, little, dear voluptuous sister these days. Same as ever I hope. (I had to say that cuz I wanted to use that $64 word.)

When did you happen to decide to build a new screen porch? That old one is new to me. Did you get a few extra dollars last week or something?

Today we cleaned up the stoves, that is we cleaned the protective coating which they had on them. Had to clean two stoves and it took both of us all morning to do it. During the afternoon we have to finish digging our bunkers. Maybe if we go slow enough we won't have so much to fill up. I take it for granted we will follow up and cover them.

We go on days the day after tomorrow. Will probably see a lot of crummy cinemas. Something like the one that is playing tonight, "The Dance in Egypt." Will sleep tomorrow cuz I'm working all night again tonight. Love, Shaggy Dog.

—m—

Sept. 23, 1952

Dear Mom, Dad and Sis,

As you know, this FDC is set up in a building. If you stepped in here this very night you'd swear to God you were in the States. We've got these big tables in here to set our situation maps on, and likewise for the firing charts. There are stands where the computers sit on. Well, you can see by the pictures I've sent home. Now they have painted all the tables, boxes, etc and even went around the walls with this Army "Green" paint. I changed my mind, we're not in the States. This outfit could be in the darkest part of Africa. This is a heck of a war here in Korea.

Just now I found out we are going to paint the top half of the walls white and also the ceiling and window frames. I'm not kidding a bit, either.

We finally finished our digging (excavating). Got our heaters all set up and ready to go except for the burners. Soon as we get the burners, we'll be all set. It's one of those nights again when I can't find a single thing to write about, so I may as well quit writing. Love, Bill

—m—

Sept. 24, 1952

Dear Mom, Dad and Sis,

The day started off real fine but ended up raining, which started about 1:30 this afternoon. They're showing a real good movie tonight, regardless of the precipitation. It's "The Winning Team" with my girl, Doris Day. Of course I have to stay in FDC cuz I'm still working nights. Tomorrow I go on days so I'll get a chance to see a few movies.

I'm sending you a picture with a fellow standing in the window of a building, which incidentally is FDC. Well, that fellow is none other than me. It's hard to tell that's why I mentioned it. The other pictures were taken at the Seoul air base where we departed for Japan. These are about the last of the pictures. Although I've still got three rolls that aren't developed.

We did a little more work around the tents today. We rigged up a few outfits which we can put our oil cans on for the winter. It took us half of the morning. The remainder of the day we raked the place and got rid of all the rocks and weeds. It looks sharp around here now. You would never know we were in a combat zone.

I noticed they got some T-shirts in the P-X today so I got three of them. I was running short. Those type of items are pretty rare around this place. I'm all set on clothes now. I also turned in a pair of boots and will be getting a brand new pair soon.

This is a short letter, eh? Love, Bill

—~—

Sept. 25, 1952

Dear Mother, Father and Sister,

I guess I'll spend the next few hours attempting to type you a brief letter. It's hard for me to type a letter cuz by the time I finish one sentence I plum forget what I'm going to put in the next sentence. Received two letters and a couple of papers from you today. I haven't had a letter from my Arkansas gal for almost a week. I must say I'm heart broken. I hope she never does write me another letter cuz I hate to have to tell her I ain't going to Arkansas to marry up with her. I know she'll cry for days at the very thought of me "snowing her." Guess you were right all along. I'm too young to get married. I've got to see the world first, and I'm done seeing Korea, or will be in a while. I have plans and I don't think marriage is in them. Then again, time will tell. Am I making sense? No, as usual.

It's been a cold and wet day today. It's not really been raining so to speak, just a fine mist. It seems to be clearing up a wee bit at this late hour of the evening. The temperature has been down to the sixty's most all day, and believe me it pays to wear a sweater to keep from freezing. We've got our stoves but no burners for them as yet so the things aren't doing us much good.

You should get a load of our bunkers and trenches now. They're all caved in and filled with water. I see now where we are going to be busy fixing them up the next few days.

(Handwritten now) I give up. I've been almost an hour at this typing and I can't seem to get the hang of it. So now I'm back to my trusty pen. To continue we had a very slow day in the FDC. Haven't fired a single mission.

You people seem to be doing quite a bit of vacationing. Gone one week out of a month it seems. I'm about ready to drop, too sleepy. Write more tomorrow. Lots of love, Bill

—~—

Sept. 25, 1952, Journal Entry:

Well, they done broke my spirit. By, "they" I mean my folks. What am I doing to that poor gal in Arkansas? Sure, I love her and I know she loves me. Why am I such a horse's ass? I'm in a mess. Can't figure a way out. Why, oh why am I so damn dumb when it comes to doing what I want to do. Why or why do I listen to dear ole Ma and Pa. What do they know? They don't even know Anita.

—~—

(During the month of September, 1952, Korea; Units of the 5th Air Force shoot down 64 MIG-15s at a cost of 7 Sabrejets.)

—~—

Sept. 26, 1952

Dear Mom, Dad and Carol,

Oh what a busy day I've had today. I ain't never been so busy in all my life. Was shooting lots of missions and in our spare time we were painting and sprucing up the joint quite a bit. The reason for all this commotion is that we are going to have a big Corps inspection the first of next month. They are really keeping us busy trying to win the blue ribbon. It wouldn't bother me if they got a black one out of the deal.

Woke up this morning and much to my amazement the sun was shining. I almost fell over. But was it cold getting up. It warmed up considerably during the day, though.

Finally, at last I get to see another movie tonight. It's been almost two weeks since I've seen a movie. Tonight we see the sensational, intriguing, intelligent, cunning, etc. motion picture named, tra, tra, tra, la, la, la, "About Face." After that big build up, it'll probably break down or something. I hope now, it will be a suave picture. I sound so naïve, eh! What does that mean? But I'm still the same uncouth person.

I've been racking my brain here trying to think. I'm contemplating writing this Arkansas gal of mine and giving her a real sweet and pleasant "Dear John—I send you, toddle home." I've got a number of fellows here giving me suggestions. I may end up by getting a pretty fair letter out of the deal. Oh well, that's what I'm thinking of doing now. Time will tell. I still have some feelings for that little Arkansas gal. No comments from the home front. I've heard enough, thank you. The ball is in my court now.

Glad you like the idea of me taking up forestry. I'm gonna try to go all the way through with this and not do like I have been doing. You know me, get something half way done and Bam-quit. It ought to make a pretty good vocation, in the woods!

You should think about taking your weeks' vacation in the Carolinas and visit Boycee and Ella. I would like to go down that a-way just to visit the country.

Till the morrow, Love, Bill

—∞—

Sept. 27, 1952

Dear Mom, Dad and Carol,

Carol sure does write an interesting letter even though it did take her four days to write it. She seems as though she likes her work all right. She'll have her own car with all the money she's making and then she won't have to drive mine. (Thank God).

I've never seen a place as busy as FDC was this morning. Had five missions piled up just waiting to be fired. Everyone running around like mad and it seemed as though they didn't know what to do next. I've never seen such confusion in all my born days. Yes, I have, but whatcha-gonna do?

During the afternoon we got the stoves set up in FDC. It's the same old story again, though. No burners and no carburetors so we can get the thing a-burning. Have to sit around and look at a cold stove.

One of the toughest feats that I perform here is getting up in the morning. It's really hard to set your warm feet on a cold floor!

That movie we saw last night, "About Face," was a good show. I hated to see it end and have to crawl back into our tents of Korea. I just saw the roster and I'm on it for tomorrow night. Guard duty, I mean. "Brrrr!" Hate the thought of it.

I was surprised to see that newspaper picture of Tom in his football helmet. He must be favored quite a bit to have his picture in the paper. Hope he makes out good. I wonder if it would be too much bother for you to send me the clippings instead of the whole newspaper. I mean when it concerns Cousin Tom and his doings on the football field. I'd like to keep track of him and how he's doing. He's big enough to be a team all by himself. Does he shave yet? I have to shave every second or third day now. Most of the time it's every second day. Enclosing a couple of pictures of myself.

Love, Bill.

—∿—

Sept. 28, 1952

Dear Mom, Dad and Carol,

We don't need carburetor here for our stoves. Leave it to the Army. We think of everything. We secure a number 10 can, fill it with sand then soak the sand with gasoline. That burns about five or six hours. What clever characters we are, eh?

I see Carol is getting right in the groove by going to the football games. That would be one game I'd love to see. Michigan State I presume is going to have a good team this year. Also nice to hear that Pontiac won its first game. I give up. I'm tired. I'm going to bed and finish this in the morning.

Well, it's morning time now and quite a nippy morning too. Guard wasn't as bad as I thought it would be at 1 a.m. in the morning. I was bundled up pretty warm though. They got our stove fixed up in the radio tent so that gave us a chance to warm up after guard. Had hot coffee all night too.

They've got some Koreans working in the area now. They work for their three meals a day and have a chance to bring the leftovers home. I never saw anybody go after food the way they do. I feel so sorry for them, these people are starving. I was walking out of the mess hall last night and had a roll on my tray that I didn't eat and before I got out to dump it in the garbage, this Korean kid came up and snatched it off my tray.

Better get this in the mail before it's too late. Love, Bill

—∾—

Sept. 29, 1952

Dear Mom, Dad and Carol,

Went and took a shower today at the Marine camp. We are not using our homemade shower anymore. The water is too cold. There is a truck leaving for the Marine's shower every day at 3 p.m. so it makes it real convenient to be taking one in hot water.

Every time I think of this I have to laugh. There is a dog around here that we have adopted as our mascot and he's the dumbest mutt ever. During the night you can flash a light on the ground and he chases it. During the day he amuses himself by chasing the shadows the birds cast on the ground. The silly thing runs himself to death night and day.

Happened to wander over to the orderly room this afternoon and by chance I happened to secure a magazine. A rare item. It was the fishing yearbook for this year. I wanted to see that book for quite some time, and I finally got it.

We're burning wood in our stove now. Made a grate for it out of wire. Works pretty good. At least it takes the chill out of the place.

That's all. Love, Bill

Sept. 30, 1952

Dear Mom, Dad and Carol,

Got two letters from Anita today. Nope, didn't write her that Dear John letter. Not yet. I need some time to think about it.

So you're going on another vacation again? Don't you people ever stay home? It would have been a nice trip for you to go to Washington D.C. or North Carolina but Father is just like me. We want to go to northern Michigan for the hunting and fishing. That's the best relaxation there is, by golly. Your letter got me homesick when you were talking about the deer meetings being held and what not. Be glad when I'm home to join in and all those activities at Oakland County Sportsmen's Club.

It was a big day again today. I'll witness three more of them before I leave. Yep, it was payday. I received the tidy sum of $74. I believe I may pocket this too in case I get to go on R & R. But I just found out there are quite a few guys ahead of me so I don't' know whether I'll be able to go. I don't' care too much about it anyway. But then I'd like to send a few more items home from Japan, so I guess I would like to go on R & R.

There's one thing I'd like to know. Is my bird still hanging around the gun cabinet? I'll sign off and write tomorrow when I have time on my hands. Love, Bill.

Oct. 1, 1952

Dear Mom, Dad and Carol,

Went through inspection today all right. The inspecting officers stayed in FDC all morning and watched all the procedures. They were really checking close on everything today. Everything was going fine until noon. Then all heck broke loose! Black clouds appeared at noon and before you know it hail started coming down and winds up to 60 miles an hour. The funny thing about it was it only lasted ten minutes and then the sun came out again and the sky was clear and it was pleasant. It was the oddest thing I ever did see. Later we got word that a building blew down in Panmunjom. So it was a fierce wind!

I finally received my study book on forestry. It's quite interesting. Read it until chow time and darn near starved cause I was late getting there and they didn't have much left to eat. But I made up for it at supper tonight. We had chicken and I made a pig of myself. Had a big drumstick and wing, carrots, peas, two helpings of spuds and three pieces of apple pie. So you see what I mean about making a pig of myself. I was hungry.

Learned something encouraging today. Our points have been extended to 38. What a blow, eh? Say for my Christmas box, you can enclose food, food and whatever else you want, fruitcake and stuff like there. Use your imagination and try to make it so I have a little Christmas over here. Know what I mean, jellybean?

Lots of love and kisses, your favorite son, Bill

Oct. 2, '52

Dear Mom, Dad and Carol,

Working nights again tonight. Sitting by the stove and keeping myself fairly comfortable. Got plenty of wood piled up in here so I guess we'll keep warm through the night. I have one good consolation though if the wood happens to run out. My schedule just runs till 3 a.m. and the other guy has to sit up until morning.

We were issued our winter sleeping bags this afternoon and two extra blankets. My worries are over in regards to sleeping warm now. That bag alone is darn near warm enough to keep you comfortable.

Tomorrow is the big Corps inspection. Once a month we have to go through this. Everything has to be spotless! I've got it lucky cuz I get to sleep tomorrow morning during the inspection in view of the fact that I'm working nights. But the inspections are good in a way cuz they keep the area in general worth living in. It's always clean. I guess there are more advantages than disadvantages.

I've got paper over in the tent to write on but I forgot to bring it up so I sneaked a few sheets of paper to write this letter on. I guess it doesn't make any difference what kind of paper I use anyway.

Why did Father sell his bow and arrow? I thought he was going to play Robin Hood for a while and practice to shoot a few deer this fall. I'd like to buy a good bow when I get home and practice a while with it. I may find that is one of my hidden talents.

(Bill did become a good archer and went deer hunting with a bow and arrow every year. He was a member of the Ford Motor Company Archery Club and won several medals and trophies.)

Enclosed you will find $110 which you can add to my account. I don't believe I will be going on R & R so I'll send the money home instead of carrying it around in my pocket. Starting next month you should be getting $75 in my allotment. If you don't, let me know. Think I'll call it a letter now. Love and kisses, Bill.

—m—

Oct. 3, 1952

Dear Mom, Dad and Carol,

Had a pretty full day today. Started out early this morning in the truck, roving through the mountains looking for ammo boxes at all the firing batteries. We went to all the outfits up on the line and found nary a box. They're using them all themselves. We wanted the ammo boxes to build a wall around our tent. While I was up there I saw an air strike and also watched the firing batteries kick out a few rounds. Boy that air strike was really interesting—watching them dive and drop their eggs.

In the afternoon I stayed in the tent and studied. After I finished my evening meal we took off for the USO show. Yep, they had another one again. Nobody I've ever heard of before. There were a few singers, a dancer, juggler and a rope spinner. The rope spinner was a girl, a cute one at that. Wow!!!

There was a guy here today that got a big box from home. It contained all kinds of canned goods, tuna fish, spaghetti and more food! So there's a suggestion for you and future boxes for me.

The guy that's working with me tonight and I hauled a few logs back from the mountain and spent a couple of hours making fire wood out of them. These axes we have, well you might as well use a hammer for all the good they do. We are the best-equipped soldiers in the world. He.he.he.

Hope you enjoyed your trip. Love, Bill

—m—

Oct. 5, 1952

Dear Mom, Dad and Carol,

Neglected to write last night, due to my unfortunate honor of being on guard duty. So I'll attempt to scribble off a few lines this morning and get it in the mail before it goes out. The mailbox was empty for me yesterday. Letters have I not!

You've never seen more beautiful nights than we had the past few nights. The moon was just as full and big as ever and the sky was as blue as ink. The moon lit up the sky like daylight. Really nice and I don't mind walking guard on such nights.

Had another movie that I didn't even bother to go see. It was "The People Against O'Hara"—Spencer Tracey. I probably didn't miss much. Instead I hit the sack to get some sleep cuz I have to work again tonight. It is a never-ending circle like a person is awake and running around all the time.

We (the other guy and I who have to work tonight) are going out to fetch some wood and chop it up for kindling to burn tonight. About time for the mail now, so best run this over. I gotta take off for church this morning, too.

I usually wash, brush my teeth, and comb hair, etc. *before* I go to church. You sorta misunderstood me in one of my previous letters.

Love, Bill

—w—

Oct. 6, 1952

Dear Mom, Dad and Carol,

I'm working again tonight. We work every other night this week. I'd just as soon be on the days, it ain't quite so tiring. Received your letter today, the one from Niagara Falls. You seem to be having a pretty enjoyable time cruising around. Bet that's pretty country all the way up and around the Soo. By the sound of your letter I guess it costs a fortune to buy anything in Canada.

Went to church in the morning then came back and waited around till noon so I could go and eat. Then being Sunday I rested and waited for supper. During the evening I played a couple games of volleyball. Us enlisted men played against officers. The officers went away mad again cuz we beat them three games straight. They really do get peeved.

After that the guys and I who are working tonight hunted logs and cut them up for firewood. Reminded me of when I went to Grams chopping wood, I mean, for her stove. I still can't figure out how she didn't burn her hand or arm when she put her arm in the stove's fire to stir the wood around. Amazing! That's some Gram I have.

It's not really that cold tonight. It's one of those beautiful nights. Strange but it makes me hate Korea all the more.

I hear Mickey Rooney is going to be here Friday or Saturday. Hope I get to see the old boy and his show. Love and Kisses, Willie.

(Oct. 6–13, 1952, Korea: Chinese Communist Force Attack on Western & Central Fronts. U.S. 51 KIA, 348 WIA.)

Oct. 7, 1952

Dear Mom, Dad and Carol,

I'm writing this letter a little earlier tonight just to be sure I will be able to get it out. I missed last night because we started firing at 7:30 p.m. and continued through the wee hours of the morning, which was about 4 a.m. We got those ole Joe Chinks, or a good amount of them. It was fire, go, go, go. Can't tell you the missions, but we hit the target at some interesting spots in North Korea. Was worn out at day break.

I really needed some sleep and got it at 7 a.m. until noon today. I believe we are going to be at it again tonight. We're going to keep a full shift on all night. Ole Joe Chink went on a rampage last night, and that's why we may turn the tables tonight and regain a little territory.

There's been bombers and fighter planes (jets) going over here all day practically in droves. The gooks are die-hard fighters; you'd better believe it.

Now for some local news. We got another radio in our tent today. The one we had wasn't that good. Now we made a nice big antenna and stuck it on a pole and the radio plays good. It's a little Philco portable.

I would like to let you in on an interesting fact. When the full moon appears, Joe Chink makes a push, and when the moon is on its last leg you can well expect him to kick again. It never fails. The moon is starting to disappear now.

We sure are having some beautiful weather lately. Haven't seen a cloud in the sky for a long time. We got three new guys in today. They came down from the firing battery. Instead of bringing inexperienced personnel in FDC they send guys from the firing battery, and send the recruits to the firing battery for experience.

We're starting to put up our day room now. It's a big, long room that looks like a Quonset hut. It's approximately 80 feet long. It's getting to look like state side here now. I guess they consider it a morale booster; because we can hang out there, write letters and so forth.

I received the folder of Niagara Falls in a letter from you yesterday. According to the folder the falls looks really pretty. But you say they're not worth going to see, eh?

Guess, then I won't go. I'll go to Agate falls or something. Also received the post card.

Boy that radio of ours is picking up some wonderful music. Missed another good movie last night, had to work. The movie was "Pat and Mike."
Lots of love, Bill

—∿—

Oct. 8, '52

Dear Mom, Dad and Carol,

Received two letters—one mailed from the Soo and one from Paradise. You sound like you were really enjoying yourselves. I just reread the letters. Good, you did take movies.

As for Korea—what we have here is the "shovel age." I won't know what to do when I get home if there isn't a shovel in my hands. I heard another rumor today. Those 38 points they are talking about are only going to last till the end of October or November. That means I'll slip out of that deal. Never-the-less I still won't get out of here until January with 36 points. That's around the 15th of the month. I've only got three more to go. It isn't so long.

I thank God we go on days tomorrow. I've worked every night during the past week. I'll be glad to get a good nights sleep. Every night we have been firing like crazy. It's the other shifts turn to stay awake.

I'd like to make one more request, and that's for Christmas cards. Just a box of ten or so would be enough. I'm missing another good movie again. It's "Jumping Jacks" with Dean Martin and Jerry Lewis. It seems to me we see the crummy shows when we're on days.

Now we've got to build racks along side our tents to support 50-gallon drums for our fuel oil. We used to have 5-gallon cans and had to fill them up every five or six hours. This new way is going to be better. I'm listening to the movie and it is distracting my concentration on this letter. Everybody seems to be having a good laugh.

Well I guess I'll quit for now. Love, Bill

(Oct. 9, 1952, Korea: "Cherokee" Strikes. 7th Fleet bombing campaign against battle front enemy supply facilities. The Navy is assisting. 51 KIA, 348 WIA)

Oct. 9, 1952

Dear Mom, Dad and Carol,

There wasn't any mail for the battery today let alone me. That's the worst it's been so far. I gotta go on guard again tonight at 8 p.m. Only got about 14 or 15 more guards to pull. Time is getting shorter. One of the guys that came down from the batteries into FDC is from Detroit. He hardly ever goes to Pontiac, and I of course very seldom went to Detroit, so there wasn't much for us to talk about. Well anyways I've got another Michigan guy here.

We got our elements for the stoves today and have them all set up. Tomorrow we have to roll a couple of 50 gallon barrels of oil down here and get these stoves in operation. That's gonna be a job. Also during our spare time we did some more fall cleaning in FDC. Practically remodeled the place. Also we built a pit out on the side of FDC to put the small generators that runs our FDC Army radio. The Major said they make too much noise sitting on the ground. They got crazy ideas in their heads.

I didn't have a chance to finish the letter last night cause I had guard so it wasn't finished to go out in the morning mail. So as it stands I will write the last half of this letter tonight. I was looking at the new Pageant and they have a few pictures of Ursula there in it. Even though she's 30 years old and has two kids I think she's really beautiful. The heck with Marilyn Monroe and the rest of them.

I'll finally get to see a movie again, "Glory Alley." It will probably be a dumb show. Daddy seems to be having quite a time shooting a few "Pats". And you, Ma, you do more work on vacation then you do at home.

Write more, soon, Love, Bill

Oct. 11, 1952

Dear Mom, Dad and Carol,

Received one letter today that was from Fred. His letter took a month getting to me. He had the wrong address and I believe it went around and around to Hong Kong. He's griping about the Army too.

Had a busy day again. Took inventory of the whole place in here, and that was something. I'm hugging this stove right now. It feels good. It's cold, but not that bad. But standing near the stove and soaking up the heat feels so good. I just finished listening to a beautiful song. It's "If you love me half as much as I love you." Rosemary Clooney sure can sing.

It's so darn hard for me to even fill half a page. There is nothing to write about. It's just the same old stuff, every day. I imagine you all get just as tired of hearing it as I do doing it.

Next day . . . Got up this morning and the frost was on the pumpkin. First time since I've been here. Don't know whether I told you or not but we have to keep our stoves turned off at night or else have a fire guard stay awake at night watching the stove. Since that's too much trouble and loss of sleep for a guy we let the stove die down and one guy gets up really early and lights it. So when the rest of the guys get up, it's nice and warm in the tent.

In about half an hour the movie will start. This time it seems to be another crummy movie, "Francis Goes to West Point." They fooled us and it starts at 7 instead of 7:30. I'll write more tomorrow, Love, Bill

(Oct. 14–25, 1952, Korea: Operation Showdown/Battle of Hill 598 (Sniper Ridge), 7th ID battles. The Chinese near Kumhwa, the right leg of the Iron Triangle, and suffers 2,000 casualties.)

Oct. 13, 1952

Dear Mom, Dad and Carol,

I got the picture folder of the Upper Peninsula of Michigan today. Very nice of you to send it. I enjoy looking at the pictures of the old tramping grounds. Also received a letter from Mrs. Gross, Fred's mom. Sit down when I tell you this. She's gonna have another baby! That's right. She said it would be a pretty nice family with six boys in it. She's expecting about March. Fred called her up a few weeks ago and said he almost cried when he found out. He's going to have a brother that is 21 years younger than him.

Nice to hear that you all got home in fine shape with your two ducks. Also sounds like a pretty good deal you got from Van Camp buying his chickens. It was a surprise to hear that he's giving up farming. After all those years. One never knows.

I haven't heard from Anita in a week. Of course I haven't written to her but four times in the last month. I think maybe she's paying me back some of the same medicine. Who cares? I'm still thinking about that Dear John letter, but—

No, my hair ain't bleached. That's my natural color, what I was born with, remember? You forget so easy! You mentioned hand warmers. Well, you could send me one in a Christmas box. Very excellent idea. Send what you want. Surprise me.

We've got out day room all built now. And the sidewalks all put in, bunkers all dug, every other thing all finished and I guess we should be set for a little while. Our Captain will think of something else for us to do, no doubt. Till tomorrow, love, Willie.

Oct. 16, '52

Dear Mom, Dad and Carol,

I got guard duty again tonight so I'm starting this letter a little early in the day. It's four o'clock now and that hillbilly music is about to start on the radio. I just got back from taking a shower a few minutes ago, I feel like a million bucks now. Those showers do wonders for my morale. Funny, such a simple thing as hot water and soap, lathering up can make a man feel like life is worth living, even in this hell hole.

Spent the morning sleeping cuz I worked all last night. It was cold this morning when I went to bed so I slept in my winter bag and when I woke up I was sweating.

Gets pretty warm during the day. Well, here it is almost 8 p.m. already. I was interrupted at 4:15 for a Troop Information program. They had a discussion on the condition of India. I was so interested in it I hated to leave. Kidding. What boring topics they choose to discuss. I just got off guard and it's pretty darn cold.

Mom, I received a little book of 10 souvenir colored pictures from your friend, Mae Kitto. Got to write to her tonight and thank her for them. Well, I guess I'll hit the sack and get some much-needed sleep. Lots of love, Bill.

—~—

Oct. 18, 1952

Dear Mom, Dad and Carol, I missed writing yesterday because I worked all night. I got a heck of a cold now from walking guard the other night. You know the kind of colds I get, well I got one of them. I was in so much misery last night and that's why I didn't write.

I've got some nice background music this afternoon while I'm writing you this letter. Listening to some good hillbilly music. They just played two of my favorite songs—"Mountain Dew" and "Let Ole Mother Nature Have her Way." Guess I'm just a hillbilly at heart. It cheers me up to hear that music.

> *(Bill would not mention it to his parents, but he enjoyed hillbilly music because it brought Anita closer to him in thought.*

He was still confused about writing her a letter and breaking off their relationship. In his heart he did not want to do it. He said he would write her a "Dear John" letter just to appease his parents.)

Tonight I get to sleep without being disturbed, meaning guard. Boy was I ever tired this morning. I came off duty at 8 a.m. and three minutes later I was in the sack and sound asleep at 8:10 a.m.

They're playing "Too Old" now. I sure get a kick out of some of those songs. It's evening now. Played volleyball for a while but I shouldn't have done that cause I got all sweaty—that didn't help my cold much.

Got a good show on tonight but I'll have to miss it cause I've got work. "We're not Married" is the show with Marilyn Monroe.

So the Army finally caught up with Bob ha! What will Carol do now? He'll probably be lucky enough to be stationed at Fort Custer.

Well I gotta go to work now. Write more tomorrow. Lots of love, Bill.

—w—

October 19, 1952

Dear Mom, Dad and Carol,

Started off the day again this morning on the right foot by attending church. I washed, brushed my teeth and combed my hair before I went to church. I think God is getting my messages, cause the days are going by faster and faster.

This cold of mine is getting a little better it seems. I'm sniffing constantly all day long and every time I sniff I think of Dad. He used to look at me so disgustedly every time I sniffed as though I should let it run down my puss instead of sniffling.

We're making new charts in FDC now and it's keeping us pretty busy these past few days. That's really a job to log down charts. Also had to log down a big map which comes in sections and we had to put them all together. It's like a giant puzzle. We got it all done now and got all our battery positions plotted and everything's all set.

I still have three rolls of film to get developed. I'll have to catch someone who is going on R&R to get the film developed for me. It will take me a month to send the pictures home. I must have a slew of them there now. Have you started to put them in my book? Will my book hold all the pictures? Maybe I should send another photo album home.

Well I guess I'd better get my bedding from outside and fix my bed and get a little shuteye. You know, counting today, it has been 10 months and 12 days since I left the states on the 15th of December 1951.

Guess Michigan State's team is really doing good, eh! Undefeated so far. Are they eligible for the Rose Bowl? Write soon, Bill

—w—

October 21, 1952

Dear Mom, Dad and Carol,

Received some photos of home. I noticed the picturesque dirt piles along the street and the grass growing between the sidewalk. Quite a good picture of sister Carol, all dolled up in a new dress and it's too bad I can't see her shoes cuz no doubt they are the latest style and new! What a voluptuous girl, eh! Just about the best sister I ever had. Best looking, too.

Father is still inquiring about whether I'm going to make it home by Christmas. Well here the best answer I can give you. Much to my disappointment, I won't be home for the holidays. I'll leave here sometime in February, only four more months. Not too bad, I guess. Could be worse.

Don't worry about me and the fighting. But I suppose it doesn't do a lot of good to tell you that. Isn't human if you don't worry. I guess I'm worrying about you at home and those flying saucers.

I just hope we don't have to move cuz we have the perfect setup here. Considering the circumstances, I have nothing to complain about.

That box you sent by first class mail must have taken the long route and changed to 3rd class cuz I ain't seen hide or hair of it yet. Should be coming along soon, I guess (I hope.)

The Christmas box will probably speed through in three days. Can't figure out the mail service. Guess I shouldn't try.

Now that I'm thinking of it, I might as well say it. Brace yourself. I'm running out of envelopes. Yep that's right. I put that request sort of indirectly, but you get the drift.

To change the subject I'll write about deer hunting. There is going to be a three-day doe season in Michigan I understand. But can you get a doe and a buck? One of each?

Getting back to Father now. He is really working on his movie camera, eh. That's a good picture of him taking movies. And if Niagara Falls is no more than that picture might as well watch water come out of the garden hose and make rainbows.

I might as well say this right now. In another picture how come there's no kindling in the basement? I thought I told you before to get some chopped. I had a silly dream last night. I dreamed I was at G.M.C. and hired into the accounting department and when I got there they all started chasing me out. I was running all over the plant and I couldn't get out. Crazy dream.

Received a letter from Fred a while back and he is still cooling his heels in the states. Guess someone has to stay back there and hold down the soft jobs. It's raining here like the dickens. So I hear it's supposed to continue for three days before it lets up. I don't know how accurate they are, but I hope they're wrong.

In a few minutes I get off work and then I'll go to the tent and write a few more letters. So till tomorrow, Love, Bill

—~—

October 22, 1952, Journal Entry:

Don't worry, I keep telling my folks. What's to worry about? Yesterday we had an unidentified aircraft about 100 miles from camp. Couldn't catch it on the screen until it was in shouting distance. Near miss. It passed us. But we sure held our breaths. Our sky search is usually very dependable and can spot a Joe Chink closer than 100 miles.

Not that I'm saying our spotting method is ancient, but tracking this fighter wasn't up to snuff. Too many "near misses" for me. I know those Chinks would love to bomb FDC. Say, aren't we the

brains of this damn war. Anyway, that's what the Major keeps telling us.

—m—

October 23, 1952

Dear Mom, Dad and Carol,

I will get right down to it now and answer your letter because I won't have any time tonight, cause I have guard, again. To change the subject, I think my Arkansas gal, Anita, is pissed off. She still writes but not too often, and her letters sound different. I think something is wrong. No, I didn't write her that "Dear John" letter.

A bunch of PX rations came in and here I am sitting with no money. I guess I'm too much of a miser. I send it all home to save—and leave myself with nothing. Well the money is better there than burning holes in my pocket here in Korea. Soon I'll be home and counting all my money.

They sure are tearing up the street there. It looks worse than when I left. They should build an elevated road so then they can dig from now till dooms day.

"Are you Teasing Me?" is playing on the radio. It's the Number One hillbilly tune. Ah, that sweet music! Make me feel gooood.

Do you listen to the "Bob and Ray" program? They've got one of the craziest shows ever. Today they advertised an alarm clock. They don't ring or play music. They nudge you. You cuddle up with the clock every night. I laughed and laughed. Write soon, Love Bill

—m—

(Editor's note: Bill mentions that "Anita's letters sound different." This may be the time she discovered she had to have her leg amputated.)

—m—

October 24, 1952

Dear Mom, Dad and Carol,

When I get a newspaper in the mail, it's about as much of a blast reading it as your letters. Had a relatively humid day today so to speak. It got up a might over 70 degrees. Maybe it wasn't so warm but after several coolish days and then have one like today, it seemed warm, anyway. I kept myself busy today. All morning and most of the afternoon we cut up some old salvaged tents and nailed them on our tent sides so as to make a double wall. I guess it is supposed to serve its purpose as a good insulator or something. There is going to be three inches of air pockets between the two layers of tents. I suppose you are wondering how we can nail it to the tent. Well, we don't. We have frames built up all around the tent and we nailed the tent from the top frame down to the floor. We'd better keep warm this winter or I'll want to know the reason why.

Later this evening, I was engaged in harder work. We are setting up a basketball court. Had to dig holes to set up some 6x6's and nail the backboards and nets on them. That required a bit more work. I'm getting to be quite an industrious worker, strange as it may seem.

I still haven't received the box you sent by 1st class mail. It's probably on the boat 1st class. Instead of riding in the bottom of the pile it rides on top. Ha! The End. . . . Love, Bill.

—∞—

Oct. 25, 1952

Dear Mom, Dad and Carol,

The enclosed three photos and the picture post card were nice. Those photos were funny. That expression on your face struck me funny even before I read the back of the picture. Seeing you dressed in your night or I should say evening clothes made me think of those PJs that I sent home. Has Carol ever worn them? Or are they more or less a showpiece.

Later—I laid down just for a minute and before you know it I was sound asleep. I missed half of my hillbilly programs on the radio.

Now it's night again and I'm working at FDC. I'm going to leave in a little while and go hit the sack. I'm so tired. I really need my sleep. I may go to Seoul tomorrow because I have to get a new crystal for my watch and buy a few things. I don't know what.

And you mean you never heard of Pageant Magazine? It's just like Reader's Digest only with pictures, and better, I think. Well I'd best leave now and hit the sack. Love, Bill

—ɱ—

(Oct. 26–28, 1952: Battle of the Hook, 7th Marines, 70 KIA, 386 WIA, 12 MIA, 27 POW.)

—ɱ—

Oct. 26, 1952

Dear Mom, Dad and Carol, We're firing quite a bit tonight, again. Busy as all get out. Those Joe Chinks are getting a good taste of Uncle Sam's medicine! We have maps and charts all over the place. It's amazing how well we all work together, get things done, even when the night is busy. But we all know what to do, and sometimes I believe we can read each other's mind. It's kind of spooky, but it's the truth. How we can reach those charts and maps and pin point the targets, and get them right on, only God knows, and he's not telling. That's what this police action is all about. The Captain says it takes a lot of guts to be here and it takes a lot of concentration on our part to get it right, dead on. Sometimes that Captain can say the nicest things. Sometimes—

I went to Seoul today for a few hours. Left this morning at 8:00 a.m. and had a two hour drive before we arrived in the big city. I got a real good look at it for the first time. And believe me it's really bombed out. They're done quite a bit of rebuilding but never-the-less you can still tell it's a war-torn city. I rode around most of the morning on various buses and it's a surprisingly large city, covers quite an area.

I took my watch to the PX and had a new crystal put in it. The other one was smashed to bits. It only took about ten minutes and 85 cents of my money. Had a pretty good time just walking around. It was nice jut getting out of the area. Right behind the PX in Seoul the Koreans have set up a make shift shopping area, looks like a flea market. They sell the things they make dirt cheap, too. Some of the things for sale were cigarette dispensers made of wood, Korean and American flags, hats, all kinds, fatigue caps for us soldiers. They were flashy hats and some guys bought them cause they would not mess up their hair.

They sold us back our cigarettes for a buck a pack. We only paid 11 cents a pack in camp, but some of us guys would run out and so we had to shell out the buck cause we needed the smokes. Something really unique were brass dishes made from our own artillery shells. And there were some ladies selling something, but I'm not telling you what. And I wasn't buying any. I did give one of them a dollar, but I didn't want anything in return. No, thank you. She looked so young, and in need of some money. Poor kid. What they do is really very sad. That's war! I wonder how we would react under the same conditions?

Other neat stuff that they sold were clothing made from our own GI blankets. They sure know how to improvise. I did tell you that the Korean kids were all dressed in cast off fatigues that we give them.

I called up Curly from Seoul, too. I heard him loud and clear and we talked about a half-hour. It was nice talking with him again. He sounds the same as he always did. He said he was trying to get down to Seoul two weeks from this Sunday. Hope he makes it out and I hope to make it too. Sure would be nice to see him again. I couldn't think of anything to talk about but managed to blab about something.

Boy what a dusty ride it was coming back from Seoul. I'll be chewing dust for the next two days. I ate lunch in the snack bar and had three hamburgers and a malted milk. Substantial food, eh?

We're firing quite a bit tonight, again. I'm writing this letter in spurts, you might say. Took me about two hours to write this much, cause we were so busy. Guess I will quit now. More tomorrow, Love, Bill

p.s. How do you like the stamp I put on the envelopes. Hubba, Hubba means hurry up or go fast in Korean. Quaint. Got two other stamps (different).

—✵—

October 27, 1952, Journal Entry:

I keep thinking about that Korean girl I saw in Seoul, selling herself for 50 cents. Yes, 50 damn cents! I gave her a buck. Didn't want anything in return. What the hell is this world coming to? She couldn't have been more than 13 years old, no kidding! I wanted to get ahold of the 'powers that be' and shake them, or do something more drastic, give them a good beating, one they would never forget. What the hell are we doing here in Korea? Tell me, please. Someone tell me. I get so damn mad! Soldiers were lining up to fuck her or the other girls. The girls were just kids! Make up on their faces and dressed in rags. These kids really know that this war is a hell on earth.

October 28, 1952

Dear Mom, Dad and Carol,

Received the OCSC (Oakland County Sportsmen Club) magazine and a letter from Anita and that's it. What a letter she wrote me today, Wow! She was telling me how much she missed me and longs for my return and missed my letters terribly when the days pass with no letter from me. She's even getting her mother in the deal. Her mother asks Anita about me and why I don't write. I must be quite a romantic Don Juan when I write letters to her. Oh well, that's life I guess.

I didn't take another expedition to Seoul today. I hit the sack and tried to sleep cuz I worked last night. It was a little cool in the tent, but not too cool. I climbed in my warm sleeping bag and "snap" just like that I fell asleep. But in a half-hour I was awakened by a pesky fly. I snuggled down in my bag and got away from the fly but I started sweating. Had to come up for air and challenge that fly again. I managed to get about two hours sleep, fifteen minutes at a time. My arms are sore from swatting at that silly thing. They sure are illusive. I hit the shower at 2 p.m. came back and listened to hillbilly music, ate a chicken supper and here I am at work 10 p.m.

We're gonna build some doors for out tent tomorrow so I have to look forward to that after work. Toddle do for now. Your favorite only son, Bill

p.s. Is father getting his hunting stuff piled in the corner yet? Probably, without a doubt, the answer is affirmative.

October 28, 1952, Journal Entry:

Another letter from Anita, and it made me feel like crap. Why am I doing this to her? This is driving me nuts. So if I write to her, whose to know? I can't get her out of my mind Sometimes her letters sound so sad. She really loves me, I know. Why am I such fool? Or have I asked myself that question many, many times? This war is screwing me.

I'm tired of playing these games with the gal I love. She's sweet kid and I think she is the one for me. Tell me, God?

October 28, 1952

Dear Mom, Dad and Carol,

The mail seems to be coming just every other day for me. One day nothing, the next day two or more. I don't care, just so the mail keeps comings. It's 3:30 in the morning right now. I guess this is my last night to work nights this week. I hope so because I get so darn sleepy working this night shift.

I had to go to Seoul again yesterday. The first sergeant took about five of us down in a truck to tear apart boxes and load some lumber on the truck so he could bring it back and fix the orderly room. I'd like to go down there myself and get a load of lumber to fix a floor in our tent but what-cha-gonna-do? I ain't the boss around here. I just work here.

It was a nice day for driving around. I went down in a $2^1/_2$ ton truck and came back in a jeep. I don't remember too much coming back cuz I fell asleep. In comparison with those trucks the jeep rides like a cloud. It wasn't too hard to fall asleep. I won't know how to act when I crawl into a civilian car.

You asked in your letter about Fred. Well, he's still in Georgia. Looks like they're going to keep him there for the duration. You also wrote that Pa isn't going hunting because of a sore foot. If you know him as I do-all aches and pains disappear when the words hunting or fishing are mentioned. Those are the magic words!

Oh yeah, congratulations Pappy, you done killed a pheasant! When pay day gets here I'm gonna buy some shells and do some road hunting. Not going in the field, too many land mines. So I'll send you a picture of me with a brace of pheasants. (Ha).

It's getting busy now and I've got to work on reports that have to get out pronto! Love from your son, Willie.

October 29, 1952

Dear Mom,

Received a letter from ya-all today concerning this new acquaintance of Father's namely this Italian woman. Well, I don't know exactly what to say about that. The one and only way you'll be able to win Daddy back I guess is to study up on your Italian accent a little and start squashing grapes in your bare feet when he comes home from work. Be sorta inconspicuous about it though. Have spaghetti every night for supper and hand him a bottle of wine every time he helps you do some thing. Try using a bit of garlic, maybe behind your ears, instead of perfume. Tell me if it works.

You know sending stuff first class isn't any different than parcel post. I still ain't got that box you sent on the seventh by first class mail. I hope my Christmas cards get here in time. If they're too late I may be able to add a notation and say they are Happy Easter cards.

Don't worry about what you send me for Christmas. Whatever it is I'm sure it'll be the best and most welcome gift I ever received. I only wish I could send you all something.

We finished making our door tonight, or rather this afternoon. Makes it pretty nice in the tent now. The wind doesn't seem to whistle through so much. It actually felt pretty warm in there, but I don't know how warm it will be in the winter. Did I tell you we got some new and better stoves for FDC? Shaped like a rectangle. It will be a lot warmer than our old pot bellied stove. Write tomorrow, Love, Bill

—∞—

Oct. 31, 1952

Dear Mom, Dad and Carol,

Halloween today. Have to go out and pull a few pranks on someone tonight. I believe I'll put on a mask and go trick or treating. I should have a jolly good time knocking on tents and collecting food and stuff.

I missed writing last night because I had guard duty on the second relief. That's from the hours of 8:00 to 10:00, then from 2:00 to 4:00. Boy I'll tell you I'm really tired, beat tired. I'm writing this letter a little early tonight because I want to hit the sack soon as I get off duty at 8:00. All of a sudden four hours have gone by and here it is 7 p.m. already. We started shooting at 3:30 and just quit a few minutes ago. There was no let up, I'm telling you. Mission after mission. I'm really glad when it comes time to leave so I can lay down and rest my weary bones.

Concerning my camera, one day I was gonna take some pictures with it and when I pulled it out of its sturdy constructed case the lens and all the works fell apart in it. There are four tiny screws that hold it together in front and now-no screws, no camera. I took up those three films a while back and I am getting them developed now. But I believe the camera has seen its day.

We had a brief thunder storm and hail shower this morning but it has cleared up now. Also today I got paid. You should get $75 out of this month's pay. That's all for now. Write soon, Lots of love, Bill.

—w—

Nov. 1952, Korea: About this time Cpl. Bill McCoy, of Benton Harbor, Michigan, attached to the 179th Infantry, Medical Corp. was on the front line. He said, "For six months I lived in bunkers and rode shot gun as an aide man in the jeep. I helped one soldier out of a mine field. I shouted to him, 'You're in a mine field!' He looked at me stunned, he was on patrol out there. Then he stepped on a mine. I watched as his foot blew off below his boot top and one hand flew into the wind, gone. One of the other medics said to follow his foot steps through the mine field and I did. Guess he knew what he was doing cause we didn't step on any mines. Well, we got to the wounded soldier, put him on a stretcher and slowly followed the foot steps all the way back to the jeep."

—w—

Nov. 1, 1952

Dear Mom, Dad and Carol,

Received the box today containing the Christmas cards, envelopes and fudge. What a surprise to get the fudge! Yum, yum. Those envelopes came just in time too. I'm almost out. Nice Christmas cards, too. Makes me kinda, sad or I should say real homesick too even looking at them I received a letter from Anita today. You'd think I was the only guy in the world. I know I'm handsome and all that but gee you know, such flattery.

It has been a real nice day today. The sun shone bright and warm all day. It looked just like spring. But I know it wasn't cuz I'd be home. I'd better not be counting my chickens before the eggs hatch. We have a nice big full moon again tonight and that means more than likely that Joe Chink will be a kicking again. Ole Joe goes by the moon, I guess.

New moons are his specialty. But we got in some new spotlights—wow—what a surprise for Joe Chink!

I'm in my tent now. Just got off duty at FDC. I put the cap on my pens and walked over here and then tried to take it off and it wouldn't come off. I finally ended up soaking it with water for ten minutes then me and another fellow each grasped and end, with a struggle we finally pulled it off. I was all set to send it back and get a new one.

I'm listening to the "Hit Parade" now for the first time since I left Japan, when I went to the school there. Half of those songs I've never heard. For instance there's a really cute one called "Jambo Laha" or almost like that and two others "Lonesome That's All" and the prettiest one I've ever heard called "You Belong to Me." You must get that one so I can sit and listen to it when I get home. I believe it's Joe Stafford who sings it. Number one tune is coming up now—"Wish You Were Here." That's real pretty too. I suppose these are some of Carol's favorites, eh?

Well I'll sign off for a while. Love and kisses, always, Bill

—w—

Nov. 2, 1952

Dear Mom, Dad and Carol,

I started out this morning by attending church and went to communion. Came back and worked in FDC most of the day. In the afternoon I came down to the tent for a while and painted the door. What color you ask? We made it an olive drab. Color designer, I'm not. That's the only color we got! We here in the Army are like Henry Ford. Remember what he said? "I don't care what color we paint the Model T, just so it's black." The pen still seems to have a little water in it from when I soaked it last night to get the top of it off it.

I got some pictures back today that I had developed. The majority of them came out very good. I'll start sending them home now. They are all taken with my camera. The ones of me in my long underwear were taken at 10:00 at night and the only light is the one we have in the tent.

It sure is a beautiful night out again and it looks just as bright as day. I can imagine what is will be like when there's new snow on the ground and a nice moon like this. We'll have to wear sunglasses or moon glasses on guard. The lights are going out very soon so I'm short of time. Write again tomorrow. Love, Bill

—᠁—

(Nov. 3, 1952: Hill 851: Heartbreak Ridge Area held by the 2nd Bn, 160th Inf, Regt. 140th ID, withstands North Korean attack. U.S. 19KIA, 54 WIA)

—᠁—

Nov. 3, 1952

Dear Mom, Dad and Carol,

I have just time enough tonight to scratch off a page before the lights go out. Today I received a letter from pop and also received the box you sent first class mail. It took quite a time getting here but all was in good shape. The Halloween candy got here a few days late but never-the-less it was all welcome, every bit of the stuff.

The big inspection is here tomorrow morning. A colonel is going to inspect FDC all morning and I'm on duty. He's going to ask me 1000 questions and I had better know the answers.

I bought myself a camera today. Paid $17.00 for it. It's a Kodak Duaflex II camera. It's pretty nice and it didn't cost too much. It's a 620 so in the next box you send me try to enclose a few rolls of 620 film. I'm going to bring the other camera home, too.

Show tonight.? Yes, I saw "Captain Horashio Hornblower." Good movie. Oops! No lights, that's it. Love Bill.

—᠁—

Nov. 4, 1952

Dear Mom, Dad and Carol,

The letters from ya all have been coming through pretty good lately. One letter a day instead of three one day and none the next two days. The weatherman has been treating us very well lately. Certainly is surprising to have such nice weather in November. Wish the snow would hurry and get here though. I should be contented with this warm weather but you know, I always want something different and when it gets here, I wish it were back as before. (Figure that one out!)

Today we worked around FDC. We didn't have the inspection as planned because they postponed it for two days and then two more days and then I'll be on the night shift so I'll slip out of that one.

Our backyard at home probably looks pretty bare, without a doubt. You're hollering now about having to buy coal, why don't you burn those trees you logged? Better than burning them outside and catching the telephone pole and wires on fire.

Nice to hear that Carol is beginning to enjoy her work now. She's a lot better off than if she hated every minute of it.

Do you believe all that stuff about Ike coming to Korea and stopping the war? Why didn't he come before and stop the war. Maybe we'd all vote for him. Bet Stevenson will win. Can't think of nothing else to write about so will quit for this time. Love, Willie

—w—

Nov. 1952, Korea; First Lt. Vayden (Andy) Anderson, of Stromburg, Neb. was a commanding officer assigned as co-commander to the 84th Engineers, B. Company. First Lt. Anderson said, "My first job was to get my men to drive piling for the X-Ray Bridge (X-Ray was the code name.) It was dedicated July 13, 1953 and named the Sgt. Libby Bridge, a hero who commanded a tank, saved his buddies and was killed in action. Lt. Victor Swanson was co-commander of B company.

The bridge was adjacent to the Carson, Reno and Vegas battle zones. Sgt. Libby was awarded the Medal of Honor posthumously.

—w—

Nov, 5, 1952

Dear Mom, Dad and Carol,

Seems funny to hear that you people back there are knee deep in snow when we here are still running around in short sleeves during the day.

I just about died laughing when I opened your letter and saw the picture of myself. Looks as though I wanted to make a face but didn't do it.

Today I received two letters from you, the box containing the envelopes and tablet and a paper. Also got a letter from Anita. Can't answer them tonight because we have a movie and I have to go see it, "Fearful Fagen." Probably some silly show of some kind.

Well tomorrow is the inspection of FDC and we have to work during the inspection. The only reason for that I guess is because we are the best!

Well, as of now it looks as though "Ike" is going to be our president.

The big package you mailed me should be here sometime the end of November. It'll get here in time anyway.

I understand if you get home anytime after 21 months you get out right away. If before 21 months you stay 24 months. Sounds screwy to me! I've got my Christmas cards all addressed already. Waiting for time to send them.

Enclosed is the picture of "Ears" Ahnen. Love, Bill

—⁓—

Nov. 6, 1952

Dear Mom, Dad and Carol,

Received no mail today but I guess I can't gripe much because I got a mess of them yesterday. So to show you how busy I've been lately, I got those papers last night during mail call and I haven't had time to open them yet. I got guard duty tonight and I want to scratch off this letter before I go to bed.

I gotta write Anita a letter too or she'll be getting plenty mad at me. I've been promising her for a long time I'd write more often but it seem as though I can never get any more than one a week off to her.

We had that inspection this morning and went through it with flying colors. That officer went through everything and lo and behold he couldn't find anything wrong. Our Major and the rest of the officers were pretty proud of us, I guess. Here I am taking the cake and eating it too. We did great!

We've got a U.S.O. show coming here to the battalion tomorrow morning. I guess it's put on by the special service branch of the Army. Tell you more about it tomorrow. I got a lot to write about but I'm gonna go to bed. I'll start a letter tomorrow afternoon and maybe I can get one off a decent length. Good night, Love, Bill.

—∾—

In Korea, Psychological warfare; Staff Sgt. Ernie DeVincent, of Benton Harbor, Michigan, was assigned to psychological warfare while in Korea. "We'd drop leaflets. In the pamphlets we'd ask them to surrender. Those that surrendered, we'd take pictures of them when they were in the POW camp south of Seoul. Some of them were shipped to an island off of Puson. We took the pictures to show the Red Cross the treatment that the prisoners were given by the United Nations. It was humane. We were fair with those soldiers." DeVincent was part of the Princess Pat Canadian Light Infantry.

—∾—

Nov. 7, 1952

Dear Mom, Pop and Carol,

So you got a letter from me in four days eh? I guess that little stamp on there did some good. About the fastest I get letters from home is seven days. The two I got today were dated the 31st and 1st.

We never did see that U.S.O. show today. Here's why—I witnessed the first snow flurries this morning. It started at 7 a.m. and continued through till about 9 a.m. A little stayed on the ground for about an hour then it melted. Thinking back, I've only seen snow three times since I've been in the Army. Once at Camp Chaffee, once in Japan and now today is the third time. It's strange why we haven't gotten more snow. Well anyway folks that's why we didn't see the U.S.O. It snowed.

Oh yes, I must tell you about our doughnut and coffee wagon that we have now. The way I understand it is that the Special Services runs it and we're supposed to have the honor of getting coffee and doughnuts in the a.m. and the p.m. I guess they don't know there's a war on. They might as will make it as nice as possible for us because we will be staying here until we get our 42 points.

Good old Anna Rosenberg is touring Korea. When she sees that we are getting coffee and doughnuts and having it easy here she'll up the points for sure.

Maybe Ike will make a pretty fair president because he has a pretty good idea what it is all about. As for Anna she doesn't know from nothing!

What's this I hear about the family? Getting on the lazy side and don't even want to get up in time to go to work any more? Sure is a pretty good Greyhound Bus Depot they built in Pontiac. The town's changing since I left. I better sign my letter pretty soon cause I have a few to catch up. I've got four letters here from Anita that I haven't answered yet. She no doubt will be peeved for me not writing in over a week now. Love you, Bill.

(Editor's note: Anna Rosenberg was regional head of the U.S. War Man Power Commission and regional director of the Selective Service board. She also regulated the amount of points required for discharge.)

Nov. 8, 1952

Dear Mom, Dad and Carol,

I did get a letter from Curly today. He seems to have a good deal now. Doesn't do much work and gets up when he wants to. He's got it all over me. I worked last night so my morning was spent sleeping and during the afternoon we did a little work in weatherproofing FDC, the building that is. Tried to plug up most of the holes and cracks.

The old timers tell us that Korea has some fierce winters and we'd better be ready for them. Frost bitten fingers fall off, no kidding. It's worst that the upper peninsula in Michigan in January.

Won't be taking many showers in the winter. So, I went and took a nice shower, came back and did the wrong thing, went out and played basketball and was sweating when I got through. More than likely I will catch another cold. Just got rid of the other one about four days ago.

I'm in the tent now listening to the radio and waiting to go to work in an hour. Just have to work two hours (till 10:00). Then came back and go sleepy bye. I have to make a special trip to Seoul tomorrow and get a sole on my boot sewed back on. That's the only place I can get it done. I've got a new pair of boots on the way and hope they'll be here in a few more weeks. May call Curly up again tomorrow when I'm in Seoul. I broke the crystal on my watch again. Just had one put in two weeks ago.

Will quit now and rest my eyes before I go to work. Love, your son, Bill

—~—

Nov. 9, 1952

Dear Mom, Dad and Carol,

The big thing today was my trip to Seoul again. I didn't want to go; in fact I hated to make the trip. I had to get my boots fixed. I have one pair of boots and the soles were falling off of them. I also took my last roll of film up to Seoul. I'm going to wait for someone to go to Japan on R & R to develop that roll of film. Seoul does a very poor job of developing film. You don't get half of the pictures back you give them. I think the GIs developing the film keep the good photos and send them home as their own. Who knows?

By going to Seoul I missed the special service show that was staged this morning. I hated to miss it cuz they said it was a good show (those who saw it, said so)

Well I've finally decided that I'm going to break off with one of my faithful writers. Yep Anita. I'm gonna send her a Dear John letter. I just can't see keeping a correspondence with her when I have no intention of seeing her anymore. Go ahead and say it. I've been wanting to do it for a long while but I just didn't want to break her heart. Just before Christmas too. Now I won't get a present from her. Love Bill

—~—

November 9, 1952, Journal Entry:

No, I don't think I'll write Anita a "Dear John" letter. Saying I will is just a smoke screen to keep my folks off my back about her. I can't break it off with her, I just can't. I love her. Sure, I have intentions of seeing her, and being with her, all my life. What is this game I'm playing with my parents? Who told them what to do?

They told me stories about their courtship when they were living in the UP. Pop told me he'd follow Mom home from nursing school. Even carried her books. Once he drove by where she was walking home and backed his car up and drove very slowly following her. She laughed and finally got in the car with him. He was a clown, still is, always joking. I think this Anita bashing is my Mom's idea. She wants me to marry a Pontiac girl, any girl as long as she's from Pontiac. Whatcha gonna do?

—m—

Nov. 10, 1952

Dear Mom, Dad and Carol,

You know I still don't feel up to prime from that ride to and from Seoul the other day. I swear I'll never get in another truck until I leave for home and then I'll gladly get sick.

I gotta work all night again. Seems as though it's coming around often but it was three days ago since I worked all night. Time seems to be going fast. It's the 10th of November already. Before long it'll be Christmas the time for Christmas cheer and cards. Now I'm not helping myself a bit by saying all that stuff. There are quite a few men in this same boat so I can't say much or be feeling sorry for myself.

I got another letter from Anita today and now I just ain't got the heart to write her a Dear John letter. I'm a soft hearted lad. I'll just tell her—"I ain't sure about you and me so don't keep the candle burning in the window."

I guess you all are right about Anita, best wait till I get home. I'm too young to think of marriage. Isn't that what you've been telling me for months and months?

But somehow I know there is something going on in Arkansas with Anita. Her letters have a different tone to them. Maybe it's because I don't write often, and maybe it's something else. I just don't know—but I do know she sounds different.

I just worked around the tent all day and cooled it. I cleaned up my footlocker and straightened everything up and that's the essence of my day. I guess I used that word right. What a jovial fellow am I, or demented. Whichever way you want to look at it.

So Father's getting in shape for deer hunting by walking to Bill Meluis' house. About all the good a little walk like that will do him is to make him a little tired and hungry so he'll eat and lay down and sleep. So what good did it do? You never notice how tired you are when you're on the trail of a deer anyway. Love, Bill

—ᴍ—

1952, Korea: Cpl. Joe Butkus, of Fairfield, Conn. was one of the soldiers who helped construct the building for the truce talks in Panmunjom, north of the 38th parallel. (Cpl. Gust Anton, of Coloma, Michigan, who was an Army photographer during the Korean conflict, returned to Korea in 2003 at the invitation of the South Korean government. He said the truce building was still standing in 2003.)

—ᴍ—

Nov. 11, '52

Dear Mom, Dad and Carol,

Only had three letters for the whole bloody battery. Probably will get some tomorrow. Slept all morning. I shouldn't say all morning cuz them darn flies were bothering me again all morning. They are the most illusive creatures ever I did see. It's too warm during the day to be covered up in a sleeping bag but you have to do it to keep away from them flies. An endless circle.

If you send me a roll of 16 mm film I can get a reel of pictures of me. There's a guy here that bought himself a camera and said he would run off some film of me and 16 mm is the size camera. You got a 16 mm camera, right? Or is it an 8 mm?

I've got guard again tonight so I'll cut this letter very short and write a longer one tomorrow. I'm pressed for time.

It rained all morning but it's cleared up pretty good tonight. Hope it stays that way till I get off guard. Till tomorrow, Love, Bill

—ᴍ—

Nov. 12, 1952

Dear Mom, Dad and Carol,

A little while ago I just about laughed in a captain's face. One of the guys here has a cold and he keeps right on sniffing and I could see it was getting on the captain's nerves. Little things always bother him. Presently he said, "Haven't you got a handkerchief? Blow your nose and stop that #@*!# sniffing!" Struck me funny. I thought about Father right away.

We did the stupidest things we've ever done yesterday in a pouring rain. We were scheduled to fire the machine guns out on the range. They didn't change their schedule a minute. Raining buckets and here we are marching out there to fire. They could have waited until today because it was nice out today, all day. Didn't get a thing out of it except get soaking wet.

I'm sitting here in FDC and really making myself feel at home. Sitting on a chair with my feet propped up on a stool, boots off and feet next to the warm stove.

Remember the day room I was telling you about that we just finished building? Well, it seems that the Corps. now wants to tear it down. Our Battery Commander went down to Seoul today to headquarters and is going to try to talk the big brass into letting us keep it. Hope he succeeds. I'd hate to see it go cuz we have a nice warm place to see movies.

I start working days tomorrow again for a week. I'm supposed to be going on R & R this month sometime but I think I'll pass it up. No Money! By the way did you receive the $110 I sent home out of the September pay? Didn't send any in October. If I'm not mistaken you also should have gotten a $75 allotment check. Keep me informed on this. Till tomorrow, Love Bill (miser)

—∾—

Nov. 16, '52

Dear Mom, Dad and Carol,

Today marks my 16th month in the Army. I'm sliding downhill and got a good start. Only five more months to go, or eight at the most. Like you say I may as well stop writing about that before I have the whole page wet.

You write that Carol was late again for church? I remember I used to get mad and also threatened to leave her behind but I never did. Always waited for my slow poke sister and missed mass sometimes. I went to church this morning. Been going pretty regular lately. That priest we got here is a Number One guy. When he preaches a sermon he gets it to you and you understand every word. Sure love to hear him. A very understanding fellow.

This afternoon we took off for the showers and decided to hitch a ride down there and ended up walking half of the way. It started to rain when we were out quite a ways but some good hearted fellow come along and offered us a ride. Very considerate of him.

I suspect it will start snowing any time now. It sure has been getting mighty cold lately. We finally got issued some of our winter clothing. Got a parka and heavy liner for it, a winter fur hat and some gloves which resemble "choppers" and the last item was a scarf or muffler. We're supposed to get our boots pretty soon, too. Swampers is what I call them. They call them Shoe Pac's, rubber bottoms and leather tops. Daddy and I had them at home for hunting.

You asked whether I had a buddy here. Well, not a special one. We all seem to be close friends. Maybe a few special friends, like the fellow from Detroit. Wong is his name, or Enno, he's an Estonian, born here. He's a very good guy. Then there's Pete, also a very good guy. He's Greek and can talk your left arm off. As a whole you can't find a better bunch of fellows. We all get along real well. No sense in fussing and fighting. And with me, the Finlander, we're our own League of Nations.

Saw a real good movie last night, you all must see it, too. "One Minute to Zero" with Robert Mitchum and Ann Blyth. Gives you a very good idea of what Korea is like. It gives me a basis for my combat stories. Ha.ha.

So that Italian Madame Butterfly is still chasing Father? What cha gonna do? Sit in the bedroom and sob and cry? No, make some spaghetti. That might win Father back. But maybe not. Don't do anything to remind him of Italy.

Have you finally resorted to using my field glasses to see pictures and read? Why don't you weld the lenses together from the field glasses and wear them. Probably be cheaper than buying eye glasses. You could paint the rims red or some such color. They sure would look becoming. People will ask you where you got dem lovely specs. And you can tell them they were part of your son's field glasses. What a jovial time you'll have.

Did I tell you about the inspection? Just found out we came out on top, as always! Out of 25 points, FDC got 25 points! That Battery as a whole lost a few points, but we still came out on top and won the Plaque. Big deal! Love, Bill

—~—

Nov. 17, 1952

Dear Mom, Dad and Carol,

We got a movie tonight so that will take up the majority of the evening. A good one is playing again for a change. "Lovely to Look At" and Red Skelton is in it so I imagine it'll be on the humorous side some what.

It has been a very changeable day today. Started off this morning by being real foggy and looked like rain. Then it cleared up to a beautiful day and now it's cloudy again and feels like snow. You hardly know what to expect around here this time of year.

Well today is Sadie Hawkins' Day ain't it? No girl asked me to go to the dance tonight. How about Carol? Did she get up enough nerve to ask anyone or not?

Our FDC quarters looks sharp now. Got the walls painted white, half way up, and the other half (down side) is olive drab. It looks like I don't know what! I'm afraid to say, or better yet, I best not say anything.

Just had mail call, no letters today. Well I guess I'll wind up this letter. Enclosed are a few pictures. I took 4 or 5 of the pictures of the sign. I did it just to find out how the camera works. It's got a range finder and a time setting on it. It's really takes wonderful pictures. I believe I may be able to use the 616 film. I doubt it though, but I may be able to sell or trade them. Love, Bill

—~—

Nov. 18, '52

Dear Mom, Dad and Carol,

Received the clipping concerning my camera. My camera looks like that only its got a chrome strip running diagonally on the side of it, and it has a range finder and a light adjustment for it on it. I should say it looks the same except for that. Mine cost $17.50. Of course, that's with all taxes off. Tax free. Originally it would have cost $22.30 according to the prices here. (no flash attachment)

What wonderful news your letter brought. Father got a promotion! Well all I can say is that he sure has earned it. I don't see why he should be so nervous though cuz he knows all there is to know about it . He's been acting as a General Foreman. What a blow to hear John got demoted. They sure have made some changes in there. I wonder what I would have been doing if I had still been at the old grind. Probably been graduated from hoods to fenders or some such thing.

There's one thing I'd like to know that I've asked before. Did you ever receive that check I sent home quite a while ago? Approximately two months ago, I'd say. I sent a money order for precisely $110. Did you receive it yet? I'm getting worried about my "mula". I still got the stub. Good also to hear you got the $75.00 allotment.

Things here have been the same so not much to say about that. I don't know yet whether we will have a Christmas tree. Hope we can. Our battery commander is kinda moody, so I hope he's in a good mood about that time. Till tomorrow, Love Bill.

—~—

Nov. 20, '52

Dear Mom, Dad and Carol,

I neglected to write yesterday. I had guard last night. I like to get to sleep soon as possible when I have guard. Only the third relief gets to sleep in the morning till noon so those on the first and second relief have to get there sleep when they can. I'm working all night tonight so I have a chance to sleep again in the morning. I love working the night shift.

Our coffee and doughnut truck has finally started up in business today. I laid down this afternoon and fell asleep and woke up just a few minutes too late to go over and get some coffee and doughnuts. I didn't care anyway, it's probably like that stuff they get off the wagon at the plant back home.

Had another moderate day today, weather wise. At night it goes down to 20 degrees above zero, but during the day it seems to climb up to around 60 degrees. Sure wish I would have had them woolen socks last night on guard. We got the parkas and the whole works and I keep pretty darn warm except for my feet. They freeze. Are you sending me some hunting woolen socks by airmail? Sure could use them. All I can say is I better be going home pretty soon cuz I can't think of anything to write about anymore.

Every once in a while I get a writing streak but it ain't tonight. Got a letter from Grama yesterday and she still thinks I'll be home for Christmas. No use talking or getting into that subject. Till tomorrow, Love Bill.

—w—

Nov. 21, 1952

Dear Mom, Dad and Carol,

What a surprise to hear that you slept all night while just you and Carol were home alone while Daddy was away hunting and without no chains or bolts on the door. You sure are getting brave. That Pin Point Hill you were referring to is way over the East coast. We have a few problems every now and then in our section but no bullets of any kind since Bunker Hill.

That reminds me of the song "Too Old to Cut the Mustard Anymore." Pretty cute song. On this hillbilly song parade I listen to every afternoon "Mountain Dew" usually follows "Too Old." I missed most of my hillbilly program today on-a-counta I went to the shower this afternoon at 2:30 and never got back till 4:30 and the program lasts only from 4:00 till 5:00.

Of course, I talked with some Marines and heard their stories. Seems one of them is in love with a Korean gal and wants to marry her. You know that the Army, Marines and Navy frown on this, I mean marrying Koreans, but they are not as strict as they were in World War II.

Well as this Marine told me, it's not the Marines that are objecting to him marrying this gal. It's her family. The Koreans are very strict about marriage. They have to marry their own kind, I mean from the same village, or else they are outcasts. I wrote you about that young Korean mother who drowned her baby and herself. It has something to do with generation of pure blood. Anyway, it's too complicated to write in a letter. I wished him luck.

I walked back from the shower which is about two miles for the sole purpose of hoping to see a pheasant or something to shoot at. I circled around one mountain side but all in vain. Took a shot at a blue jay. Yesterday afternoon a big cock pheasant flew directly over the battery area about 25 feet high. Would have been a beautiful shot with a shotgun. There are a million pheasants around here. Did I tell you about the deer a couple of guys shot about a month back? It was just a small one. I don't guess they get too big over here anyway. The pheasants don't even seem as big as in the states.

Saw another interesting thing this evening. Something I've never seen in Korea—Geese. A big flock of them flew over here heading south about supper time. I guess cold weather and snow will be setting in pretty soon. It has been too nice here for the month of November. It was considerably warm today.

Carol and you sure are a pair of silly ones if I ever did hear of any. You say, " I got $80, what do you want for a Christmas present?" And Carol says, " A coocoo clock." Ha ha ha.

A lot of these guys here, when they are writing letters just sit around with a blank look on their faces. Many times they ask me what I can find to write about. I don't call myself a good letter writer but at least I can get a few pages out and that's a page more than the other fellows can do.

I go by the old proverb you taught me. "Just write as though you were talking to the person."

Those items you mentioned that you're getting Pa and Ma for Christmas would sure be ideal gifts. (This sentence concerns Carol.)

That would have been funny if you (Carol) and Mother would have bought a new house while Father was hunting. If you haven't already done it we should plan to surprise Father like that next year. Won't that be fun?

Did you see Red Skeleton in "Lovely to Look At"? I thought it was really a wonderful movie. Till tomorrow, Love, Bill

—~—

Nov. 22, '52

Dear Mom, Dad and Carol,

As a matter of fact I didn't receive any mail today. There are a lot of boxes and packages coming in the mail now. For the past five nights there have been at least 20 boxes a night. Me? I not-a-even getta letter. (Italian accent).

I may as well pour out my heart to you instead of walking around here like I got a complex. For the past two months I've been put in for Corporal and never made it yet. Two months ago no one in FDC got it though they were put in. This month one man got a corporal rank one got PFC. You see they got a certain allocation for the battery and they aren't allowed to exceed it. There are so many men here that deserve more rank but they just can't give it to them. It's very possible I may make it about this time next month. I thought they gave rank out easy in Korea but I sure have found out differently. I've been doing a corporal's job for quite some time but—ah well, enough of that.

The morning I spent in dream land and the afternoon I laid around the tent till 3:30 p.m. when at that time I played basketball till 4:45 which is mail call. Then I went to chow and came back just as hungry. Be glad when Thanksgiving is here so I'll know what it's like to be filled up. More than likely we'll get a pretty good chow that day.

I'm going out about two weeks before Christmas and secure a Christmas tree which we will set up on a table. What kind of trimming did you send me? We in FDC are thinking of drawing names and also have a grab-bag. A really jolly Christmas.

Tonight being Saturday night I must get to bed early so I can get up and go to church in the morning. I got a letter from Curly three days ago. I ain't answered it yet. I'm just too darn lazy to write anymore. I also owe Grama a letter from two days back—I'll get caught up one of these days.

A week ago three of us sent our names into a platter spinner program called "Music Box" and he read off our names and played the song we requested. I wonder how many guys in Korea that I know heard my name? He even pronounced it right.

Well so much for the day's diary. Love, Bill

—ɯ—

Nov. 23, '52

Dear Mom, Dad and Carol,

I feel jovial tonight. Started off the day again right being as I went to church. Also being Sunday, recreation activities commence early in the morning and continue on through the day. Recreation consists wholly of basketball. This afternoon, I found myself involved in a good game against the Marines. They just happened to be walking by and the five of them challenged us like fools. Naturally, as always, we won.

The day finally dwindled away and here I am at work, and further more nothing to write about. I'm tired, I guess that's the reason. Can't think straight, let alone trying to keep my eyes open. How do you like this paper? I'm experimenting with this new type and it has not met my qualifications. I'll use it as scratch paper in FDC.

I've two hours to stay awake yet and I got to sleep at 2:30 a.m. Seems like all I live for over here is to sleep and eat. Oh well. Till tomorrow, Love, Bill.

—ɯ—

Nov. 24, '52

Dear Mom, Dad and Carol,

Anita wrote me again. I'm still waiting for her answer to the Dear John (sorta) letter I wrote to her. Maybe it wasn't strong enough, the Dear John one I mean. She wrote me four letters since I wrote that one and she still loves me. What a heck of a fix I'm in.

Had a day of intermediate rain today, and all of a sudden tonight it's turned cold enough to snow. The temperature sure did drop fast. Might have snow for Thanksgiving but I doubt it very much. I remember this time last year I was at home waiting for Thanksgiving dinner. To tell the honest truth time has really flown by. Dec. 7th will be a year since I left and it really doesn't seem that long to me. I imagine for the big dinner coming up you'll have turkey and all the trimmings, and have seconds and thirds on all of it.

I'll no doubt eat like a pig and won't be able to walk back to da tent. I remember the times at home when I ate so much I couldn't straighten up. Had to lay down for a while. I don't believe I'll be that bad now.

Had an unusually easy day today. One of the guys that went to Seoul got a checkerboard and now we have a new game to amuse ourselves. A person goes nuts, demented, if he doesn't find something to do with his time. Time actually goes slower when you sit around. Just as soon be working. Getting late, and should write to Grama. Till tomorrow, Love, Bill

—ɯ—

Nov. 25, 1952

Dear Mom, Dad and Carol,

Stood out there in mail call for five minutes and never heard my name called. This makes two days I ain't had no mail from home. This morning when I got up it was raining pitchforks. It looked like it wasn't going to clear up for days but by eight o'clock every cloud in the sky was gone and the sun was beating down radiant beams of energy. Really have some changeable weather over here. Yesterday I figured we'd have snow any minute but today, don't guess we'll see it for a month.

I'm working all night again in FDC and tomorrow night I get guard duty. Then the next day I work during the day. They got me busy for a change and you better believe I'm gonna sleep the majority of the day tomorrow. I got the second relief guard and you don't get hardly any sleep at all, maybe about four hours at the most.

Boy I'm glad my time is getting shorter and shorter I swear I'd go nuts if I had seven or eight more months to do. As it stands right now I've got but a little over two months 'fore I leave. Expect to pull out sometime in February. You rotate with 38 points but I'll have 39 at the end of February so I suspect I'll leave somewhere around the mid part of the month. I really shouldn't be counting my days like that cuz something will go haywire and I won't be home when I expect to be. Won't be enough replacements or they'll start juggling the points again.

The days seem to fly right by. For instance today I laid around the tent. In the afternoon I took a shower, then went to FDC and relieved another fellow so he could go take a shower. What interesting and exciting days I endure here. I'm not telling you all the excitement that happens at FDC. It's secret stuff.

Well I best close now. It's about time for the other fellow to wake up and my turn to sleep. Till tomorrow, Love, Bill.

Nov. 26, '52 (Wednesday)

Dear Mom, Dad and Carol, Finally received one letter from you tonight. Mail from home sure has been slow coming. Suppose they are pretty busy because Christmas is almost here. It shouldn't slow up the regular mail though.

Got guard duty again tonight. Was gonna go to bed and get my beauty sleep because of the fact I have to spend the first two hours of Thursday walking my post. There's some good music on so I thought I may as well stay up and listen to it and write ya all a letter at the same time.

Big deal about this President elect "Ike" eh? Over the news now they said that "Ike" regrets to announce that he won't be able to spend the Thanksgiving holidays with the boys in Korea. He has to stay in New York and eat his turkey dinner.

Tomorrow we don't have reveille in the morning due to the holiday. We get to sleep till 7:30 a.m. if we don't want breakfast. I can't afford to miss that breakfast cuz they may have eggs cooked some other way but fried, and they might even make a decent pot of coffee, which I doubt.

I found out we are having turkey, which is customary, pumpkin pie, assorted candy and nuts, cranberry sauce and some other things. I was talking to one of the cooks and he said they got plenty of food.

How much difference in time is it between here and there? I know we are a good part of a day ahead of you. I don't know how much though.

What a silly record that must be of the people laughing and trying to play a trombone. I'd probably laugh myself sick If I heard it. Well I'd best hit the sack now.

Enclosed is an excerpt from Anita's letter. I'm being conceited. I know I'm good looking, anyway. She told me so. Love Bill

Part of Anita's letter, Written in Purple ink

"Oh yes! I meant to do this before but I got started on something else. But here is what I wanted to say. Thanks for the nice picture of yourself, Billy. I got the letter just before I went to work and all the girls down at the theater thought that guy in the picture (you) was the "handsomest" thing they ever saw. And of course, I agreed. Of course they meant you, Billy, who else?

Well Darling, I guess I had better close and go to bed. I am tired and sleepy and tomorrow will be a long, long day again. Answer soon. Love and kisses, Always, Anita"

Nov. 28, '52

Dear Mom, Dad and Carol,

I can't remember whether I wrote you a letter yesterday or not. It seems as though I did but then on the other hand I have four fingers and one thumb. Just in case I didn't write I'll try and tell you the menu that was on order yesterday for dinner. Turkey, spuds, pumpkin pie, ice cream, salad, shrimp, nuts, apples, tangerines, and some other vegetables, too. It was a good meal. I had a drumstick that was nigh as big as a chicken. Really filled myself up. That was the Thanksgiving Day all wound up with the exception of the movie. They had a very good one for the occasion—Lana Turner and Fernando Lamas in "The Merry Widow." It was a very good picture. I enjoyed it very much.

Tonight I went to a USO show. I just got back from it just a few minutes ago as a matter of fact. It was one of the worst shows I ever did see, I swear. They had a violinist that tried to be funny but just wasn't and a couple of singers and tap dancers that were awful. I could sing and dance better than they did. It was a relief for it to end. 'Twas torture to watch. Should have stayed in bed, which reminds me the lights just went blink and that means lights out in five minutes so I'd better sign my name. Love, Bill.

—∞—

Nov. 30, 1952

Dear Mom, Dad and Carol,

Received two letter today from ya all dated the 18th and 19th and yesterday received two dated the 21st and 22nd. They seem to have it a little screwed up.

Just made an easy dollar now. A guy here offered to bet me he was on 2nd relief guard and I said first. We argued a bit then the dollar bet came up. I never knew for sure, but anyway I came out on the good end. They only reason I could have made that small bet was cuz we done got paid today. Within the past hour to be exact. Took in the tidy sum of $49. You never did tell me yet whether you received the $110 I sent home just before my increase in allotment came through.

I have to go chop-chop now so while I'm gone I'll try to think of something else to write about.

Just back from eating my ham chunks and apple pie. I just remembered that I best tell you that I received the Christmas box you sent (tonight). Boy those canned goods came in just fine shape. I don't exactly know how to say it but it sure is wonderful to receive all that stuff. The hand warmers-Number One. I had one out this afternoon and fired it up. They work fine. Made me feel kinda lonesome to be unwrapping those presents. Brings me back to the other Christmas times I spent at home.

I didn't go to that Scottish Show USO you mentioned, so you won't see me in the newsreels. Didn't you use embellish wrong? You're embellishing the room in the house but how can Father embellish his deer stories?

You should eat cold hamburger if you get the hic-cups (flash!)

Concerning those pictures you inquired about-yes, that building is our FDC and those tents are the ones we live in real quaint, eh?

Who is the other dame pictured with my sister? Some new girl friend? Will Carol have a new boyfriend when I get home? Yes, I do joke, don't I?

Well enough gabbing for now. Love, Bill

p.s. This place is kaleidoscopic. Look that one up.

—∞—

December 1, 1952

Dear Mom, Dad and Carol.

What a night to have guard duty. A steady light rain coming down now which has been going on since noon. If it would clear up I could walk my next two hours in a beautiful romantic moonlight night. A little light from the moon shines through but not much. Boy, my feet are soaked. At the present time I'm sitting practically on the stove and trying to get some of my clothes dry.

Received one letter from you today. So Father is back and brought a deer with him too. I'll have to wait for the story from him to find out who shot it. I hope he doesn't blame it on his new rifle. Better have a better excuse than that for me.

Had a little excitement here today that I feel may be worth writing about. Sorta on the humorous side, too. Several pheasants glided over the Battery area today just after dinner and there happened to be a few officers outside at that time so they ran to get their shot guns (four officers) and commence to pursue the pheasants. The major stayed back with a pair of field glasses. The whole thing lasted about 15 minutes. The major guided them to the pheasants by means of hand signals. Flutter-Flutter, two of 'em took off and kept on going regardless of the three shots fired in their direction. I am an eyewitness. The officers on the hill took five more steps and up goes two more shots, they got one, when those shots were fired. I counted six pheasants that took off at the time. I counted a total of ten pheasants and they only got one. I would have been in heaven standing in the midst of ten pheasants going every which way. Well, so much for that. Love, Bill

p.s. Good to hear you did get the $110.

Dec. 2, 1952

Dear Mom, Dad and Carol,

Big news today! It snowed and it's still on the ground regardless of the sun shining all day long. It's really been chilly and even chillier tonight. We got word that it is going down to zero tonight. Quite a cold snap that has hit here.

It's been averaging about 20 degrees all day. I wired my 616 camera together and took some pictures of the snow. I'm going to try and send the undeveloped rolls home cus they do a much better job of developing there than here. Most of the time the developing shop in Seoul only gets half of them developed. Not very efficient if I do say so myself.

I spent the majority of my day in FDC next to the stove. Sure am glad I haven't got guard tonight cuz I'd freeze my toes off, I believe. That's the only place I get cold is my feet. We've got enough clothes now to keep warm in 52 below except for the feet. Pretty soon we are going to get Swampers (snow boots)

I'm in the tent right now and rather than sit on the stove and try to keep warm, I'll get into my sleeping bag with my hand warmer in the bottom of it. I don't play hero and see how much cold I can stand here. I have to put another blanket on. I've heard some tales about toes and fingers falling off because of frost bite. Till tomorrow, Love and stuff, Bill

Dec. 4, 1952

Dear Mom, Dad and Carol,

More cold, brrrr! Concerning those socks you sent me, don't feel bad cuz you sent me the wrong kind. I sure can use them. My socks are getting pretty well worn and got a few darns here and there in them. If my time left in Korea wasn't so short I'd be worrying about stuff like that. About two more months from now I hope to be thinking of getting home so who's worried about socks? I hate to think about it cuz then the time seems to drag by. The rotation drafts are starting up again. This month of December we got three of them. These are the first big rotations we've had since July.

Boy has it been cold here these past few days. Dropped to zero the night before and last night it registered two below. You can believe I've got my hand warmer in the bottom of my sleeping bag. That warmer works fine. One of the guys in FDC received a hand warmer today from home and two cans of fluid were enclosed. May be against the law but never-the-less it got to him. I'm using lighter fluid in mine. It seems to work.

Ever hear of Thermo boots? That's what the front line infantry soldiers are getting. Some of the guys back here got them too. They are mainly the guys who are on the work crews or on survey. They are the best boots ever for keeping your feet warm. If I can I'm gonna buy a pair when I get home and use them for deer hunting. If I can talk one of the guys into it, I'd like to borrow a pair for guard. That would be the only time I'd have use for them.

From what I gather around this place President-elect "Ike" must have passed around here today sometime. I doubt very much if he would get this close. Some of the G.I. soldiers might even razz him. You know everyone doesn't love the ole boy. Quite a few men over here aren't happy with him. At least he fulfilled his promise to make a trip to Korea.

You know I told you about the floor we got in our tent. Well it's elevated about four inches above the ground. And it was nice during the summer months but now that winter has set in all the cold air rushes under and up through the floor and Brrrr! Lumber is really difficult to obtain here but we have managed to get enough to construct a little wall from the floor to the ground and I was actually surprised at the results. It's 90 percent warmer in here now.

Soon as we shove a little more dirt around the cracks it should be all right. Always improving and modifying around this place but it's all for us.

That box I received from you a few days back sure has been coming in handy lately cuz our chow hasn't been up to par. Well you know me anyway. There aren't too many people that can give me enough to eat. If I had my way about it we'd have a least five meals a day. Best quit talking of food cuz I'm getting hungry again. Before I came to work I finished a box of crackers and cheese. The first thing I want when I get home is two quarts of milk and a box of graham crackers. Funny thing to be craving.

So you're getting to be a "Bob and Ray" fan now? It must be catching. I can hardly wait until 12:30 for 'em to come on and the days I work and I can't hear them, I'm very disappointed. They are good.

Just glancing over your letter again I see you said that you didn't know that we could wear any kind of socks. Over here in Korea we can wear argyle socks and blue and red striped underwear, even orange and black sweaters, and sweat shirts. It's what we got showing or our outer garments that counts.

When you mentioned the storm door in the letters and the wind blowing it open it made me laugh. Remember how it always blew open and then Crash! Another window gone and Father got pretty disgusted. Now, how many door windows have been replaced?

I believe I am going to use some of those white envelopes you sent me a while back. I'm sure I have enough envelopes to last me till I leave here.

I wrote Anita a Dear John so I'm not writing or receiving any letters from her. That cuts down on envelopes.

You know I may have a couple of thousand bucks at hand when I get out of the Army. What a miser! I should leave it in the bank to collect interest. I've been thinking seriously about my schooling when I get out. My mind always seems to turn to Hydraulics and Diesel. That interests me more than forestry and other subjects. I know Father would like me in Conservation and I wouldn't mind it myself but I gotta do what I like to do. Hydraulics is the coming thing and it interests me. Now back to you again. What do you think?

I wonder if I'll be able to get this long letter in the envelope? I'll try. Love, Bill.

—w—

December 4, 1952, Journal Entry:

It wasn't really a "Dear John" letter. I just told Anita we should think about our relationship and when I come back we could take it from there. I really care for her.

She knows that I do. I keep thinking about her all the time. Lately, her letters sound so sad. I know there is something going on in Arkansas that she is not telling me. Damn!

—w—

December, 1952, While Bill was in Korea, Paul Balasick, of South Haven, Michigan, was completing basic training at Fort Knox, Kentucky, as a tank gunner. His journey to Korea was by way of Seattle to Japan. (He traveled on the same ship that Ahnen was on in 1951.) In Korea, Balasick was assigned to Company A, Tank Battalion with Captain George S. Patton, junior as his commanding officer. One day in formation Captain Patton asked Corporal Balasick what sorority he belonged to because his hair was long. After formation, Balasick raced to the camp barber and got an official GI scalping.

Balasick's older brother, Ernest, was on the island of Marianas when the A-Bomb went off during World War II. He was killed in action on May 28, 1945.

—w—

Dec. 5, 1952

Dear Mom, Dad and Carol,

Well I'm back to the old-line paper once again. I'm working all night tonight and I plum forgot about bringing my regular writing paper up with me. Paper is paper I guess no matter how or which way you look at it.

This morning I got up and greeted another bloody cold morning. It sure isn't getting a darn bit warmer around here and that's for sure. If we put water in our little washbasins at night to use the next morning, all we find is a solid cake of ice. During the day light hours a field jacket will keep you plenty warm, it's just the nights that are cold. We did more work on our tent today. Slowly but surely we are going to get it fully winterized.

I received the box today containing the socks and fruitcake. Haven't eaten any of the cake yet but before the sunsets tomorrow I'll already have it sampled. It looks real good and probably tastes fine, too. Wish I had some now cuz I seem to be getting just a little bit hungry but I'm the only one up in FDC so the cake will have to wait. I'm really getting sleepy now. I can hardly see the lines on the paper. I wrote a long letter yesterday so I'll cut this one short so I can go to bed very soon. I can't think straight. Write again, tomorrow, Love, Bill.

—m—

Dec. 6, '52

Dear Mom, Dad and Carol,

Father, I bet that sure was a thrill killing that bear. When you run across a bear in its hole I guess it would be a little easier shooting it than if it were 10 yards away looking you over. The only thing I remembered when I was there is that I had legs and I put them to use. I can still kick myself in the rear end for not shooting the bear or even the deer I saw not three minutes afterwards. I may have another chance next year.

Had another big battery inspection today or this morning to be a little more precise about it. Due to the fact I worked last night I slept all morning and all through the inspection, too. We now are attempting to winterize our FDC building. The floor in this building is also elevated about three feet and sits on a cement foundation. It's been here umpteen years for all we know and the foundation has quite a few hole and gaps in it which enables great gushes of freezing cold air to seep through the floor. So today we went once again to the river to get some sand and piled it up against the side of the cement. You'd be surprised at the difference. It really is a lot warmer in here now. We plan to do the same thing to our tent whenever we can take another journey to the river for more sand.

I hope all your fish don't die before I get home to see them. You know Mom I really hate to say this but I forgot your birthday. The most I could have done is wish you a Happy Birthday and I didn't even do that. It's a late one but Happy Birthday anyway.

We get our mail right away no matter what it is or what time of year it is. They don't wait until Christmas to hand out the boxes. About that "Lazy Susan" thing, what is it for anyway? You put your meal in it and instead of revolving the plate you just have to turn the Lazy Susan to what you want? When I first looked at it I thought it was a flying saucer. You didn't help me much by sending me a picture of it so I'll send it back and let you clarify it a bit more.

Also received the daily paper and a copy of O.C.S.C. magazine. Sure hope Pop does well in that new job of his. Like Mother says it won't be long before you take over Bill White's job. And Carol too. I guess she's really slaving away and trying to pay her bills.

About time for me to go on guard now so I will close. It is a bitter freezing cold night. Did I say it was cold? It doesn't get this cold even in the Upper Peninsula of Michigan, believe you me. Will sign off for now, Love, Bill.

—⁓—

(About the bitter cold in Korea: Dec. 9, 1952 When Pvt. Gust Anton, of Coloma, Michigan, was assigned to Co. B. 84th Engineers Const. Battalion on the Imjim River behind battle lines of Vegas, Reno and Carson, there weren't winter sleeping bags available so he slept on a bare cot between several blankets and shivered and froze during the nights until a sleeping bag was available. When he arrived, a soldier, Leonard Balbat, hailed him by a nickname Gust used in grade school. Gust and Leonard had been friends through grade school and high school. Later, Gust discovered he was Leonard's replacement. Company Commander, Capt. Goldsmith assigned Gust to the job of assistant battalion photographer when he discovered that he had experience as a photographer.

—⁓—

Dec. 9, 1952

Dear Mom, Dad & Sis,

The night before I had guard duty and I was so cold and tired when I came off of my first two hours that I couldn't stay awake to write a letter so I says, I'd put it off until tomorrow. Then tomorrow came and cuz I worked all night in FDC and we were busier than a, like you say, a one-armed paperhanger. We had many, many missions.

So that brings me up to the present time once again. Also received the woolen socks yesterday in the package. As a matter of fact I used them on a little jaunt down to the showers today for the purpose of trying them out and they kept my feet very warm. Sorta of a test for when I walk guard the next time.

I sprained my thumb this afternoon. I may get the Purple Heart for it if I work on it. I just found out I have to work all night again tonight. I don't give a hoot anyway cuz I get to sleep in the morning. I work till two o'clock then wake up the other guy on nights and I sleep till 6:30 in the morning. Then I get off duty at 8 a.m.

Well I haven't got too many more weeks to go to keep this up. I hope not any more than 10 more weeks at the most. I sure will have a lot of movies to look at when I get home, eh! Umpteen reels there by now. I'm racking my brain now so best I sign off and till tomorrow. Love, Bill

—~—

Dec. 10, 1952

Dear Mom, Dad and Carol,

Father looks like the proud hunter in that photo you sent me where he was posed between the bear and deer he shot. I say that bear sure looks to be a monster of a beast. The deer ain't small by far, either. How is the meat? Tough or lean? A big one like that I would suspect it to be like shoe leather. Also got the daily newspaper, thanks. I get it about four times a month and it's good reading what's happening back home..

This morning I spent in dreamland and this afternoon after 3:30 I played basketball up til mail call, which is about 4:45. Tomorrow we go on day duty so that will be a week of mental anguish. I just live for every other week. I'm referring to the off duty days. The new quota came down for rank. I'm in for it again, but will I get it? That's the $64 question. Time will tell. I'd tell them they could keep it but I realize I'll get a bit more money. Well it's about time to hit the sack. So, si-a-nara. Love, Bill.

—~—

Dec. 11, 1952

Dear Mom, Dad & Sis,

Anita sent me a Christmas package. That's the packages she sent me just two days before I wrote her the Dear John letter. Well, it really wasn't that, just a "let's see what happens when I get back" letter. You sounded as though you didn't believe I wrote her. Well, I did!

Sure she loves me. She started writing about her plans when I get home. I can read between the lines and saw marriage all over the paper. That's what scared me off I guess. After being away from her for over a year the journey down yonder to hitch up with her-I just can't see it. With all these women waiting for me at home why should I break their hearts by marrying up with some other dame?

I found that picture of the bear and deer, that I thought I lost. It's the one where they were mounted on the car and all set to make the long push home. Come to think of it I bet those guys were plenty busy explaining the kill to the many others who were on the ferry coming back home. Probably will be a few more hunters in the area next year looking for the mate to that bear.

You mentioned about the fellows having all those pin ups in your last letter. We believe in uniformity, too. Other tents have them, so naturally we do too. To mention a few pin ups—Marilyn Monroe, Liz Taylor, Debra Paget, Debbie Reynolds, etc., etc.

Looking back to Thanksgiving once again. Yes we did have plenty of turkey that day, and tonight for supper we had turkey, too. I couldn't say whether it's still leftovers or not. Probably not.

My word, don't tell me you are finally breaking down and purchasing a new stove (electric, that is). Did the last burner finally wither away or what enticed you to get it?

Good deal about Pop winning a prize—a car robe. That's to cover your car isn't it? Something like a portable garage? He doesn't even bother driving his car into the garage, so all he has to do every evening is spread that car robe over the car. Right? Ha!

Being today is our first day on day duty, tonight we see a movie once again. "The Happy Time" is playing tonight. Sounds like a very exciting and relaxing movie. Bah!

I can hardly wait to see what I got in the package from Anita. Did I tell you what I got in the last package from her, which was my birthday? Some cookies, which she made and to put in something extra, about 10 packs of gum. Something I've always wanted. She probably has gum and paper clips in this one. But I may be fooled, though. Just have a little while until the movie starts. It's best I sign my name about now. Love, Bill

—w—

Dec. 11, '52, Journal Entry:

Well, I wrote a 'smoke screen' letter to my folks about Anita and our plans. Sure, I told Anita we should think about our future when I get back. I know marriage is in her plans, and mine too. As for the girls in Michigan breathlessly waiting for me. That's a bunch of crap. They are all hitched or going with someone, from what my Mom says. I've already got a sweet southern belle, and I think I'm keeping her.

—w—

Dec. 13, 1952

Dear Mom, Dad and Carol,

Received the clipping from the Factory News concerning Father' promotion. Looks right good. He's even got to interview some dame for his secretary and stuff like that. That picture of him is the same one he had taken a number of years ago. Remember how we commented on it when we first saw it?

We had a big command inspection today. I haven't been about to find out what the outcome was, but if every tent stood as tall as ours did, I'm sure we passed with flying colors. Our tent was just so in uniformity, cleanliness and the whole works!

I endured one of the slowest days ever yet. Seemed like the afternoon was never going to end. We didn't fire one mission all day. I guess that's why it dragged. I got another letter from Anita. I'm not even writing her anymore. Pretty soon she'll stop or write to try to get me back to writing to her.

Best I quit for now. Got guard again tonight. Write again tomorrow. Love, Bill.

—~~—

Dec. 14, 1952

Dear Mom, Dad and Carol,

Ain't time for mail call but I will start this to be sure I get a letter off tonight. I had to rush last night's letter and didn't get a chance to say too much of anything that made sense. We got a few replacements in today. Oh, how I wish they'd start pouring in so I'll be sure of getting out of here with my 38 points. No replacements, it stands to reason, no rotation. I'd dread that.

Went and took a shower again today. Hitched a ride down and back and it didn't take much time. There are rumors going around now that a person here can go on only one R & R per tour in Korea. It's still in the rumor stage and I expect to get on R & R on the 19th of this month. If the rumor isn't fact by then I stand a good chance of going. It's too late for you to send my money. I'll find out if I'm going and in the meantime I'll borrow some from my buddy, Pete, then when you send the money I will pay him back.

I've been thinking very seriously of calling home from Japan. When I'm there I'll arrange it so that you get a day's notice before I can and it costs $4 a minute or 5 a minute if I reverse the charges. You told me once not to hesitate on reversing the charges but $5 a minute will really add up. The time limit is three minutes but you can converse for a little longer, I think. I have to decide that myself whether I should call home. I have decided! I will reverse the charges and you can draw the amount out of my mint if you like. The only thing I hate about saying "hello" is that you have to say "good bye." The call will brighten me up that's for sure.

Just got back from supper and had quite a conversation with some other guys about reversing charges so I will go to special services and they will tell me what the scoop is about reversing charges. They also will work out to have you home when I call. It will be about 8 or 9 p.m. when I call (EST), which is your time. But it will be morning over here. I would like to make it Christmas Eve but I may be a few day before. So have everyone home by that time—Carol, Dad and you.

Going to see another show tonight—"Chicago Calling". That's about it for now. Your son, Love Bill.

—~—

Dec. 15, '52

Dear Mom, Dad and Carol,

Received a letter and package of cookies and Christmas tinsel today. When we find that we have a few decorations pooled from home, we'll have a nice looking tree. We're saving all this tin foil to put at the base of the tree. The only thing lacking is lights and they are forbidden over here.

Just got back from the show few minutes ago. Saw "Dream Boat" with Clifton Webb. It was very good and funny. I enjoyed it very much.

Our delayed replacements finally come in today. Twenty-five of them. But I didn't know any of them. They were all cannon guys so they all went to the Firing Battery and left not a one for headquarters battery. We'd better be getting some more in right quick cuz my time is getting pretty short.

Come Thursday, Pete and I, plan to take to the hills in search of a Christmas tree for our tent. Thursday we go on night duty so we have all day to hunt for a tree. On Friday, I head for R & R and possibly won't be back till after Christmas.

I lost my regular writing paper and I don't feel like digging to the bottom of my footlocker for it. Just as soon write on this anyway. Well I think I'll quit for now and wash up and brush my teeth. Till later, Love, Bill.

—~—

Dec. 17, 1952

Dear Mom, Dad and Carol,

Well as far as I know I'm going on R & R the 19th, so I guess you can right well expect a call from me. I'll have to write a few notes on a pad so I won't stutter. You'll do the same I presume. It'll probably be a couple of days before Christmas, but you'll be notified of the call coming in time.

I learned another word too but haven't found a way to use it yet. "Abominable." Tonight we change shifts again and go on night duty. I'll have a chance to get a little rest before I start on my journey. We sure have been having pleasant weather for the month of December. It hasn't even been cold enough to freeze lately and during the day we have just short sleeves on.

There's another movie tonight, "Operation Secret." Sounds like a war movie or some such thing. Another hour before mail call so I guess I'll finish this. By the way, I'll try to write everyday this time when on R & R and not be like last time. And please send $50 in money order. I need it to pay back my buddy.

In regards to that last list you sent concerning the items in the box. Well, I got them all. I guess the box was never opened till it got to me.

Also just got back from the show and it wasn't too bad. Took place in the other war. Well I'll hit the sack so I can get a little rest before I take off for Japan for a few days of more rest. Till tomorrow, Love, Bi . . .

—~—

Dec. 24, '52, Tokyo, Japan
The American National Red Cross Stationery

Dear Mom, Dad and Carol,

I finally managed to get some paper so I could drop you a line. A poor excuse for not writing, eh? I can think of none better at the time so it'll have to do, I guess. Today is when we are supposed to leave to go back to Korea but I firmly believe we will get a one or two day extension. That's a rumor but it's also very probable. I hope so cuz I sure hate to go back to that place—Korea. Only another month to do anyways so what the heck.

Excluding today we stayed at a beautiful Special Services hotel. I mean to tell ya we really lived the life of Riley during our stay here. This hotel is a large, luxurious place that the Army took over just recently. Inside they have Japanese waiters, bellboys, and the whole works. I know I was really living cause when I first got there I had someone open the door for me. Then signed for my room and they carried my bag to my room. Well, to put it more briefly and simply—we didn't have to do nothing but just sit and relax.

We get up and they put clean sheets on every morning and clean up the room. Then comes the fantastic dining room. Looks like a super deluxe Howard Johnson. They sure have the place fixed up beautifully. They set a menu in front of you and you can eat what you want. But the only trouble was I had to figure out which piece of silverware to use. They have five different kinds of forks, knives and spoons in front of you. Plush carpets, lounging chairs, all this and more for two bucks a day!

I sent home a couple of packages too. They'll probably be there before this letter gets there. One box was a jacket, and the other one another jacket and tie and some jewelry. That jewelry is supposed to be real expensive stuff. Enclosed is a little pamphlet that will tell you all about it, better than I can.

I also took a few pictures here too and had some developed that I had taken. They didn't come out very good but will send them on the way anyway. I believe I'll save the other roll of films and take them with me when I come home and have them developed in the states. They'll do a better job there. Tried to make a call too and the telephone lines were so full I couldn't do it. Sorta a let down, as I wrote and told you. What cha gonna do? Will write more later. Love, Bill

—~—

(Dec. 25: T-Bone Hill, 38th Inf. Reg: 12nd ID, repels Chinese Communist Forces during an intense battle.)

(Dec. 25, 1952: Hill 812, Held by Co. K. 3rd Bn. 179th Inf., 45th ID; hit hard by North Koreans.)

—~—

Dec. 27, 1952

Dear Mom, Dad and Carol,

Just got back from my R & R in Osaka, Japan. I managed to get one letter off in my stay there. You probably received it by now. Also I sent those two boxes. Hope you got them too. I really should have written more but as you found out I didn't.

Got back here and found umpteen letters waiting for me and Christmas cards, too. I was also very surprised to get a few letters from Anita and I haven't written to her in I don't know how long. She says "Please forgive me if I have done wrong." What a gal! She still loves me and I don't even know what she looks like any more. I must be a Don Juan or whatever his name is. She sounded sad or upset in her letters. I don't know what to do about that gal. Was she sad because I told her not to write too often, or was it something else that was bothering her?

(Editor's Note: This was probably the time that Anita went in for surgery to remove her cancerous leg. She still had not written Bill about her cancer or her surgery.)

I awoke to find a heavy blanket of snow on the ground. At least a good four inches of it.

For our Christmas dinner we had everything from soup to nuts. I believe I brought a menu with me and I'll enclose it. We ate as much as we wanted and I really did fill myself up. I went to Christmas mass in Japan. The church sure did look pretty all decorated. Makes me home sick.

Today they put my name in red in the orderly room and that means only one thing. I've got approximately 40 more days here! The replacements are pouring in pretty good. If I'm not home by the end of February some one better watch out.

Guess I'll finish this after the movie which I'm going to see right now. Going to see Marilyn Monroe and Ginger Rogers in "Monkey Business". Will tell you about it when I get back. Well, I'm back. It was a very humorous show, if I must say. I never laughed so hard for a long time. I've got so many letters to answer that I don't know where to start. It's getting too late now and I can't write when I'm tired so I'll attempt to tell you a bit more tomorrow. Love, Bill.

—ɯ—

Dec. 29, 1952

Dear Mom, Dad and Carol,

I think I told you yesterday I was going to send you a copy of the Christmas dinner menu. But I forgot, so I'm enclosing it now.

I have guard duty again tonight. They sure don't waste any time in putting a man on after he gets back from R & R. What have I got to gripe about though? I'll pull guard every night as short as my time is now. It's a beautiful night out again tonight. The moon is almost full and has a nice blue sky for the background and a nice white blanket of snow here. Altogether it makes the night almost as bright as day.

Yesterday was one of the longest days ever I did spend in Korea. The reason was that I just got back from R & R. I thought I'd never see the end of the day.

There are a lot of good programs on tonight. I wonder if I'll ever get this letter written. Just listened to "Charlie McCarthy" now, "My Friend Irma." I have so many letters to write and don't know where to start. I'm off duty (days that is) till Thursday, so maybe I can just get a few answered then. Have to hit the hay, now. Love, Bill

—~—

Dec. 30, 1952

Dear Mom, Dad and Carol,

So you think I don't know what a car robe is? It's a robe you put on a car after you wash it. Isn't that right? Isn't it something you cover up the car at night?

Thank everyone for writing me those notes wishing me a Merry Christmas. All that talk you hear about us having cold weather is almost right. True, they have it super freezing on the east coast and central front but over here on the west coast the weather is just cold. That snow we had a few days ago is all melted now. Wonderful weather! We have all our winter clothing just in case it does get freezing cold here.

Reading over Father's letter I gather he is satisfied with his new job. That's good to hear. Nothing better than enjoying the work you're doing.

Some character hit upon a plan concerning the movies they show us and it certainly sounds good. From now on they are going to show the movie twice to give us unfortunate soldiers who were on duty a chance to see it the second time around.

Word has reached me through a Christmas card that Bob Boner has re-enlisted and is now on his way to Korea. Serves him right for re-upping. Guess I'll cut this short and try to write a few more letters, which I owe.
Love to all, Bill.

—~—

Dec. 31, 1952

Dear Mom, Dad and Carol

Got a box from the Warreners. Don't say anything but why are people sending me puzzles and games? I'm 22 years old, not five. They did send me a nice box though. I appreciate the thought behind each one of the boxes I received.

Tonight a snowstorm hit us. It was beautiful all through the day though. Just all of a sudden it came up and already we have almost an inch of snow on the ground. If it keeps up we won't be able to get out of the tent.

It's New Year's Eve tonight and I work all night at the FDC. So I'll be a good boy tonight. I remember last New Year's Eve I was sitting outside the post of Yokohama, Japan waiting to unload and be imported into these strange lands. Just think a whole year has passed while I have been in the strange land of the Orient. Sounds Oriental, eh?

I heard a bad rumor today. They said something about the points being raised to 40 now. Gads! I'll never get out of this place. I best take out citizenship papers and purchase a nice rice paddy and retire over here. I couldn't thing of anything else to write so I played a game of checkers to relieve my mind, and the tension. So long for now. Love Bill

—m—

January, 1953, After completing training as assistant tank driver and gunner in Japan, Sergeant Harvey Williams, of South Haven, Michigan, began his duties in Korea supporting the infantry. He hauled ammo to the front lines. He was the lone survivor when the tank he was in was blown up, killing his tank commander and the other soldiers.

—m—

Jan. 1, 1953

Dear Mom, Dad and Carol,

Brrrr, I mean to tell you it was cold last night. Got another cold snap here now, hope it doesn't last too long. I'm playing it safe tonight. I'm putting my hand warmers in the sleeping bag. You better believe I'll be warm. I'll insert another "Brrrr" here because tomorrow I have guard duty. Again the hand warmers will have a work out.

Even though today was New Year's Day nothing spectacular happened. Just another routine day. They didn't even have a movie tonight. Guess it was considered a holiday cause we didn't have to get up for formation as we usually do at 6:30 a.m.

In Warrener's box that I received yesterday I got a small checkerboard and it's been the main attraction here. I took it to FDC and when we're not busy we play checkers. Matter of fact two guys are playing checkers right now. I get the winner of the next game.

We got some more replacements in today. I love to see them pour in like they have been lately. Our battery is just about up to strength now so I don't believe they can hold me back due to a shortage of men. It's my turn at the checkers now. Lots of love, Bill

p.s. later. What happened? I won the game!

—~—

Jan. 3, 1953

Dear Mom, Dad and Carol,

I ain't been feeling too good the past few days. I think I got dropsy and heart trouble. Yep-I drop down and ain't got the heart to get back up again.

I had third relief guard last night and believe me that was one of the most tiring nights and coldest night I have endured in Korea. That relief guard pulls the ungodly hours of 10 to midnight and then again 4 a.m. till 6 a.m. in the morning.

After I finished that you can believe I went straight to bed and never woke up until noon. This afternoon I was in the tent resting cause I have to work all night tonight. As a matter of fact that's where I am now, in FDC starting my night's work.

I suppose you heard the sad news, that radio's beloved hillbilly singer, Hank Williams died. For the past two days now about all you hear on the hillbilly stations are songs dedicated to him and his records.

We've been having some cold weather the past few days. Sure wish it would warm up. I'm beginning to detest winter. Sounds like everyone got some nice gifts for Christmas. Which reminds me. Haven't you received the boxes I sent from Japan? I was hoping Carol would get that sun lamp she wanted. Then even I would get a suntan in the middle of winter. When I get home, that is. Write soon, Love and kisses, Bill

—~—

Jan. 5, 1953

Dear Mom, Dad and Carol,

Received a letter from you yesterday and it was the one that held a money order for $50. I found that I didn't spend as much money on R&R as I expected so therefore with my pay at the end of the month I had enough to pay Pete the 60 samalios I borrowed and still have a few extra bucks for myself.

I now find myself financially able to carry myself through the month so I will enclose the money order ($50) in this letter and hope it reaches you OK. I don't rightly know if I had to sign it or not, but I did.

All day long yesterday we all worked at FDC putting in a floor. That is putting a floor on top of the one we had in here. You better believe it makes it a lot warmer in here now. Before we did this, we (mainly me) who worked nights had to sit on top of the stove to keep from freezing. I'm not exaggerating any either. Now with the double floor it keeps it a bit warmer.

The big thing around here now is the coming Corps. inspection. Everyone has to run around like crazy to get the place ready. The place here looks cleaner than a nursery in a hospital. If we don't pass something is radically wrong. The whole thing is a pain in you know what. That's about it.
Till tomorrow, Love, Bill

—w—

Jan. 6, 1953

Dear Mom, Dad and Carol,

My long lost Arkansas friend, Anita wrote me a letter. She said that she will continue writing to me as long as I don't tell her to stop. Real nice of her, eh? I should at least have the heart to write to her cuz she ain't heard from me now for three weeks.

Somehow we managed to pull through the inspection today. We never had a lecture by our Battery Commander this evening. So there is a good possibility that we pulled through but we now have to undergo another inspection by the Corps. tomorrow. The inspecting General did us the honor this morning.

Seeing as how I have to work all night, I spent the day cooling it. Tomorrow is the last day and then we go on day shift for another week. The only good thing about working days is that at least you can get a good night's sleep, uninterrupted.

Saw a very good cinema this evening, "Henry's Full House." It was funny, sad and happy and a few other extremes. I guess I'm going nuts over here, or something.

Pete and I are pulling the grave yard shift tonight so I will finish this letter in the early morning hours about 3 a.m. Later—It is now 4 a.m. in the morning. What an ungodly hour for writing a letter, eh? I am still unable to think of anything to write about so I will sign off till tomorrow. Love, Bill

—m—

January 6, 1953, Journal Entry:

Just got a short time here and I'm going crazy. Why do I keep sending Anita those mean letters? I don't want to break off with her. She knows it and I do too. What am I doing? Following my folks' wishes. Shit! I think this Korea is getting to me and I'm going bonkers. What's wrong with me? What's wrong with Mom and Dad? Why do they want me to wait? I have feelings. This pressure is unbearable sometimes. I just can't lead my life the way they want me to lead it. I can make up my own mind.

—m—

Jan. 9, 1953

Dear Mom, Dad and Carol,

I caught myself a bad cold yesterday and this morning I went to the Medics to get fixed. Got my temperature taken and it was 100 degrees. The doctor put me on quarters. So I've been lying around all day. Hope to get it extended and have quarters tomorrow too.

I was supposed to pull guard last night but they took me off. I feel a lot better now, and it's been a nice day. The topsoil has melted and made a layer of mud around the area. If I didn't know it was January I'd swear it was spring around here. Seems funny that we are having nice weather and on the other side of Korea they are freezing in knee deep snow.

Till tomorrow, Love Bill

—m—

January 10, 1953

Dear Mom, Dad and Carol,

I say it sure was nice to find out just what our Christmas tree looked like. With a bit of imagination and the few needles which I got in the mail today I can see it in my mind. Your tree was quite a bit taller than the one we had here and much more bushier. I could tell by the needles it was all that and a lighter green than the one we had here. I also might add that you did have more decorations.

A person couldn't ask for a better day than the one we had today. It was really beautiful. I actually got a touch of spring fever. I think someone is fooling us and it'll probably rain or we will have a blizzard, cuz good things never last around here.

I was put on quarters two days in a row. Really cooling my heels now. That little rest really felt good. Got up when I felt like it and slept when I felt like it. Now I'm ready to tackle the world. Probably I'll be taken off come tomorrow and I'll have to go back and work again. Wish I could get on quarters just one more day though, just to rest up after my two day rest. Makes sense doesn't it?

You received only one box so far? Well, I sent two of them. The one you got had the smoking jacket in it. It's not a Coolie coat. The other box coming has a nice jacket in it for me. I can wear it when I get home.

I had to laugh when you wrote and said you saw Carol rummaging through her drawers at 2 a.m. in the morning. What a silly thing to do.

Come to think of it, that jacket may be a Coolie jacket. I don't know. Take it for what it looks like is all I can say. Till tomorrow, Love, Bill

Jan. 11, 1953

Dear Mom, Dad and Carol,

The day is drawing to an end and I am getting sleepy. So I will go to bed. Good night. I figure I'd better write a little more than that. I didn't get any letters at all today. Guess nobody wants to write to me no more. How strange it felt to get back to work again, after two days off of rest and relaxation. It got me all tired working for a full day.

Saw a silly movie last night, "Let's make it Legal." Didn't care too much for it. The fellow from Detroit that I was telling you about just got back today from spending 51 days in a hospital in Japan. There was something wrong with his eye. He collected his three points per month while he was gone. I sure wouldn't mind getting sent away for about a month.

I can't think of anything to write now so I will wrap this letter up for today and enclose a few pictures to make it a little thicker and interesting. Love, Bill

—m—

Jan. 12, 1953

Dear Mom, Dad and Carol,

Finally received word from you that you got my jacket. I was getting worried for fear it was lost in the mail. I'm gonna be a mighty flashy stud when I sport around in my new Ford or Chevy with the Bee Bop jacket on.

I'd like to be home watching some of those home movies you're talking about. I could throw in a few words along with your narrative. Great stuff!

The weather here has changed for the worse today. It got real cold, brrr! Cold enough for a nice blizzard anytime. Something happened tonight in regards to the meals. We've been having some pretty rotten chow lately, and tonight they honored us with a big turkey dinner with all the fixings. I about fell over when I found out about the big feed. Probably be in the same rut again tomorrow night though.

Tonight is movie night. "The Thief" with Ray Milland. It's slow at FDC so I may be able to go see it.

To answer your question: Never have been on Rte.#33 or Rte.#23 going from here to Seoul.

Well I guess a few pages a day will be a sufficient amount. And so here are the few pages. Till tomorrow, Love, Bill

—m—

January 14, 1953

Dear Mom, Dad and Carol,

Two more days from today and I will have been in the Army for exactly 18 months. Only a little while longer to go now.

It's still cold out!. Looks like winter came back to visit us for a while again. Hope it doesn't stay too long cuz that warm weather we were having sure was nice. Got a real good show tonight that I must see, "Rainbow Over Your Shoulder." My Detroit buddy says it's a real good movie. He saw it twice while he was in the hospital. He also gave me a brief rundown of the movie and it sounds pretty good. The day has come that I have been anxiously waiting for-Wednesday. That's the day we change shifts and we now go on night duty. For a week I can lay around and catch up on my sleep.

Did I ever tell you about the Mental Giant that came in FDC while I was on R & R? He's just a kid but sure has got the brains. He comes from Arkansas. He can do any type of mathematical problem. Nothing is hard for him. He's got brains he hasn't used yet. Also he is a good checkers player. We've stood him up against everyone in the battery and he's conquered them all. He is unbeatable. I think his mind has outgrown his body or something.

It's about time to attend the movie so I will sign off now, Love, Bill

—∞—

Jan. 15, 1953

Dear Mom, Pop and Sis,

Anita sent me another letter. She sure is persistent. She wrote me a real mushy letter this time. She's trying to get me back on the same track. I've got a weak heart but I may be able to hold out might longer, yet. You all are right, I should wait until I get home before making any decisions about Anita.

I've been thinking lately of getting myself a car when I get home. Gotta think about getting myself adjusted to civilian life again. Cars, clothes and other luxuries. I got a lot of living to do. I also want a new car. I believe I'll be able to do it all right. Now I'll ask Papa's opinion. Should I get a Chevy or a Ford? What are the prices?

We're remodeling our tents today, and tomorrow too as a matter of fact. We lowered the tent for the purpose of trying to keep more heat inside and by the same token we are building new doors cuz the others had more cracks in them than wood. We also got it now so the wind doesn't blow under the floor. It's starting to get warm in these tents, finally. We need it warm cuz it's getting mighty cold outdoors. I've got guard tomorrow night. Brrr!

Walked a mile and a half to take a shower today and found it closed. What a blow, had to come all the way back just a bit dirtier than when I left.

So Bob enlisted in the Air Force? I wish I had done the same thing. He'll have a better deal than the Army life. That's about it for now. Love, Bill

—∞—

Jan. 15, 1952, Journal Entry:

Will you tell me why I keep mentioning Anita to my folks? Crazy, that's what I am. The more I mention her to them in my letters, the more I get that "wait until you get home before making any decisions." Crazy, that's what I am. Or did I say that? Why am I so mixed up about Anita, about my life? I can't talk to the guys here about it. Sure, I tell Pete some things, but not everything. He tells me to take it easy. He tells me she will be there when I get out. He tells me to stop worrying and to stop giving Anita a hard time. Guess Pete is right. I should cut out the crap and send her a loving letter.

—∞—

January 18, 1953

Dear Mom, Dad and Carol,

We've been pretty busy lately. I'm working all night tonight and haven't time to answer all those letters. I just hope to get this one finished.

We're doing quite a bit of firing and have to do quite a bit of work seeing I'm the only one awake. Makes time fly by anyway.

We're making new doors for our tent should have them finished by Sunday, but by the way we've been poking along, it doesn't look like we will make it. All day long they've been playing music on the radio. It started this morning and it's going to continue indefinitely. It's for the March of Dimes. Everyone who sends in money can request a song. They are going to continue until all the requests are played. They mentioned on the air that they have enough requests for four or five more days. So you can imagine the money that is piling in. I wasn't too observant but the tune I thought was most requested was Patti Page, "I came to your wedding," and Eddy Fisher's "Any time." And quite a few others in that era, that I can't recall. I'll be a little more observant tomorrow of the ones that are most requested and give you a run down of the hit tunes over here.

This weather seems to be warming up and we are starting to play basketball once again. I know cuz I ran myself ragged last night at basketball. Lots of fun and exercise. The other day six of us took a walk through the hills and took a few good pictures which are being developed now. A few more treasures to put in my album when I get home. Enclosed are some more. Well, that's it for now. Love, Bill.

—m—

January 18, 1953, Journal Entry:

Short timer, that's what they are starting to call me. Hope they don't up those points. It seems I'm always a few points behind them. I was the only one awake at FDC and damn did we have the missions. Something's cooking in Chink land. What do I think about when there's a lull? Well, there wasn't one, tonight. I had to keep my wits about me, and all my ducks in a row, as Pa would say. I'm in a situation here in Korea where I can't stand it. But I can't get out of it, not just yet. So I have to tolerate it. Shit, it's become my life! I like it when we have tons of missions. Keeps me from thinking about myself. In this work speed and accuracy are what it's all about. Speed, that's what I want. I want to get the hell out of Korea, fast!

—m—

January 18, 1953

Dear Mom, Dad and Carol,

Received a letter from Curly. According to his letters he's doing all right over here for himself. The only thing he's not satisfied with is that he won't be leaving here for another five or six months. In answer to your question, I will have 39 points at the end of February and have a good chance of leaving here during that month. But, you never say you're sure of anything when you're in the Army.

Had quite a hectic day today, in sports that is. I washed my things last night, so I lost the morning by sleeping through it. At noon I finally dragged myself out of bed, went and ate, then played basketball and ping-pong all afternoon. Yes, ping-pong. They try to make it as nice as possible around here by giving us a few recreational facilities. Also got our day room fixed up real nice. Put a floor in it and just got it completed a few days ago. The next thing I look for is wearing a Class "A" uniform on the weekends. That will be the last straw.

Saw a movie tonight. "Untamed Frontier." I gotta write Mrs. McHenry a thank you note for the box I received from her yesterday. Golly, she sure is extravagant, a six pound ham, fruitcake, etc. you know mmmmmmmm-good is the word. Love, Bill

—~—

January 19, 1953

Dear Mom, Dad & Sis,

Another letter from Anita! My mind is all mixed up. Don't know what to do about that Arkansas gal. She says she really, really loves me. When I get home, we shall see.

So Father is all excited over getting a new Buick ? It will be nice for me too. Come home and jump into a new car and sport myself around town. What color you getting this time? I'd like to have a new car waiting for me when I get home but I suppose there is no chance of that happening.

Had another beautiful day again today. Can't kick about the weather we're now having. Got a box from Grama yesterday, too. She had quite an array of stuff in it, too. A nice package. I shall cherish them until I leave for home. Those socks sure look nice after those olive drab. "Candy Yeller" is what I call them.

We finally got our tent all fixed up. Pretty nice in here now. I won't mind leaving it all though I'm not that attached to the tent. I'm pretty sure I made corporal this time. I'll know for sure tomorrow or the next day. Till then it's still PFC.

It's getting late now so I'll sign off. Love, Bill

—~—

> Jan. 19, '52, Journal Entry:
>
> *Yes, I'm going to write her and tell her I'm coming to Arkansas when I get out. First, I'll get me a new car and then off to see my*

gal. That's what I'll tell her. She is for me and I'm for her. Yes, I know she really, really loves me. Same for me. Still, her letters sound sad, maybe because I've been putting her through hell, with my smart ass letters. That will change.

—᠁—

January 20, 1953, 11:30 p.m.

Dear Mom, Dad and Carol,

I wanna tell you I'm just all pooped out today. My hands are even tired so that it's work to hold this pen. I'm working all night tonight, too! I've got till 2:30 a.m. to stay awake, I can't rest my weary bones for a while.

The letters are starting to pile up on me. Yet I never seem to have time enough to get any of them answered. Didn't get any mail today. I just got letters from two weeks back to answer yet so—so what.

This morning we had to unload lumber off a truck and stack it all up in the proper piles. That washed up the majority of the morning for us. Then this afternoon we had to put in a tent and build a floor for it. That's the afternoon shot. Too much work for me in one day I guess.

I was looking over the pictures of the different styles of new Chevrolets. It's really a sharp looking job for that year. The one I like the best, and the one I'd love to get is that Bel-Air streamliner. My eyes caught that picture the first thing and I say to myself, "That's the one I want." A pretty Chevy like that wouldn't look too bad sitting next to a Buick would it? It's been sort of a changeable day today. This morning started out beautiful then towards noon I thought it would rain, and just before twilight it looked like snow. So what ya gonna do?

You know they're still going strong with old melodies on the radio and playing requests sent in for the March of Dimes. It's been constant music on the radio for nigh on to a week and it may last another week. I don't mind it though cuz I like to turn on the radio any old time and hear my favorite melodies. I finished the ham you sent me for Christmas and everything else you sent me and today I dug into the six and half pound ham that Art and Lydia sent me. We get three fairly square meals a day. I should say square meals but they never seem to fill me up. You know me, I can eat a full meal every two hours. I'm hungry now. I guess I'm getting food on the brain. It is now Jan. 21, the whole day is gone and I'm starting a new one. This month seems to be fleeting right by. Till tomorrow, Love, Bill.

—∞—

January, 1953, Korea: 270,000 Chinese and North Korean troops man enemy lines.

—∞—

January 21, 1953

Dear Mom, Dad and Sis,

Received one letter from you today. I must say you sure surprised me concerning the price of the new Buick and mostly the depreciation of our old one. The way I see it, it sure doesn't pay to buy a Buick unless you have a few hundred grand stashed away somewhere. You might as well buy an Olds '88 as a Buick at that price. I believe I've decided I want a Chevy.

After the evening meal a few of us guys pooled our food and had another meal about 7:30 p.m. along with a game of cards. Had quite a feast, ham, fried chicken, canned fruit, cake, cookies, etc.

From your letter you don't like the idea of me smoking those "filthy weeds" ! Won't it look charming when I'm clad in the smoking jacket and puffing away? So father quit, eh? Guess that leaves only me.

Your son finally made Corporal. I'll be going in a few weeks and now they give it to me. Oh well, I got it anyway. Till the next day, Love, Bill

—∞—

January 22, 1953

Dear Mom, Dad and Sister, Boy, we've been busier than heck in here today. Our battalion commander was up on one of our outposts and he was sending us targets to fire at and we were adjusting our guns on targets all day long. Really a hectic day.

Our major here in FDC asked me when I was going home. I told him Feb. He then asked me the number of points I will have at the end of Feb. I responded with 39. I gotta have 40 so it looks like I'll be here in March, too. I get sick and tired of jumping from month to month and them just keeping ahead of me.

Today, the 22nd I have been away from home exactly 18 months and 15 days. And it will be two more months before I see home again. I'm counting the days, and getting more lonesome by the day.

Got a movie tonight, so will cut this short. The "San Francisco Story" is playing tonight. Till tomorrowwwwwwwwww, Your son, Bill

p.s. That wasn't our battery that got strafed (according to the dictionary strafe means rapid fire from machine guns in low flying planes). We were in that position originally. Glad we moved.

—~—

> January 22, 1953, Journal Entry:
>
> *We were lucky! Just missed getting strafed by the Gooks. Just missed! Moved at the right time. Those unlucky bastards that took our place got it. Moving, that's what we do, one step ahead of Joe Chink.*

—~—

7 p.m. January 24, 1953

Dear Mom, Dad and Carol, I neglected to write you a letter yesterday cuz I had guard last night and I chose to sleep after, cuz I worked all night. I'd like to go to bed but they have a very good movie playing tonight, "Because of You" with Jeff Chandler and Loretta Young. It's seems as though I'd get tired of seeing a show every other night but actually I look forward to them.

I can't think of anything to write about that happens around here because it's the same ordeal day after day. Just come in here and work from 8 to 8 and then take off till the next day. Although they are hectic days I may be able to endure for a while longer. I have 36 points at the end of January and at the end of February about 39 points. And 42 hopefully at the end of March. As it stands presently we have to have 40. So I know as much as you do now. Sometime in March I can tell you a bit more. You hear as much news at home about points as we do here, so———

Enclosed you will find my income tax return. I don't know where to send it so I'll send it home. They took income tax out of me until I got to Korea. So the money that is taxable was what I made in Japan. I guess all I have to do, or what you have to do is send in one of the copies. I don't know if I have to sign it.

Please send me about three or four rolls of 620 film. I can't get any here. I want it to take pictures on the way home. Love, Bill

—w—

(Jan. 25, 1953: Operation Smack. Assault on Spud Hill by elements of the 31st. Inf. Regt.)

—w—

January 25, 1953

Dear Mom, Dad and Carol,

Went to church this morning and got back at 10:30, so that cut the morning short. The afternoon went by pretty fast cuz we fired quite a few missions today.

That show I saw last night was the best one yet. Really a tear jerker. I wouldn't mind seeing movies like that every night. If you only knew how it feels to step out of a show like that with it fresh in your mind and then realize you are still in Korea instead of home stepping out of a theater with your girl.

I'm getting absent minded lately. I forgot to enclose the income tax thing yesterday so; will do it now. Will you send me Allan Barrow's address again? I done went and lost it before I had a chance to write him. I believe he's not far from here. So be it. Love, Bill

—w—

Jan. 26, 1953

Dear Mom, Dad and Carol,

So you're looking at a Pontiac now? A good car I think. It's a little out of my class such as the Buick is or else I wouldn't mind having one myself. What does Dad have against them? I'd like to see one sitting in the yard when I get home.

Carol had me fooled too. I thought she'd be moping around the house while Bob was in the Air Force. But no use living a dead life while he's gone though. You can still wait for him and have fun.

It's been a very nice day today as far as I know. I've been inside most of the day doing my part in this conflict over here. Movie time again tonight. The "Black Castle" is scheduled for this evening. I don't believe I've ever seen a show as good as "Because of You". It was wonderful.

You know I've been thinking about school after I get out. There's quite a few in Michigan that teach forestry classes. There's one in Roscommons isn't there? I'm sure there is one in the upper peninsula somewhere. One of the guys here was telling me there's one in Houghton, Michigan. I'd be in seventh heaven up there. Wish I knew where to write and get some information. Love, Bill

—w—

Korea, January, 1953: Air Force Staff Sgt. Gerald Matt, of Chicago, Illinois, was crew chief of a B-36 Bomber, the largest airplane ever built, with ten engines and a 230 foot wing span. Matt and his crew maintained the bomber's engines. According to Matt, in 1953 he flew in the B-36 over China and North Korean once a week carrying Atomic bombs. (none were dropped) The mission took 35 hours round trip. On one mission, three engines malfunctioned (shut down). They were the reciprocating engines in back of the plane. The plane eventually landed safely in Fort Worth, Texas. Matt, who now lives in Allegan, Michigan, said that the B-36 had a tail rudder that towered five stories high. The B-36 weighed 165,000 pounds when empty of fuel and 450,000 pounds fully fueled. The Air Force maintained 37 B-36s during the Korean conflict, added Matt.

—w—

January 27, 1953

Dear Mom, Dad and Carol,

This makes four days in a row that I haven't received a letter with the exception of yesterday, when I got one. I'm putting a few more pictures in the envelope again, today. I've been thinking of all the pictures I will have to paste in my album. I won't mind it though, because I'll be home.

"I'm Yours" just finished playing and now Eddie Fisher is singing, "Wish You Were Here." Both very beautiful songs.

You know Mom, you couldn't ask for better days than we've been having here as far as the weather goes. Seems odd to me that they're having such cold weather just on the other side of Korea. I don't know whether it's due to the nice weather, but the shows have been getting better.

How's Pop been getting along with his new job? With my father turning one of the big wheels in the plant, it's without a doubt everything is running real smooth. Have you decided what kind of car you're going to get? And what color? Why don't you get a fire engine red convertible? I wouldn't mind driving it around a bit. Will it have a radio in it?

Time to hit the sack, now. Till tomorrow, Love, Bill

—m—

January 28, 1953

Dear Mom, Dad and Sis,

This morning I really had a tough time climbing out of bed. I would have given 20 bucks if I could have just laid there till noon. But we have to get up at six and make the morning formation every morning except Sunday. The only thing I ever bring to the mess hall in the morning any more is just a cup and spoon. The eggs they have aren't worth consuming. They've got bowls there so I just have coffee, toast and cereal, a fairly substantial meal.

The movie I saw the other night sure was the "berries." It was one of those eerie Frankenstein things called "Black Castle." Tonight we have "Horizons West" or "West Horizons." Can't remember which way it went.

FDC is still under construction. The porch we used to have is now boarded in and made into an extra room. Got some kind of plaster board on the walls and ceiling and pretty soon we're going to do the same to the FDC room here. It'll really look sharp in here in a few more weeks.

Today is the last I work days, tomorrow I start nights. The letter I received from Carol was real nice. I sure enjoy getting letters from my sister. If she writes like that to everyone she'll be assured of getting an answer.
That's it for now. Love, Bill

—m—

January 30, 1953

Dear Mom, Dad and Carol,

About those new cars and what I was talking of buying. The reason I'd like to get a new one is that I've paid for someone else's troubles about four different times and I'd sorta like to start on something that no one else has had their hands on before. Yeah, I know what father is saying, "You can sit behind the wheel of a custom made job and have it ruined in two days." Ain't that what he's saying? I'd like to have a new one, but if I can't afford it, I guess I can't.

Now about that picture that you sent back to me. It sure wasn't me in the picture cuz I took it. I hate to admit that I took a bad one like that but I did. The names I've got written on the back are correct. While we're on the subject of pictures that one you sent me of the house sure was a beautiful shot. Makes me homesick to look at it. That weeping willow sure did grow out a lot. Cutting that thing back just makes it grow all the bigger. You must have really had a storm. I haven't seen snow like that for two years now. It snows one day here and it's gone the next. But the cold weather sure doesn't go with the snow. As I told you before, it snowed here a few days ago and it's gone already but it's still cold. Real cold!

I had guard last night and I found out just how cold it was. A few degrees below zero. We keep our stoves turned off during the day to conserve fuel and during the course of the day our water freezes over in the cans. It must not be too warm here, eh? Now I wish for warmer weather and when it's warm I wish for some of this cold weather. Either I'm hard to please or something.

I'm working all night tonight. I had third relief guard last night and when you pull that relief you can sleep in the morning. I hit the sack right after chow last night and slept until 10:00, walked from 10:00 till twelve, slept again till four then walked til six. Ate then went to bed again until noon.

Now I work again tonight until 3:00 a.m. and will sleep in here (FDC) until breakfast then go to bed until noon. I'm getting enough sleep—in stages—that is.

According to your letter you seem to think I'll be home in February. I hate to say I'll be home in March cuz I don't want to disappoint you. But the way it looks here, I'll be leaving in March. I have to have forty points. If they raise it to forty two I'll still make it in March cuz I'll have forty two points at the end of March. It's very disappointing, isn't it?

I went and skipped right by and didn't mention cars. I did want to mention the one you all are going to buy, that is if you ever get around to it. I didn't think you'd ever get a Pontiac. The luck you had with the Buick of yours I wouldn't trust driving one of those very long. It sure was a lemon, wasn't it? You know those pictures I sent home and said that one man might have been Ed Murrow. Well it could have been because I took that picture in Seoul, Korea, where he was supposed to be and not in Tokyo.

I didn't receive the box you were sending me. This is the first time that's happened. It should be here soon if you sent it the last part of December.

Well, I guess this will be about it for now. Till tomorrow, Love, Willie

—₩—

January 30, 1953, Journal Entry:

Guard! And to top it off I worked all night at FDC. Double time, and no pay for overtime. That's a joke, son. Sleep walking, I'm so dead tired, I can't see straight, so sleepy, but I have to go on. This is a bitch. So cold I froze my ass off! These Korean winters are ten times colder than northern Michigan. I can swear to that. And not having much heat in the tent. Thank God for my winter sleeping bag. I know, I should be thankful I'm in a tent. I know. I know. Think of those boys at the front. I saw them, I know.

—₩—

January 31, 1953

Dear Mom, Dad and Carol,

They gave us some new rules today concerning the stoves in the tents (sleeping quarters). They have to be turned off now at 9:00 in the morning and not to be lit again till 4:30 in the afternoon. It'll save quite a bit of oil but in the mean time we will freeze during the day.

Got paid today. Big deal! I think they overpaid me this month cuz I drew 95 bucks across the table. With simple addition it means I get a total of $170 this month and a corporal rating doesn't make that much difference in pay. I'll probably just get $10 next month. You'll be getting a money order in the mail from me in a few days. Have you been getting my allotment okay? Hope so. I wrote too much yesterday, so will cut it short today. Love to all, Bill

—∾—

(Feb 3, 1953, Hill 101/Ungok. 5th Marines conduct a raid and sustain 15 KIA, 55 WIA)

—∾—

Feb. 3, 1953

Dear Mom, Dad and Carol,

I worked all last night too. I came here (FDC) at 8:30 last night and from then until 1:30 in the morning I worked. Had to make some overlay situation maps for the Colonel. He trusts my work. Always asks me to do the maps. Guess I know what I'm doing. We were super busy on the missions!

I woke up the other man here at 2:30 a.m. and during the hour that elapsed I was so tired I couldn't see to write. T'was a real chilly night again, but I expected it to be a might warmer tonight cause the sky is overcast. I don't like this freezing cold weather. Guess I'll be coming home just about the right time. Be just about summer. I may as well be pessimistic. Face life as a realist.

My buddy, Pete, and I have been gabbing about cars and the subject of what kind of car you were gonna buy has been discussed. I was surprised when you finally ended up with a Pontiac. All I can say is that you surely got a good deal. All those "extras" and for only 24 bucks. Not bad at all. You got a radio in it too, that's what I'm happy about. Won't I look sharp in a new Pontiac when I get home?

When you said something about how I would like to work in a jet engine plant got me to thinking. Yep, my mind is still changing. Haven't quite grown out of that yet. One of my characteristics, I guess.

Got another letter from Anita again today. I can't seem to wash that Arkansas gal out of my hair. Guess I'll have to write her a strong letter to the point and end it all. She can't figure out why I don't write to her. Mom, you were right. I have plenty of time for serious stuff. I've got all those gals in Michigan waiting for me!

One more day before we go back on days again for the week. During the past week I have been playing quite a bit of ping-pong. We've got a nice table in the day room. Just got back from seeing "The Winning Team" with my girl Doris Day in it. Very good show. Till tomorrow, Love, Bill

—m—

Feb. 4, 1953, Journal Entry:

What kind of a game am I playing with Anita's heart? Who am I kidding? I love the gal, and I'm being mean to her, so that makes my folks happy? You betcha! Why don't they want me to marry her? Beats me. As I've said many, many times they don't put any hold on Carol and Bob, no matter how often they fight. What gives? Why the double standards? Is it because she's from Arkansas? They don't even know her. Well, I'll play their game for a little while longer. Damn it, I don't want to mess up my life any more.

—m—

Feb. 4, 1953

Dear Mom, Dad and Carol,

I've been thinking about that tube that blew out in your TV set. I hope it isn't the picture tube cuz I at least want a halfway chance of seeing TV when I get home. Probably be a little while before you get a picture tube?

You sure did humiliate me again by putting Pfc. on my letter when you know darn well I'm now a double barreled Cpl. Yes, it means I get a bit more money now. About a 25 dollar raise. Now along with my longevity I'm drawing $150. That four years I put in the Naval Reserves helped me out a little bit didn't it? In other words as a CPL. I'm drawing a sergeant's pay.

Here's the money I said I was going to send, $50. Each penny adds up doesn't it? The weather warmed up a little today. Probably due to the cloudy sky. The nights aren't quite so cold either. Say, while I think of it, did you get that income tax thing I sent? Hope so. I sent it a while ago. Guess all you have to do is send in that piece of paper and wait to get the money back. Love, Bill

—m—

Feb. 6, 1953

Dear Mom, Dad and Carol,

You insulted me again. In one of your letters you called me a Pfc. Of course, in the other one you scribbled the proper handle and so you are forgiven.

We got FDC all fixed up now. Looks pretty sharp with the walls all lined with this brown smooth poster-board stuff. Got a big long window in front. Picture window, I guess is what you'd call it. The captain said to me "Maybe you'd like to stay here for a little while longer." I looked at him sorta funny like and he knew what I meant without saying it.

You seem to be wondering about the flu epidemic here. We done had our shots and sure needed them. About everyone here had them including me.

Those hit tunes you wrote about; well I've never heard them. We're just a might behind here. Those shacks you asked about in the pictures I sent you? Well, that's where the Koreans live. Those are their houses. Not what you'd call America houses, like in Pontiac. Here are a few more photos for the album.
Love, Bill

—m—

Feb. 7, '53

Dear Mom, Dad and Sis,

We were very busy firing missions in FDC yesterday. This ain't no police action, this is war! Haven't you heard?

I also had guard duty so that took up the majority of my time. I got a letter from you yesterday but nothing today. Woe is me. After the two warm days we had it has begun to turn cold again. It fell down to about zero last night. It isn't bad though because we have a warm place to sleep and a nice place to work. I pity those soldiers out there in the firing batteries. But as comfortable as it is here at FDC it won't influence me to stay here any longer than I have to. It ain't quite that good.

I have been sleepy all through the day. Had second relief guard duty last night and only managed to get about four hours sleep. They've got a show playing tonight but I ain't even gonna go and see it. Too tired. I'll hit the sack right away. "The Thief of Baghdad" or something like that is playing.

Wish I could explain to you how FDC is fixed up but it'd take umpteen pages, besides some of that stuff we are not suppose to talk or write about it. Maybe, I can fill you in a little when I get home if I don't forget by then.

I thought you all had already decided on a Pontiac, and here you haven't even ordered one yet. Gonna keep me in suspense a while longer, eh? I've got about five rolls of film I haven't developed yet, so these aren't all the pictures I have. I'm going to take them home with me and develop them there. Do a better job at home, anyway. Enclosed are a few more. Did you receive the money order yet? So lonesommmme, Love, Bill

—~—

Feb. 9, '53

Dear Mom, Dad and Sister,

I got a Valentine card from Anita. That girl sure is thoughtful. Before I forget it I want to wish you all a happy and pleasant Valentine Day.

Also I am celebrating in an ironical sort of way my second anniversary when I took my physical for induction into the Army. February 14, that is. Today I have been away from the training ground exactly one year, two months, twelve days and twelve hours. Long time, eh?

You said something in your letter about you're glad I'm not getting all the cold weather these past four days that's not holding true here. It's been dropping down to below zero at night. Brrrrrr. But the days seem to be getting a little warmer. So it'll give us a chance to thaw out a little.

Well, I don't know what to say about little sister. Carol and her idea about getting engaged to Bob. Personally, I'd say no! It'd be just as wrong as two left shoes. She's too young for one thing to be married, I mean. True, there's no sense in being an old maid but why tie yourself down when you're 18? It's the same old story. If you love each other, you'll wait. It's up to Carol though, I guess. If she thinks she wants to settle down it's up to her, but I'm against it. She should wait for a few more years.

Say, isn't that what you keep telling me, and I'm four years older than my sister. You say I'm too young to get married when I mention the subject. Why isn't Carol too young at eighteen? Well, I'll sign off for now. Till tomorrow, Love, Bill

—ɷ—

Feb. 10, '53, Journal Entry:

Talk about double standards—my kid sister, Carol, just 18, plans to get engaged. Whamo! My folks think that's fine and dandy. But I just have to mention Anita's name and whamo, they say I should wait. Maybe when I'm 80 I can get their permission to marry. Hell, I don't need their permission. I'm almost 23 years old, and I'm here in Korea fighting this stupid war. I can do what I want and when I want and that includes marriage.

—ɷ—

Feb. 10, '53

Dear Mom, Dad and Carol,

I'd be darned if it hasn't started snowing this afternoon. It started in about three o'clock and now three hours later, it's still going strong. By morning we should have quite a bit of snow.

Had another hectic day again today here in FDC. Can't tell you too much but we had firing missions after firing missions. That's what happened.

It's really hard to write a letter when you don't receive one. This is the shortest letter I've ever written but—I'm lost today. Love, Bill.

—ɷ—

February 11, 1953

Dear Mom, Dad and Sister,

Now maybe I can fill out a full page after getting some mail from you. I notice by one of the clippings you sent that Charlene's husband is home from Germany now. Are you going to have my picture in the paper when I come home? I'm getting to be a publicity hound. You can write up my army career along side of the photo—Bill Ahnen, who has spent fourteen months in the Far East Command. Two of which were spent attending school in Tokyo before coming to Korea to serve in a Fire Direction Center in an Artillery Unit, etc. etc. etc. You know, write it really good.

The snow I wrote about the other day is all gone now. It sure didn't stay long. The cold weather either, thank God.

The nightshift starts tonight for us and I'm working with my Detroit friend, Wong. We get off at noon today to sorta rest for the long night ahead of us. First of all I went to the showers and then I came back and slept till five o'clock. I feel pretty wide-awake now so I guess I can pull an all-nighter. I'll sleep half of the day tomorrow and then probably do work detail to fill out the rest of the day.

Saw a good movie tonight, "Springfield Rifle" with Gary Cooper.

I suppose you have hit on a good idea for me to wait until I get home before I decide about the school business. I don't know too much about it myself. It's just that I've been getting a few ideas in my head. No use coming home with a blank mind, might as well have some constructive thoughts. Well, I'm out of words, again. Love, Bill

—~—

Feb. 12, 1953

Dear Mom, Dad and Carol,

This afternoon we were on details cleaning up the area and getting the place ready for another inspection, which is supposed to come off in the near future. This inspection will be a pain in the neck is all I can say. When I went for mail call this evening the first sergeant informed me that I have guard duty tomorrow night, again. What a pleasant thing to look forward to, eh? It's third relief so I'll get to sleep again all morning. How nice.

They pulled the unexpected on us today. By that I mean a movie. We usually have them only every other day. It was just TV shorts they showed tonight. Had three different films—"Meet the Champ," "Hit Parade" (Feb. 2, 1952, about a year old) and "Jack Benny." Benny is quite a card on television. I like this program. Have you all gotten a TV set yet? If not, when I get back I'll have to go somewhere else to watch Jack Benny.

My little sis, Carol, is doing a lot of gallivanting around. Ain't she? Just think if she were married she could stay home, be the little housewife. Wouldn't that be nice?

If you mark the packages you send me "fragile" they'll throw them around a little more than usual. They do things in a haphazard way. Anyway, I like crumbs, instead of cookies. I seem to be quite a faultfinder today so I'd better quit writing and stop telling you all that crap. Time to go back to the tent anyway and go to bed. Love, Bill

—~—

Feb. 14, '53

Dear Mom, Dad and Carol,

Well, finally got the news that I have been waiting for, and I'm sure you have, too. I guess about the simplest and best way I can say it is, and I quote: "You can now cease fire on writing me any more letters and what not. Your baby is coming home to Mama!"

I'll be leaving Korea the 24th of February, which is just ten days from today. I'm excited as a little boy with a pretty new penny. They went over the points and found out that I had just over 39½. I thought I had only 39 and here I have 40 of them, I've been tearing around here like a chicken with no head.

The weather here has been pretty nice lately. Hope it stays that way till I leave. I just hope we have half decent weather on the ocean cruise, not like the trip over through storms.

I gotta work all night again tonight and also Tuesday night. That's the last time though. That's all I can think of now going home. What else is there to say? Wouldn't it be terrible if they found out I only had 39 points? Gads! Why be a pessimist. Tain't good.

That box you sent in December got here a while back. I thought I told you that I received it. The nut bread was moldy too. Had to throw it away. But the rest was in fine condition. I haven't got that other package with the film, yet. If you sent it airmail, I should get it tomorrow. I've been expecting it for the last two days.

That's all for now, Love, Bill

—~—

> Feb. 14, 1953, Journal Entry:
>
> *Happy day! I'm on my way, home! I can't believe it. Home, eh! Been smiling and laughing all day. Best I keep myself alive for the*

short time I have here. Don't want to spoil my homecoming. God, thank you!

—∾—

Feb. 15, 1953

Dear Mom, Dad and Carol,

Another day has passed which means another day less. I slept all day today. It being Sunday we didn't have to perform any work details. I didn't go to church either cuz I worked last night and I slept all morning, and afternoon. I was tired.

Tonight I saw a very wonderful movie. It was a lot different than any other I have ever seen. It was "The Miracle of Our Lady of Fatima." I really enjoyed that movie.

I am back in the "hole" again, that is the FDC headquarters. Our shift works from 8 until 10 p.m. At that time all but two of us leave and go back to the tent, Guess who has to stay? Yep, me. Can't think of anything else to write.

When I get ready to leave Korea don't expect a letter from me every day. I'll probably be really busy until I get on the ship and once on the ship I can't send any mail. But you'll know I'm on my way home, so I guess that should be good enough.

Till tomorrow, Love, Bill

—∾—

Feb. 16, 1953

Dear Mom, Dad & Carol,

Only eight more days to go now. I just found out today that six days prior to my departure I am officially relieved of duty in as far as FDC is concerned. No more all-nighters. I've got those six days all planned out, too. One day I'll get everything all straightened out and packed up. The other five days I'm a gonna rest. For a year now I've been getting up at 6 for reveille but now I can cool it in bed till I feel like getting up. It's going to be okay the last days, right?

I was mighty happy to hear you got another allotment check of mine. They seem to be doing okay as far as that goes. Tomorrow night is my last night to work and I probably without a doubt will have to pull guard duty, too. One more time.

It's a funny feeling to be finally leaving. It's hard to explain. I want to go home more than anything in the world, but I hate to leave all my buddies back in Korea. Buddies, I've lived with so long. Till tomorrow, See ya soon, Love, Bill

—∿—

Feb. 18, '53

Dear Mom, Dad and Carol,

Didn't write a letter yesterday cuz I was too tired. I worked all night in FDC for the last time, I might add. As of today, I am relieved from duty at FDC. So I'll lay around and try to enjoy life for the last few days in Korea. There were too many missions and we were working our butts off. Can't tell you much more. Today a unit of M*A*S*H nurses and a couple of doctors rode through on jeeps going to the front.

I should have written last night but I couldn't keep my eyes open. I was so tired. This morning I slept and this afternoon I took a ride with one of the truck drivers up to one of the firing batteries. I wish I had a role of film with me so I could have taken some pictures of the guns.

Your box came a little late. I received it this afternoon after I got back from the battery. The cookies were in good shape, plus the film. I thought for a while I wasn't going to get the package, but it finally came. Good.

So at last you got the Pontiac, eh? Now I've got some transportation when I get home. We'll, guess I'll go to bed now. Write again tomorrow, Love, Bill

p.s. See you all soon.

—∿—

*Korea: More than 500 women served in Mobile Army Surgical Hospital (M*A*S*H) units in Korea. One of them was Capt. Jane Thurness, Army nurse.*

—∿—

Feb. 19, '53

Dear Mom, Dad & Carol,

Went and wrote you a letter the other night and forgot to mail it till after the mail done went out. I guess I shouldn't say I forgot because that wouldn't really be the proper excuse. The thing is, I didn't get out of bed till noon and I'm not exaggerating the least bit. You see I've been relieved of duty now so I have nothing to do but loaf and sleep.

I forgot to put the letter out for someone else to mail so there it stayed till I got up at noon. Tonight, I'm pulling guard duty, my last time, I might add, so I'm going to stay in the sack til noon again tomorrow. That's the quickest way I know of to pass the time til I'm out of here.

This afternoon I went and took a shower, then came back and played a few games of ping-pong. At four o'clock I had to drop everything and come back to the tent and listen to my hillbilly music on the radio. My evening consisted of pulling my first two hours of guard duty and watching a movie. Had a very good one playing again tonight, "The Pride of St. Louis." I don't give two hoots and a holler about baseball but I thought the show was pretty good anyway.

Did I tell you that I'll probably come home a civilian? This is the way I think it goes, but I'm not sure. If you have less than twenty months in you have to stay for the full twenty-four months. But if you have twenty or more months in you are discharged when you return to the states. That is you'll be shipped to a camp, then discharged. I think I'm right but couldn't swear to it.

I suppose you are wondering just how long after I leave here I will be home. I may be able to give you the approximate time but not precise. If I have good connections all the way through this will hold pretty true to form.

Within a week after my departure here, I should be in Japan and on my way to the ship. Within two to three weeks I'll be in the states so I figure I should be home in approximately a month. In other words that means March. See you soon, Love, Bill.

Feb. 20, 1953

Dear Mom, Dad and Carol,

I slept all morning again and this afternoon I passed my time away by cleaning both our stoves in here. Boy the days are sure going slow for me. I don't know what to do with myself. I've got my footlocker and everything else all straightened up and packed. I could leave on a moment's notice, any old time.

I just haven't a thing to write about. So, to bed early, then three more days. Love, Bill

—~—

Feb. 21, 1953

Dear Mom, Dad and Carol,

Might as well write another short letter to let you know that I'm getting a little more excited as the days draw near to the big one. Tomorrow morning I have to go to supply and turn all my stuff in with the exception of my bed, of course. I have to sleep in it the next few days. Also I will turn my carbine in and get me a M-I rifle to carry back to Japan.

I've been carrying my clearance papers around all day and having different people sign them. Won't be long now before I'll be all set to move out. I slept all morning today. This afternoon played a bit of basketball in between times when I was having the papers signed. Tonight I'll spend the evening away by watching a movie. "Buccaneer" is showing tonight. Sounds good enough to pass away two hours, anyway. Love, Bill

—~—

Feb. 22, 1953

Dear Mom, Dad and Carol,

Had to get up early this morning and turn in my clothes to supply. Couldn't sleep till noon like I'm going to do tomorrow morning.

I hate to brag any but I'm a "Jack of all trades". I came in here today and the guys were trying to fix the radio and all were about to give up when I strolled in. I put my brain to work and within ten minutes—it played like a new one. I told 'em it would be a dollar an hour for lessons though! Can't afford to give away my talent.

I played basketball again all afternoon. Had quite a few exciting games. I guess I'll be pulling out just in time now. H.Q. Battery is going on another one of those practice maneuvers in the morning. Remember when I told you about the others I went on? Going to bed now. See you all soon. Love, Bill

—~—

Feb. 23, 1953

Dear Mom, Dad and Carol,

This here is the last letter you'll get from me while I'm in Korea. Sounds good, eh? Just think, within a month I'll be knocking at your door. I'll be pulling out tomorrow morning. I shot the morning again today and this afternoon is really going slow for me. Went and took a shower.

Wrote a letter to Curly and it's only 4:00 now. I can sit here till five and listen to hillbilly music. That's always one way of passing the time. These fingernails of mine sure have been tempting the past few days. I'm all on edge about leaving here and I'm just about to bite them all off. Got about another hour until mail call so guess I'll just hold up on this letter until then.

I heard some talk that they are starting something new. Instead of going to Seattle, we will go to the east side of Mississippi, embark at New York. That'll mean thirty days on the ocean. You go around through the Panama Canal that-a-way.

Just my luck, I'll probably be the one to make that trip. I'll be very disappointed if I do. I didn't like the ocean coming over here and that took fifteen days, so fifteen more days wont' help none. I'll find out pretty soon.

This is my last letter from here. I'll probably find time along the way to write though. There ain't no mail box on the ocean, I hear tell. Love, Bill

—~—

The Crossroads, Army Service Club #52
Sasebo Replacement Depot,
Camp Mower, Japan
Friday, March, 1953

Dear Mom, Dad, Carol,

Here I am at Sasebo. I sure wish they'd get us out of here. It's getting to be very nerve wracking.

I went to the movies last night and saw, "The Snows of Kilimangaro." It's a great movie, lots of wild animals and exciting scenes. We sure have the life of Riley here now but I just can't seem to enjoy it at all. I keep thinking of the long, horrible boat ride back home. Docking in Frisco wouldn't be that bad, but if we have to go to New York, yee, gads!

We had an inspection this morning at 9 a.m. Now our day is free. Then tomorrow they may decide to have another inspection-again. The Army can't live without its inspections, I guess. I think I'll take a hike over to the snack bar and get a cheeseburger and malt. I just have to wander around and stuff myself with all this food.

Till tomorrow, Love, Bill

—~—

The Crossroads, Army Service Club #52
Sasebo Replacement Depot,
Camp Mower, Japan
March 4, 1953

Dear Mom, Pop and Sis,

Sorry I haven't written to you sooner but we have been so busy around this place that I didn't know whether I was coming or going. The first night I got here (in fact none of us got any sleep). Stayed awake all night processing and what not. To start at the beginning-I left the 159th at 3:00 in the afternoon of the 24th of February, Saturday. I was in Inchon, Korea, that evening and stayed there three days before we finally got on the ship "General Meigs" and docked here in Sasebo, Japan 32 hours later. We just finished processing last night which included new clothing issue, record checks, etc. etc. etc. just to mention a few of the things.

I am now all finished processing and am awaiting a ship to take me back home. When it will get here is beyond me. From all the talk I hear we may be staying here another month. They are rumors but probably true.

Another thing is that I may get a ship that goes around to New York. That will take about 30 days (one month on the ocean). What a horrible thought but it's just my luck to get on a ship like that. This I know for sure, I'm going to Fort Custer, Michigan, to be discharged when I hit the states. That's good. Anyway even if I have nothing else worth raving about. Look at me. Going home and still griping about how this Army is run. I should be overjoyed but I suppose I'd gripe even if they handed me a million dollars.

They have some nice activities to keep you occupied during the stay. On the post they have a Service Club which offers just about everything. Movies, PX, bowling, etc. It's not so bad here considering. I could be on my way home if the big wheels would only get us on a ship. Before I forget, do not write to me for a while because I will not get the mail. I won't be here long enough for that. I'll write to you but don't write me. When you don't get a letter for a few days, you'll know I'm on my way. If I land on the west coast or east coast, I'll call you. I'll also call from Battle Creek, Michigan and maybe you can come down and pick me up.

Another thing that is really nice here is that we can take a hot shower just whenever we please. I've been taking one every day. Even though I despise the ride on the ship, I am patiently waiting to get on that thing. Now if I can find some stamps, I will mail this letter. Lots of love, Bill.

—ʍ—

March, 1953, Kumhwa, Korea: Cpl. Leon Emanuel Miller, of Benton Harbor, Michigan, was attached to the 9th Korean ROK Army as part of an air-ground liaison team for front line troops. According to Miller, they were given orders to pull out during the combat, but that never materialized. They held off the North Koreans and made a name for themselves on White Horse Mountain, north of Kumhwa.

—ʍ—

The Crossroads, Army Service Club #52
Sasebo Replacement Depot,
Camp Mower, Japan
March 8, 1953

Dear Mom, Dad and Carol,

Well, I finally got my orders. When I'll be leaving or such as that I don't know. Probably will be tomorrow sometime. After all this time wasted here I more than likely will be stuck on a ship that goes to New York. It's a ticket home I guess, one way or the other.

Went to church this morning and when I got out it was time to eat dinner. Had chicken and I never in my life saw anything that was as tough as that was. I fought with it for ten minutes or so and finally gave up and lost. Everything else was good, but I just couldn't master that chicken. Went to the show last night and saw "Clouded Yellow." It was pretty good. Nothing out of the ordinary.

I suppose I'll have a little mail at home waiting when I get there. So far I've filled out about 15 change of address cards so I presume they'll know where to forward my mail.

(Anita's two letters were waiting for Bill at home.)

I had sort of a crazy dream last night. I dreamed I just got home and the first thing I did was get the movie projector out and start running off all those reels. Never said hello or nothing.

I'm going to scribble off another letter to somebody so hope to see ya all soon as possible. Lots of love, Bill

—ııı—

(March 9, 1953, Korea: A 7th ID 34-man patrol loses 20 KIA, 2 MIA, and 12 WIA in Chinese Communist Forces ambush. A 2nd ID 34-man patrol also loses 12 KIA and 5 MIA in another ambush.)

—ııı—

March 9, 1953

Dear Mom, Dad and Sis,

Still here. May be a couple more days yet before I leave here. There are lots of fellows on the same orders that I have and they are going out on the west coast so I stand a very good chance of not going way around to New York. It's more than likely, we'll go to California which I won't mind in the least.

Got up bright and early this morning about 5 a.m. ate breakfast and then back to barracks. I then laid down on the bed and fell asleep and never woke up til dinner.

This afternoon I had to pull three hours of Fire Guard. That's the only thing about staying around here is that we have to pull all these details all the time. I don't know what I'll do tonight. I already saw the movie that's on tonight.

Might as well go to bed early and be ready to greet the happenings tomorrow, come what may. Here's hoping I get out of here soon. Lots of love, Bill

—‰—

The Crossroads, Army Service Club #52
Sasebo Replacement Depot,
Camp Mower, Japan
March 10, 1953

Dear Mom, Dad and Carol,

Don't look like I'll ever leave this place does it? Doomed here I guess. It's plenty boring just sitting around with not a thing to do. I don't even have anything to write about. Just going to scribble a few lines to let you know I haven't left as yet.

I laid around all morning and slept. This afternoon I wandered around the compound here trying to find something to do but couldn't, so I came back to the barracks and read a bit. I'm now at the service club horsing around and that's it. I may leave tomorrow then I may stay for another 30 days. Oh well. Love, Bill

—‰—

March 11, 1953

Dear Mom, Dad and Carol,

I'm getting disappointed at the whole setup here. I, as well as the rest of the guys, just wander around here aimlessly, not knowing what to do next. No sense in giving you all my troubles but it does make me feel just a bit better to get it all off my mind .

At the chapel here they have Rosary every night and I've been attending it regularly. Of course, that's only fifteen minutes. It's a good thing, too.

I don't believe we will be leaving tomorrow either by the looks of it. A ship came in the other day but it has gone to Korea to pick up some troops and when it comes back we'll probably get on it. It rained all last night and up till noon today. Lots of thunder and lightning. That's the first time in a long time

I've been in an electrical storm. In Korea we just had rain, no lightning. Well, that's the news of the day brought to you by the Ahnen kid. Till tomorrow, Love, Bill

—~—

(March 13, '53, Korea: Aircraft of TF77 devastate Chongin, North Korea.)

—~—

The Crossroads, Army Service Club #52 Sasebo Replacement Depot,
Camp Mower, Japan
March 13, 1953

Dear Mom, Dad, Carol,

Today be the day! I've been waiting for it for 20 long months! We are finally shipping out and probably will be on our way sometime tomorrow. I feel good all over. I've been jumping around all afternoon. We are going to Seattle so it probably won't take too long. Not as long as if I was going to New York. I figure it should take somewhere around 12 to 14 days. Seasick days probably. Also I may call you when I get to Seattle and instead of me dropping quarters and dimes in the pay phone I'll just reverse the charges and it will make it much more simpler for me. Then I'll give you the money when I get home.

Home, that really sounds good to me, and if you only knew how nice. I only have a half hour before I have to load up on the truck and be off to the ship. There are a lot of men leaving so I gather it must be a pretty big ship. I wish it had jets on it. Well, I must tear away from this letter now. Give my regards to all. Be seeing you soon. Lots of love, Bill

—~—

March 13, 1953, Journal Entry:

I can't believe it! I'm alive and I'm leaving this hell! I can't believe it. I've been jumping around and laughing all day. Thank you God! It was some experience, and something I will never forget. So, I'll put it in the back of my mind, and that's where it will stay. I'm glad

Mar-13-53

THE CROSSROADS

Army Service Club #52
Sasebo Replacement Depot
Camp Mower, Japan

Dear Mom, Dad & Carol.

Today be the day I've been waiting for, for ~~fifteen~~ (12) days. We are finally shipping out and probably be on our way on the water sometime tomorrow. I feel good all over. I've been jumping around all afternoon. We are going to Seattle so it probably won't take too long. Not as long as if I was going to New York. I figure it I'll take some where around 12 to 14 days sea-sick days too probably. Also I may call you up when I get to Seattle and instead of me dropping quarters and dimes in the slot for it's just reverse the charges and it will make it just that much ... see me anyway. I ... [illegible]

I survived in one piece. Too many died in this hell of a war, too many came back armless and legless and out of their heads. Did I thank you God? I'm going home, and I'm going back to my Anita. No more games. She's my gal and I love her. The war has ended for me and so have the games with my parents.

Bill's Korean War Letters

AFTER KOREA AND HOME

April 2, 1953 and Years Later

After Korea and Home

April 2, 1953 and Years Later

After Bill read Anita's two letters he walked downstairs and joined the well wishers in the living room. The door bell rang and he went to answer it. It was a special delivery letter for him. He signed for it and opened it there in the hallway. It was from Anita. It said:

> *"Dear Billy, I'm sure you're home by now and I'm glad you are safe. I prayed for you all the time you were in Korea. Welcome home!*
>
> *Now, I'm going to tell you something that will upset you, but I have to say it. I don't want to marry you. I thought about it and it just wouldn't work out for us. Yes, I loved you. Maybe it was puppy love. But you've been gone so long, I can't really remember what you look like, unless I look at your pictures. My feelings for you have changed. So please, do not try to call me or write me.*
>
> *I'm just a plain Arkansas gal and I can't see myself living up in northern Michigan, and I certainly can't see you down here. It was fun but we were young. Now, I know we have matured. We have both been through a war. Always, Anita."*

Bill honored Anita's wishes, he did not write, call or go to Arkansas. Months passed. His mind was confused, he didn't know what to do about Anita. He just had to put her in the back of his mind. Some day he would go back to her in Arkansas.

He would have to see her, talk to her. He still loved her.

For a while Bill worked on the assembly line at GM Truck, in Pontiac. Then his father, who was a general foreman at GM, got Bill into

General Motors' drafting school. (Bill didn't want to work on the assembly line forever.) He also took drafting and engineering classes at Wayne State University, in Detroit.

Bill lost track of his Army buddies, Curly and Pete (the Greek from Chicago) who were discharged months later. They never did get together although years later Bill often spoke of them and wished he had kept in touch. As for Ollie, his boid, he died in August 1952, a peaceful death. Bill and his Dad had many adventures hunting pheasants with Brownie, his hunting dog, in the upper peninsula of Michigan. It was what Bill had dreamed about when he was in Korea.

Bill's sister, Carol, and Bob were married in December, 1953. Bill was an usher at the wedding.

During 1953 and 1954, in his leisure time, Bill and his Pontiac buddies cruised Woodward Avenue, the main strip to Detroit, in his new Chevy Bel Aire. They usually drove into Ted's Drive-In on Woodward for a 'burger and fries' after cruising.

One evening at the drive-in, Bill met a tall blonde. She was a teenager in high school. They started dating and during the summer ran off and got married. In August 1955, she gave birth to a baby girl. The baby girl died more than a year later from a brain tumor. Their second child, a son was born in 1956. A few years later two other sons were born. Bill did not talk much about this first marriage. He just said it didn't work out. In time they were divorced. During this time, Bill was working at Ford Motor Company in the Design Center, Dearborn, Michigan, using his talent to design Ford automobiles.

In the late 1960s, Bill mentioned Anita to a friend who worked with him. He said he never wrote to her, or called her, as she wished, but she had been on his mind all these years. He could not forget her.

"Call her," the friend said. "She probably is married with a bunch of kids. Call her, and stop worrying, that's my advice. Call her now, there's the phone."

So Bill looked up her parents' number and telephoned Paris, Arkansas. It had been some fourteen years since his discharge and her last letters. On the second ring he was talking to one of Anita's relatives. He explained who he was.

"Oh, I know who you are Bill. I'll never forget you," the women replied.

Bill thought it strange that she would say that—"never forget you." But that was clarified in her next remark.

"Bill Ahnen," she began, "Anita died a month after you were discharged in 1953. She wrote you that last letter because she knew she was dying. She really loved you Bill but did not want to tell you she was dying. She had her wedding dress. Actually, I think she died of a broken heart, but the doctor said it was cancer. How she loved you!" Then she hung up.

Pearl Kastran Ahnen's Memories

I met Bill on Halloween, 1970. It was at a university party and I was on the planning committee. He was a guest. When we were introduced, we were immediately attracted to each other. We spent the evening talking and dancing. You might say instant sparks flew, love at first sight. Maybe it was because I'm short, have brown hair and brown eyes. Maybe I reminded him of Anita. I'll never know. I was dressed as a Japanese Geisha and he wore red flannel pajamas and a clown wig. Quite a pair! After we talked a while, he took off his clown wig and revealed tousled blond hair. Quickly he finger combed it.

"Warm in here," he said running his fingers around his open pajama collar. "Think I'll take off my pajamas."

"What?" I said.

He excused himself and went into the men's room. In a few minutes he returned wearing a military khaki shirt and pants. "Corporal Ahnen, at your service," he said and saluted. Then he whispered, "I was wearing this under my PJs."

I grinned and saluted back. "Geisha at your service, and I don't care how hot it gets in here, I'm not taking off my kimono."

Our courtship continued and on February 14, 1971 he proposed. We were married on April 23, 1971. When I received the letters from Bill's mother, Martha, I went on a journey of my own. I discovered Bill's "talking on paper" showed honesty, humor, compassion and revealed the heart of a very lonely, homesick young man.

Then in the summer of 1987 we started off on a long journey back into time. We were on our way to Camp Chaffee and Paris, Arkansas.

Earlier I wrote about visiting the camp and the town, but I did not mention our trip to the cemetery.

We went to the caretaker's office at the local cemetery and Bill gave the caretaker Anita's name and asked if she was buried there. In a matter of minutes after looking through several charts, he found where she was buried. He gave us directions. The cemetery was not large, and we thought we would find her grave immediately. But we were wrong. We drove around the cemetery several times. Finally Bill was about to give up. "We just can't find her," he said.

"Let's give it one more try," I suggested.

He put the car in reverse, getting ready to make the narrow turn, then he stopped. "I must have hit something. Better not try to turn here. Maybe it's a gravestone."

So we both got out and went to the rear of the car. Bill had bumped into Anita's tombstone.

Pearl Kastran Ahnen, Bill's widow

Bill Ahnen died May 10, 2002, of cancer.

Bill and his parents, Nick and Martha Ahnen

Brownie (Bill's dog)

Bill's War Medals

Bill Ahnen's Service Record

Inducted	July 16, 1951
Basic training	August 1, 1951
Completed Basic	November 19, 1951
Furlough (home)	November 19, 1951
Left Furlough	December 7, 1951
Left Seattle	December 15, 1951
Arrived Japan	January 1, 1952
Left Japan	February 26, 1952
Arrived Korea	March 1, 1952
1st R&R (Japan)	July 6 to 13, 1952
2nd R&R (Japan)	December 20-26, 1952
Left Korea	February 24, 1953
Left Japan	March 15, 1953
Arrived U.S.A.	March 28,1953
Arrived Fort Custer, Mich.	March 29, 1953
Discharged	April 2, 1953

Total time: 20 months 19 days in Army

Decorations and Awards

Korean Service Medal with 2 Service Stars

National Defense Service Medal

United Nations Service Medal

Korean War Service Medal
(awarded on the 50th Anniversary of the Korean War)

INDEX

Battles And War Related Encounters

Men And Women In Korean War (Police Action)

ACKNOWLEDGMENTS

Before receiving Bill's Korean War Letters from his mother, Martha, in April, 1971, I had not thought much of the Korean War, or as it was commonly called the Korean Police Action. For me it was just another war fought in a distant land almost two decades ago and something most people did not mention in general conversation. Wasn't it called the forgotten war?

When I read Bill's letters the war became real to me. Through the years, recording the letters, and talking to many Korean War veterans about their experiences in the war, I discovered an amazing behind-the-scenes view of what ordinary soldiers did when they were not in battle.

My deepest gratitude to the late Martha Ahnen, Bill's mother, for saving his war letters and giving them to me.

In the time that it took to record Bill's letters into "Revealed by Fire" many people helped me. Among them were my children and their spouses, Steve and Chelle Kastran and Deneen and Curtis White. They were always there for me from the very beginning. I want to thank them for believing in the book, for their love and support, for their encouragement, for reading many drafts of the manuscript, and for their knowledgeable suggestions.

Others who were there for me, and none of this would have happened without them, include:

* My grandchildren, Jessica, Drew, and Bryan for constantly telling me "never to give up." I am also grateful to Jessica for reading the final draft of the manuscript.

* Jack Sheridan, my sincere thanks. He is a computer genius, who answered all of my computer questions, and converted computer "lingo" into layman (laywoman) terms for me. He was always supportive, fully involved with the project, be it transferring text or photos into CDs or discussing the next step in the manuscript's progress.

* Kris and Penny Kramer for their backup computer expertise.

* Carolyn (Pete) Owen, my heartfelt gratitude for proof reading the final manuscript. She didn't miss one period or comma. She was there for me from day one, reading and rereading various drafts of the manuscript and making constructive comments.

* Gust Anton for allowing me to use some of his Korean War photos (he was an assistant photographer during the Korean War). Also for introducing me to many Korean War veterans and inviting me to Korean War Veterans reunions and meetings.

* Paul Balasick for use of his Korean War photos.

* The Monday night Artists' Way class members for listening to my blow-by-blow description of the manuscript's progress.

* The Lakeshore Artists' Guild members for encouraging me and boosting my morale during the writing and processing of "Revealed by Fire."

* Laura Kovarik, business instructor at South Haven High School, Michigan, for coordinating the typing of the first draft of "Revealed by Fire."

* Ms. Kovarik's students who typed the first draft—Melissa Krzemen, Crystal Jones, Renae De Rosia, and Jenna Aerra.

* George Wondergem, my gratitude for reading and proofing the final draft of the manuscript.

* Members of the Army's 84th and 62nd Engineers' Construction Battalion, who served in the Korean War. They invited me to speak and read some of Bill's letters at their reunions in Branson, Missouri in 2004, and Pigeon Forge, Tennessee, in 2005.

* Henry Seo, for inviting me to observe Korean life in Chicago's Korean Village, together with his Buchanan (Michigan) High School Korean language class and several Korean War veterans. We dined in a Korean restaurant, watched Korean dancers and young men demonstrate Korean Gum Do (martial arts). We visited the Korean Consulate General, the Korean Times, and the Korean TV and radio stations.

* The many Korean War Veterans who shared their memories of the Korean War with me.

* U.S. Marine Corporal Duane E. Dewey, Medal of Honor, a brave and compassionate man, who graciously wrote the Foreword to this book.

* Father Jim Bogdan for blessing the manuscript.

Thank you God,
PKA

Sources

* Information about the battles and war related encounters obtained from the official website of VFW of the U.S. (June/July 2000—www.vfw.org) "America's War in Korea—A GI's Combat Chronology."

* Facts of the Korean War obtained from VFW and Korean War Veterans' publications and library and newspaper research.

ABOUT THE AUTHORS

Pearl Kastran Ahnen is the author of the widely acclaimed novel, "Daughter of Immigrants." She won the Michigan Livingston Arts Council Award in Literary Arts in 1992 for her "Legends and Legacies," a collection of 50 biographies, and in 1996 for her fiction collection, "Balancing Act." She has written, edited or contributed to nine books. She is also a prize-winning playwright having written eight plays. A former newspaper editor and journalist, she was born in Chicago, Illinois, and now lives on the southwest coast of Michigan. Ms. Ahnen is the widow of Bill Ahnen.

—∾—

Bill Ahnen, born in Pontiac, Michigan, was inducted into the U.S. Army in 1951 and was discharged on April 2, 1953. He worked at the Design Center of Ford Motor Company for more than thirty years. He was on the engineering team that designed the first Ford Taurus. He spent a great deal of his free time in the Upper Peninsula of Michigan hunting, fishing, and exploring the state he loved. Mr. Ahnen died May 10th, 2002.